Persecution, International Refugee Law and Refugees

This book explores the ambit of the notion of persecution in international law and its relevance in the current geopolitical context, more specifically for refugee women.

The work analyses different models for interpreting the notion of persecution in international refugee law through a comparative lens. In particular, a feminist approach to refugee law is adopted to determine to what extent the notion of persecution can apply to gender-related forms of violence and what the challenges are in doing so. It proposes an interpretive model that would encourage decision makers to interpret the notion of persecution in a manner that is sufficiently protective and relevant to the profiles of refugees in the 21st century, most particularly to refugee women.

The book will be of interest to academics and students in the field of public international law, international human rights law, international humanitarian law, immigration law, European law and refugee law, as well as those working in the areas of international relations.

Mathilde Crépin has been working in different operations for the UNHCR since 2010, in Turkey, Thailand and Malaysia. She is currently working as a consultant for the UNHCR, based in Paris, France.

Law and Migration

Series Editor
Satvinder S. Juss, King's College London, UK

Migration and its subsets of refugee and asylum policy are rising up the policy agenda at national and international level. Current controversies underline the need for rational and informed debate of this widely misrepresented and little understood area.

Law and Migration contributes to this debate by establishing a monograph series to encourage discussion and help to inform policy in this area. The series provides a forum for leading new research principally from the Law and Legal Studies area but also from related social sciences. The series is broad in scope, covering a wide range of subjects and perspectives.

Other titles in this series:

Conflict Displacement and Legal Protection:
Understanding Asylum, Human Rights and Refugee Law
Charlotte Lülf

Refugee Law and Durability of Protection
Temporary Residence and Cessation of Status
Maria O'Sullivan

Implementing EU Mobility Partnership
Putting Soft Law into Practice
Fanny Tittel-Mosser

Persecution, International Refugee Law and Refugees
A Feminist Approach
Mathilde Crépin

Human Rights and The Revision of Refugee Law
Romit Bhandari

Refugees, Democracy and the Law
A Deficit of Rights
Dana Schmalz

For more information about this series, please visit: www.routledge.com/Law-and-Migration/book-series/LAWANDMIG

Persecution, International Refugee Law and Refugees

A Feminist Approach

Mathilde Crépin

Routledge
Taylor & Francis Group
LONDON AND NEW YORK

First published 2021
by Routledge
2 Park Square, Milton Park, Abingdon, Oxon OX14 4RN

and by Routledge
605 Third Avenue, New York, NY 10017

First issued in paperback 2022

Routledge is an imprint of the Taylor & Francis Group, an informa business

Publisher's Note
The publisher has gone to great lengths to ensure the quality of this reprint but points out that some imperfections in the original copies may be apparent.

British Library Cataloguing-in-Publication Data
A catalogue record for this book is available from the British Library

Library of Congress Cataloging-in-Publication Data
Names: Crépin, Mathilde, author.
Title: Persecution, international refugee law and refugees : a feminist approach / Mathilde Crepin.
Description: Abingdon, Oxon ; New York, NY : Routledge, 2020. |
Series: Law and migration | Based on author's thesis (doctoral - King's College London, 2019) issued under title: The notion of persecution in the 1951 Convention Relating to the Status of Refugees and its relevance for the protection needs of refugees in the 21st century. |
Includes bibliographical references and index.
Identifiers: LCCN 2020011281 (print) | LCCN 2020011282 (ebook) |
ISBN 9780367893507 (hardback) | ISBN 9781003018728 (ebook)
Subjects: LCSH: Political refugees--Legal status, laws, etc. | Asylum, Right of. | Political persecution. | Women--Crimes against. | Women refugees--Legal status, laws, etc. | Sex discrimination against women--Law and legislation. | Convention Relating to the Status of Refugees (1951 July 28)
Classification: LCC KZ6530 .C74 2020 (print) | LCC KZ6530 (ebook) |
DDC 341.4/86--dc23
LC record available at https://lccn.loc.gov/2020011281
LC ebook record available at https://lccn.loc.gov/2020011282

ISBN: 978-0-367-52825-6 (pbk)
ISBN: 978-0-367-89350-7 (hbk)
ISBN: 978-1-003-01872-8 (ebk)

DOI: 10.4324/9781003018728

Typeset in Galliard
by Taylor & Francis Books

Contents

Introduction

I.1 Background and context of thesis

'The twenty-first century is proving to be the century of people on the move.' This observation was made by Antonio Guterres, the former United Nations High Commissioner for Refugees,[1] during the speech to the General Assembly of the United Nations on 1 November 2011.[2] On this occasion, he noted that, in the past few decades, a huge number of people have been displaced on the international scene and, unfortunately, they have not received adequate assistance from recipient countries. For him, this situation was partly due to the fact that international refugee law instruments were not sufficiently protective of 'people on the move', thus leaving some grey areas as to who should receive international protection today. His concerns were again echoed in the New York Declaration in 2016, where the United Nations solemnly proclaimed: 'we are witnessing in today's world an unprecedented level of human mobility. More people than ever before live in a country other than the one in which they were born'[3] without adequate protection.

The main instrument defining who is a refugee at the global level is the Convention Relating to the Status of Refugees[4] adopted in 1951 (the 1951 Convention). It was drafted after World War II, when representatives of 26 countries[5] decided to

1 Antonio Guterres was the United Nations High Commissioner for Refugees from May 2005 until December 2015. He then became the United Nations Secretary General on 1 January 2017.
2 Meetings Coverage, GA/SHC/4024, 1 November 2011, General Assembly, Third Committee, 38th Meeting of the Sixty-sixth General Assembly '21st Century Proving to be "Century of People on the Move", Innovative Approaches Needed to Address New Patterns of Forced Displacement', available at https://www.un.org/press/en/2011/gashc4024.doc.html.
3 General Assembly, 3 October 2016, Seventy-first session Agenda, Resolution adopted by the General Assembly on 19 September 2016, New York Declaration for Refugees and Migrants: https://www.unhcr.org/57e39d987.
4 Convention Relating to the Status of Refugees, Geneva 28 July 1951, entered into force 22 April 1951, No. 2545, UNTS Vol 189, 137.
5 The 26 countries were: 'Australia, Austria, Belgium, Brazil, Canada, Colombia, Denmark, Egypt, France, Federal Republic of Germany, Greece, Holy See, Iraq, Israel, Italy, Luxembourg, Monaco, Netherlands, Norway, Sweden, Switzerland (the Swiss

address the problem of refugees displaced by the conflicts in Europe. They agreed on the terms of a common definition, enshrined in Article 1(A)2 of the Convention. They stipulated, inter alia, that a refugee is a 'person who owing to a well-founded fear of being persecuted for reasons of race, religion, nationality, membership of a particular social group or political opinion, is outside the country of his nationality and is unable or, owing to such fear, is unwilling to avail himself of the protection of that country'.[6]

In this definition, the plenipotentiaries raised the notion of persecution as a core criterion to determine who is a refugee, making it the 'keystone'[7] of the Convention. In spite of its pivotal role, the term persecution was not defined in any instrument at that time. This lack of clarification on the meaning of persecution did not raise major problems in 1951 because the interpretation of the notion was relatively straightforward. In this period, persecution was commonly perceived as a repressive act carried out by totalitarian or oppressive states. However, the evolving geopolitical context at the global level progressively called into question this approach. In particular, concerns arose as to whether persecution should be interpreted only in conformity with the initial political background of the Convention or whether it could have a flexible meaning, making the definition of a refugee more adaptable to the types of harm faced by the new 'people on the move'.

The uncertainty surrounding the notion of persecution has led many commentators to consider that it was an archaic notion that was not adapted to the protection needs of refugees in the 21st century. In this sense, Guterres enumerated new displacement patterns that have emerged since World War II, such as

delegation also represented Liechtenstein), Turkey, United Kingdom of Great Britain & Northern, Ireland (UK), United States of America (US), Venezuela, Yugoslavia. The governments of Iran and Cuba were represented by observers'. Additionally, 'At its second meeting, the Conference, acting on a proposal of the representative of Egypt, unanimously decided to address an invitation to the Holy See to designate a plenipotentiary representative to participate in its work. A representative of the Holy See took his place at the Conference on 10 July 1951'. Final Act of the United Nations Conference of Plenipotentiaries on the Status of Refugees and Stateless Persons by the UN General Assembly, 25 July 1951, A/CONF.2/108/Rev.1.

6 Article 1 A (2) of the Convention Relating to the Status of Refugees (1951) in its entirety reads as follows: 'As a result of events occurring before 1 January 1951 and owing to well-founded fear of being persecuted for reasons of race, religion, nationality, membership of a particular social group or political opinion, is outside the country of his nationality and is unable or, owing to such fear, is unwilling to avail himself of the protection of that country; or who, not having a nationality and being outside the country of his former habitual residence as a result of such events, is unable or, owing to such fear, is unwilling to return to it. In the case of a person who has more than one nationality, the term "the country of his nationality" shall mean each of the countries of which he is a national, and a person shall not be deemed to be lacking the protection of the country of his nationality if, without any valid reason based on well-founded fear, he has not availed himself of the protection of one of the countries of which he is a national'.

7 Hugo Storey, '*What Constitutes Persecution? Towards a Working Definition*' [2014] 26 International Journal of Refugee Law 272, 272. DOI: https://doi.org/10.1093/ijrl/eeu017.

'population growth, urbanization, climate change', 'food, water and energy insecurity',[8] and that are not easily encompassed by the term persecution. He noted that these phenomena contributed to the emergence of new conflicts and had not been anticipated by the plenipotentiaries in 1951, leaving some protection gaps on the international scene. During the session at the General Assembly, particular emphasis was also put on the plight of refugee women who constitute nearly half[9] of these 'people on move'.[10]

Not only are women part of population flows that are unprecedented, but they are also facing circumstances that tend to be largely misunderstood. In particular, the application of the definition of a refugee and more specifically the notion of persecution, raises some difficulties when applied to forms of hardship that are typically faced by women. Their protection needs, and the risk they are likely to face in their country of origin are often based on structural causes that perpetuate gender inequality in numerous societies and that tend to be ignored. As a result, their refugee claims are often inconsistently and inadequately adjudicated. In order to avoid these pitfalls, host countries need to adopt sufficiently protective and consistent interpretations of the definition of a refugee and more particularly of the notion of persecution in the context of asylum claims lodged by women.

Whilst some legitimate concerns can be expressed regarding the application of the 1951 Convention today, some voices have adopted a relatively optimistic view of the situation, pointing to the fact that the international definition of a refugee has a great potential to apply to various forms of refugee situations. They highlighted the flexible character of this instrument, considering that it could well adapt to the changing profiles and priorities of refugees,[11] if properly interpreted. The extent to which the definition of a refugee can fit the particular circumstances faced by refugee women is however unclear. In order to answer this question, it is necessary to understand the limitations and potential of the notion of persecution in international refugee law as well as the specific protection concerns faced by women who are 'on the move'.

I.2 Methodology

This research has sought to advance and contribute to the literature on the notion of persecution in refugee law in order to address the above concerns. In the

8 Guterres (n 2).
9 UNHCR statistics: https://www.unhcr.org/women.html.
10 Sexual and gender-based violence was reported 'to be one of the most serious threats to the protection of displaced persons' in Meetings Coverage, GA/SHC/4024 (n 2).
11 Andrew I. Schoenholtz, '*The New Refugees and the Old Treaty: Persecutors and Persecuted in the Twenty-First Century*' [2015] 16 Chicago Journal of International Law 8, DOI: https://chicagounbound.uchicago.edu/cjil/vol16/iss1/5; McAdam Jane, '*The Enduring Relevance of the 1951 Refugee Convention*' [2017] 29 International Journal of Refugee Law 1, DOI: https://doi.org/10.1093/ijrl/eex017; Hathaway James C., '*A global solution to a global refugee crisis*', Open Democracy, 29 February 2016, https://www.opendemocracy.net/en/openglobalrights-openpage/global-solution-to-global-refugee-crisis/.

present book, it will be argued that the notion of persecution remains relevant nowadays, in particular for refugee women, if the notion is consistently interpreted by taking into consideration the various circumstances of women, through a combined human rights and circumstantial approach that factors in elements of intersectionality. This requires development of a broad understanding of the root causes that structure unequal power relationships and that create the conditions for women's predicaments in their own country.

Sources used and scope of the research

This book has based its methodology on a desk review of various sources. Primary sources were considered such as international, regional and national instruments as well as soft law documents from International Organisations and reports prepared by various bodies, essentially Non-Governmental Organisations. These sources were selected based on their relevance as well as recognised authority on the international scene. A thorough legal review of relevant case-law was also conducted. The cases considered in the present book were found on various public databases[12] through thematic searches and through a systematic browsing of the relevant cases corresponding to the themes identified. A chronological approach was also taken in order to filter out the cases that were not relevant to the periods of time considered. The challenges in finding adequate case law in these databases were however not overlooked. Such sources only provide published decisions and sometimes produce limited results (overlapping with other topics). Therefore, academic reviews of specific case law were also relied upon in order to obtain some complementary insights to identify the most seminal cases in the relevant areas analysed. No attempts were made to receive unpublished cases from public or private bodies (such as lawyers or UNHCR) given the well-known principle of confidentiality applied by these entities and anticipated reluctance to share documents. The case law analysis has essentially focused on countries that have signed the 1951 Convention and have well developed refugee status determination systems. Although some countries in Africa and Latin America[13] have recently developed such processes, countries with significant asylum jurisprudence were mostly found to be common-law countries such as the United States of America (US), Canada, New Zealand, Australia, as well as some selected countries of the European Union, including some civil law countries. For the purpose of the present book, only a

12 The main databases used were: UNHCR Refworld: https://www.refworld.org, European Data Base on Asylum Law: https://www.asylumlawdatabase.eu/en, case law summaries of International Journal of Refugee Law: https://academic.oup.com/ijrl/issue, Heinonline, https://heinonline.org/HOL/Welcome, as well as the databases of national jurisdictions.

13 Alice Edwards, '*Refugee Status Determination in Africa*' [2006] 14 African Journal of International & Comparative Law 204, https://ssrn.com/abstract=1535377; U.S. Committee for Refugees and Immigrants and Asylum Access Ecuador, *Refugee Status Determination in Latin America: Regional Challenges and opportunities: The national systems of Brazil, Colombia, Costa Rica, Ecuador and Mexico*, January 2013.

few countries of the European Union were selected, namely the United Kingdom,[14] France and Belgium. They were identified based on the language in which these countries have published a significant number of cases involving the analysis of the notion of persecution, namely either English or French and in consideration of their long-standing jurisprudence on asylum cases.

Additionally, secondary sources such as academic pieces of writing were also considered. A selective approach was used in order to identify the sources that directly addressed the meaning of persecution through a legal perspective (rather than for instance sociological or cultural). In particular, a mapping of the scholarship was made in order to identity the crux of the debate regarding the relevance of this notion in contemporary contexts. Early authors as well as more recent scholars were considered. This research has essentially focused on the most prominent and recognised legal scholars who addressed the notion of persecution in refugee law as well as gender issues. This selection was done in order to circumscribe the theoretical debate to the approaches that have gained major traction amongst relevant stakeholders. The objective was to propose a practical contribution to the field rather than questioning the notion of persecution through a purely conceptual lens. However, at times, references were made to authors who have proposed original perspectives with limited influence in the academic arena or in the jurisprudence, but who nonetheless were found to shed some light on relevant aspects of the notion of persecution.

The primary and secondary sources selected were sources that mainly addressed topics relevant to urban refugees, as opposed to camp refugees. Given that the present research focuses on the application of the definition of a refugee in the 1951 Convention, it was deemed more relevant to assess the circumstances of refugees who lodged asylum claims in front of national jurisdictions, which is almost never the case of refugees living in camp settings. Partly due to the very large number of displaced individuals in short periods of time, the protection afforded to camp refugees is rarely the result of individual status determinations but is either based on the discretionary will of states or on regional and broader definitions. In particular, reference can be made to the Convention Governing the Specific Aspects of Refugee Problems in Africa (the OAU Convention)[15] in 1969, which adopted a new definition of a refugee. It relied on the 1951 Convention definition as a departure point but further enlarged the eligibility criteria by considering that the mere existence of situations such as 'external aggression, occupation, foreign domination or events seriously disturbing public order' could warrant international protection. In 1984, the Cartagena Declaration on Refugees ('Cartagena Declaration')[16] then adopted a similar narrative and added new

14 The jurisprudence considered was still in conformity with the law of the European Union at the time the UK was still a member.

15 OAU Convention Governing the Specific Aspects of Refugee Problems (concluded at Addis Ababa on 10 September 1969, registered on 31 March 1976) 1001 UNTS 45 (OAU Convention).

16 Cartagena Declaration on Refugees (adopted on 22 November 1984), OAS Doc. OEA/Ser.L/V/II.66/doc.10, 190 (Cartagena Declaration).

elements to the causes of flight, namely 'generalized violence', 'internal aggression' and 'massive violation of human rights'. Both definitions reaffirmed the primacy of the 1951 Convention but in addition, they developed a new refugee paradigm by referring to objective conditions in refugee-producing countries and ruled out the concept of persecution. As a result, they were no further examined in the present book. Major focus was placed on the international system of asylum rather than on regional adaptations of refugee law.[17]

Line of argumentation of the research

Based on the above sources, this book has first sought to establish the interpretive background of the 1951 Convention by defining the new geopolitical challenges that characterise forced displacements in the modern world. Amongst various patterns of displacement, the specific condition of refugee women was highlighted as a new challenge in interpreting the definition of a refugee and, more specifically, the notion of persecution.

In order to better evaluate the interpretive scope of the notion of persecution in particular in this context, this research has built on the existing literature and engaged in an extensive analysis of the scholarship to examine the various proposals made by many authors to interpret persecution. Other proposals brought forward by institutions of the European Union as well as the United Nations High Commissioner for Refugees (UNHCR) were also considered. The purpose of this was to explore various interpretive schemes and test them against the current background of refugee claims in order to identify different aspects of the notion of persecution that pose major challenges in applying the 1951 Convention today, in particular regarding claims lodged by women.

This theoretical exercise was also accompanied by a practical overview of relevant case law in order to survey the current state of practice through a comparative legal perspective. As previously mentioned, this research essentially focused on countries that have robust refugee status determination procedures. The objective of this review was to understand how various interpretive models examined in the book were used by decision makers and what the protection gaps are. In order to overcome these gaps and by drawing upon legal principles developed by scholars and refugee law practitioners, this research sought to identify adequate modes of interpretation that can be consistently applied at the global level and that can accurately reflect the circumstances of women. A relevant interpretive model was defined through an inductive approach that takes as a departure point the circumstances of refugees and highlights the importance of intersectionality in determining protection needs. The intersection between refugee law and human rights law was acknowledged. However, it was contended that human rights law should not be used as a formal and restrictive framework of interpretation as this field of law was in itself unable to capture the complexity of women's experiences.

17 José H. Fischel De Andrade, '*Regional Policy Approaches and Harmonization: a Latin American Perspective*' [1998] 10 International Journal of Refugee Law 389, 402.

Although the development of international human rights has helped to advance the understanding of the notion of persecution in the context of gender-related forms of violence, it should not be used in a strict manner to define the notion. Instead, it can be relied upon as one form of guidance.

It was then found relevant to engage in a specific case study of gender-related claims for three particular types of predicament faced by women, namely FGM, domestic violence and people trafficking, because such claims particularly exemplify the current interpretive challenges and the difficulties for applying the notion of persecution in contexts that were seemingly not anticipated by the drafters of the 1951 Convention. A survey of feminist approaches to refugee law has underpinned an analysis of the case law in order to adequately identify specific gaps in interpreting persecution in situations of gender-based violence.

I.3 Outline of research

In order to assess the scope of persecution and its relevance for modern refugees, a preliminary chapter first analyses the historical background of the 1951 Convention and the context of the emergence of persecution as a pivotal concept in international refugee law. This chapter demonstrates that persecution has been perceived to be a politically biased notion and that, when the definition was developed, the plenipotentiaries had a particular meaning in mind, adapted to the necessities and circumstances of their time. However, they were also aware of their inability to anticipate the multiple forms of persecution as they could arise in the future, and therefore, they intended to use a flexible term in order to make the refugee definition malleable. It is then observed that the interpretation of persecution had not posed any particular problems in the bipolar world of the cold war, but that interpretive challenges started to arise with the emergence of new displacement patterns in the 1980s/1990s. The characteristics of these new patterns are fleshed out in order to delineate the contours of the interpretive debate today. In particular, the phenomenon of 'feminisation' of forced displacement is highlighted, demonstrating that the situation of women has been particularly misunderstood in the past decades and their protection needs appear to be different than those of the male refugee population.

The second chapter engages in an in-depth analysis of the traditional interpretive frameworks that have been proposed by scholars in order to overcome the challenges in applying the notion of persecution to new refugees. These frameworks have generally relied on a basic human rights paradigm to define what amounts to persecution. In particular, Hathaway's proposal that persecution should be understood as a sustained or systemic violation of basic human rights demonstrative of a failure of state protection is considered and evaluated against other models and contemporary refugee claims. Several other basic human rights models are considered through a critical perspective in order to identify their advantages and limitations. A more general analysis of human rights theories is undertaken in order to assess whether human rights standards shall be considered relevant benchmarks of interpretation and to what extent this should be the case.

It is then argued that basic human rights do constitute relevant interpretive references because they provide objective norms of interpretation. However, a formalist reliance on a basic human rights scheme entails the risk of adopting a restrictive approach that, in addition, does not necessarily foster consistency amongst jurisdictions for various reasons that will be expounded in the following chapters. It is then further demonstrated that additional theoretical frameworks might be needed to provide adequate interpretive guidance to decision makers.

The third chapter explores more recent interpretive schemes that have been developed in the past years and that propose to enlarge the understanding of persecution beyond a basic human rights narrative. In particular, the definition provided by the Qualification Directive[18] (QD) of the European Union is analysed in depth as it sets a new interpretive paradigm. Proposals of other scholars are also evaluated as well as the general framework developed by the Refugee Agency (UNHCR). The benefits and limitations of these various theoretical frameworks are assessed against each other through the same comparative approach adopted in the previous chapter. It is eventually argued that a holistic and inductive approach, factoring in human rights norms and the individual circumstances of refugees as proposed by UNHCR appears the best adapted to the protection needs of refugees, in particular to refugee women as it has great potential for capturing the complexities of their experiences.

After a comparative analysis of the different paradigms proposed for interpreting the notion of persecution, Chapter 4 engages in a case study of asylum claims specifically lodged by women. The choice of a case study was deemed necessary in order to highlight the existence of major interpretive difficulties that exist for female refugees. As previously pointed out, the share of refugee women in the world today is significantly higher than in previous decades and brings to the fore new concerns of modern societies, often related to the negation of harmful traditional practices or the rejection of social mores. These predicaments are particularly challenging when it comes to applying the notion of persecution because they were not apparently considered by the drafters of the Convention when they developed the refugee definition. However, they correspond to the current protection needs of refugees and, as such, could be covered by the notion of persecution that was meant to be sufficiently flexible in that sense. An overview of feminist theories in refugee law is undertaken in order to identify major features of the protection needs of refugee women. This theoretical understanding of women's asylum claims is tested against the case law in order to argue that the current interpretive approaches, often based on a basic human rights narrative, obviate some circumstances of refugee women and need further development through a more holistic and circumstantial understanding of the conditions of women in certain social settings.

18 Directive 2011/95/EU of 13 December 2011 on standards for the qualification of third-country nationals or stateless persons as beneficiaries of international protection, for a uniform status for refugees or for persons eligible for subsidiary protection, and for the content of the protection granted [2011] OJ L 337/248 (Revised Qualification Directive).

Overall, the present book seeks to demonstrate that a sufficiently evolutionary and robust understanding of the notion of persecution will help to ensure the 'enduring relevance' of the 1951 Convention, at least in the current world. In particular, the 'enduring relevance' of the notion of persecution in cases of violence faced by refugee women is crucial and will be ascertained only through a broader understanding of the circumstances of refugee women. It is suggested that decision makers adopt a human rights as well as a circumstantial approach to interpret the notion of persecution, taking into consideration the various aspects of women's lives through an intersectional methodology that reveals the deeper social structures causing and perpetuating the oppression of refugee women in their countries of origin.

1 The notion of persecution, historical background and interpretive challenges in the 21st century

The international definition of a refugee was developed in 1951 in Europe in order to determine who was eligible for asylum in the aftermath of World War II. However, to define who is a 'refugee' is to restrict the number of people entitled to protection and to exclude those who do not meet the criteria of the Convention. In this sense, the development of a generic definition sets clear 'boundaries or limits'[1] to the category of people who could receive assistance in Europe. In particular, authors pointed out that the plenipotentiaries 'privilege(d) particular concepts'[2] more than others to define the contours of the states' international engagements. One might therefore wonder how refugeehood was conceptualised in this period and for which reasons. In fact, as noted by Juss, the fundamental question should not be 'who is a refugee' but 'whose refugee'[3] are we talking about and 'why do we define [refugees] the way we do?'[4]

Understanding how the refugee definition was elaborated will shed light on the scope of the 1951 Convention as well as the meaning of some pivotal concepts such as the notion of persecution. The first part of this chapter will provide an overview of the historical context in which the 1951 Convention was drafted in an attempt to explain the reasons why the plenipotentiaries chose the current eligibility criteria to develop the refugee definition, and more particularly, why the notion of persecution was introduced as an essential concept in refugee law. The second part of this chapter will analyse the current geopolitical situation to highlight the changing context of the interpretation of the Convention and in particular the major role of women in global displacement patterns. Lastly, the third part will assess the challenges that arise from these changing circumstances in order to better evaluate the scope of this notion and

1 Jean-Francois Durieux, '*Three Asylum Paradigms*' [2013] 20 International Journal on Minority and Group Rights 147, 150. DOI: https://doi.org/10.1163/15718115-02002002.

2 Sara E. Davies, '*Redundant or Essential? How Politics Shaped the Outcome of the 1967 Protocol*' [2007] 19 International Journal of Refugee Law 703, 705. DOI: https://doi.org/10.1093/ijrl/eem068.

3 S. S. Juss, *International Migration and Global Justice* (Ashgate, Aldershot, 2006), Chapter 6, 198.

4 Ibid. 199–200.

its relevance in the 21st century. It will be argued that in spite of some uncertainty surrounding the exact intention of the plenipotentiaries, it can generally be agreed that they wanted to introduce a concept that could adapt to the different profiles of refugees, including the claims brought forward by refugee women. Additionally, it will be contended that the mere existence of international standards suggests that some level of consistency is needed in the interpretation of the definition of a refugee to ensure that the 1951 Convention is implemented in a manner that does not disadvantage some host countries over others and does not encourage asylum shopping. This chapter will thus conclude that a global principled interpretive approach is needed to ensure an effective implementation of the international asylum system and more adequate protection for women forced to leave their country.

1.1 The emergence of the notion of persecution in international refugee law

1.1.1 Legal developments and the progressive conceptualisation of who is a refugee in international law

The concept of asylum is an old concept, dating back to antiquity[5] and consisting in the right of a state to grant asylum to individuals at risk of political or religious oppression. This right was for a long time the prerogative of recipient states and merely constituted an individual and political choice of the host country.[6] As a result, no coordinated plan of action existed at a regional or international level to address the plight of displaced individuals. It should be noted that prior to the 20th century, the ambit of displacements and migration was relatively modest, with a limited global impact. As such, there were very few incentives for states to develop a common system of protection. One of the first and largest displacements of population across nation states only occurred in 1685 when the French King Louis XIV made the practice of protestant faith illegal in France. As a result, protestant Huguenots fled in masse to neighbouring countries, seeking shelter in today's Germany, the Netherlands, Switzerland and other European states.[7] At that time, it was estimated that over 200 000 individuals were displaced in the space of two decades[8] and the protection responses provided by European states were based on the discretionary decisions of the reigning powers.

5 Gy Haraszti, '*The Right of Asylum*' [1960] 2 Acta Juridica 359, 361.
6 Ibid. 363: 'In the first place, let us point out that the right of asylum is the right of the State to grant asylum to persons prosecuted for political reasons. This right resulting from state sovereignty is recognized by international customary law and is a constituent of several international agreements as well.'
7 See analysis of Owen Stanwood, '*Between Eden and Empire: Huguenot Refugees and the Promise of New Worlds*' [2013] 118 The American Historical Review 1319. DOI: 10.1093/ahr/118.5.1319
8 Ibid. 1319.

During World War I, much larger movements of population took place on the European continent.[9] Given the high risk of destabilisation in the region, European countries decided for the first time to adopt a number of common agreements in order to better organise the delivery of aid. New instruments were developed under the auspices of the League of Nations, to determine who was eligible for refugee status by referring to specific categories of people. For instance, a number of bilateral and multilateral treaties were created to protect individuals who had fled the consequences of the Russian revolution in 1917 and the problems arising out of the dissolution of the Ottoman Empire.[10] Some other treaties covered different groups such as 'Latvian refugees (…) in the territory of Ukrainian Socialist Soviet Republic',[11] 'Greek refugees',[12] 'refugees in Bulgaria',[13] 'refugees coming from Germany'.[14] In these instruments, refugee law was understood as a response to the plight of certain categories of people fleeing repressive state policies. It can be observed that, in this period, the notion of persecution was not mentioned in any of the League of Nations' documents because refugees were categorised as specific groups of individuals depending on their origins. Some authors such as Zarjevski highlighted the fact that this approach was quite restrictive because it was limited 'to precisely describe already existing categories of people'[15] and did not rely on a generic definition.

9 Up to 9.5 millions in Peter Gatrell, '*World Wars and Population Displacement in the Twentieth Century*' [2007] 16 Contemporary European History 415, 418. DOI: https://doi.org/10.1017/S0960777307004092.

10 Inter alia, 'Arrangement with respect to the issue of certificates of identity to Russian Refugees', signed at Geneva, 5 July 1922 League of Nations Treaty Series (LNTS) [1922], vol 13, 237–257; 'Arrangement concerning the Extension to other Categories of Refugees of certain Measures taken in favour of Russian and Armenian Refugees', signed at Geneva, 30 June 1928, League of Nations Treaty Series (LNTS) [1929], vol 89, 47–52.

11 'Agreement regarding the repatriation of Latvian refugees who are at present in the territory of Ukrainian Socialist Soviet Republic', signed at Moscow, 3 August 1921 League of Nations Treaty Series (LNTS) [1923], vol 17, 306–315

12 Inter alia, 'Declaration relating to the settlement of Refugees in Greece and the creation for this purpose of a Refugees Settlement Commission' signed in Geneva, 29 September 1923 League of Nations Treaty Series (LNTS) [1923], vol 20,41–43; 'Protocol relating to the settlement of Refugees in Greece and the creation for this purpose of a Refugees Settlement Commission', signed in Geneva, 29 September 1923 League of Nations Treaty Series (LNTS) [1923], vol 20, pp. 29–39; 'Additional Act to the Protocol of September 29, 1923, relating to the Settlement of Greek Refugees'.

13 'Protocol concerning the Settlement of Refugees in Bulgaria' signed in Geneva, 8 September 1926 [1926], League of Nations Treaty Series (LNTS), vol 58, 245–257.

14 Inter alia, 'Provisional Arrangement concerning the Status of Refugees coming from Germany, and Annex', signed in Geneva, 4 July 1936 League of Nations Treaty Series (LNTS) [1936], vol 171, 75–87; 'Convention concerning the Status of Refugees coming from Germany, with Annex', signed in Geneva, 10 February 1938 League of Nations Treaty Series (LNTS), vol 192, 59–81.

15 Delphine Zarjevski, *A Future Preserved, International Assistance to Refugees* (Pergamon Press 1988) 12.

The League of Nations was eventually dissolved at the outset of World War II and, as new groups of refugees appeared, the old refugee treaties became obsolete. Just before the beginning of World War II and in the aftermath of the Allies' victory, the international community successively created the Intergovernmental Committee on Refugees (ICR) in 1938, the United Nations Relief and Rehabilitation Administration (UNRRA) in 1943 and the International Refugee Organisation (IRO) in 1946 in order to provide assistance to refugees. These entities adopted new approaches to international aid. The first organisation, the ICR, was in charge of facilitating the emigration of victims of the Nazi regime from Germany and Austria and considered that only individuals from these countries were entitled to receive international protection.[16] This new approach was rather innovative given that it identified refugees as individuals who could receive assistance even in their own country of origin. It was however only limited to German and Austrian refugees. As such, this definition followed the previous category-oriented and restrictive approach of the League of Nations. In spite of these limitations, it was noted by an author that the ICR developed a new paradigm, somehow defining refugees based on 'personalized criteria of political opinion, religious belief and racial origin'.[17] For this author, the ICR announced the beginning of a new phase where refugees were considered in 'individualist terms'.[18] The individualist paradigm, namely whereby refugees are defined through their personal characteristics and their own story, is the one that eventually prevailed.

After the ICR, the mandates of UNRRA and IRO established new refugee definitions that further emphasised the individualistic paradigm to define refugees. Resolutions of the UNRRA council stated that the organisation is competent to provide material help to 'displaced persons'[19] and:

> other persons who have been obliged to leave their country or place of origin or former residence or who have been deported therefrom, by action or activities in favour of the United Nations, or for the control of epidemics for the purpose of preventing the spread of such epidemics to United Nations areas or to displaced persons of United Nations nationality found in the particular enemy or ex-enemy area.[20]

16 James C. Hathaway, '*The Evolution of Refugee Status in International Law: 1920–1950*' [1984] 33 The International and Comparative Law Quarterly 348, DOI: https://doi.org/10.1093/iclqaj/33.2.348, 370–371: Refugees were defined as '1. Persons who have not already left their countries of origin (Germany including Austria), but who must emigrate on account of their political opinions, religious beliefs and racial origin, and 2. Persons as defined in (1) who have already left their country of origin and who have not yet established themselves permanently'.

17 Ibid. 371.

18 Ibid. 350.

19 Appendix I, Resolutions on Policy of the Third Session of the Council, UNRRA Council Resolution 10, 4.

20 Appendix II, Resolutions on Policy of the Third Session of the Council, UNRRA Council Resolution 71, 7.

This definition was based on a generic approach rather than referring to predetermined categories, thus it seemingly encompassed more individuals. The UNRRA definition was, however, quite complex and was later superseded by the IRO's constitution.[21] The IRO constitution still defined refugees as individuals belonging to specific groups but also through the enumeration of more general principles, such as the principle of alienage, the existence of reasons for forcible displacements, and exclusion considerations. The nature of harm prompting an individual's flight was not characterised, but a new term—persecution—was introduced to designate the objections that refugees could raise for not wanting to return to their country of origin.[22] Through this notion, the IRO further emphasised the

21 Annex I, Part 1, Section A of the Constitution of the International Refugee Organisation, 15 December 1946, United Nations Treaty Series, vol. 18. p. 1: '1. Subject to the provisions of sections C and D and Part II of this Annex, the term "refugee" applies to a person who has left, or who is outside of, his country of nationality or of former habitual residence, and who, whether or not he had retained his nationality, belongs to one of the following categories: (*a*) Victims of the nazi or fascist regimes or of regimes which took part on their side in the second world war, or of the quislings or similar regimes which assisted them against the United Nations, whether enjoying international status as refugees or not; (*b*) Spanish Republicans and other victims of the Falangist regime in Spain, whether enjoying international status as refugees or not; (*c*) Persons who were considered refugees before the outbreak of the second world war, for reasons of race, religion, nationality or political opinion.

2. Subject to the provisions of sections C and D and of Part II of this Annex regarding the exclusion of certain categories of persons, including war criminals, quislings and traitors, from the benefits of the Organisation, the term "refugee" also applies to a person, other than a displaced person as defined in section B of this Annex, who is outside of his country of nationality or former habitual residence, and who, as a result of events subsequent to the outbreak of the second world war, is unable or unwilling to avail himself of the protection of the Government of his country of nationality or former nationality.

3. Subject to the provisions of section D and of Part II of this Annex, the term "refugee" also applies to persons who, having resided in Germany or Austria, and being of Jewish origin or foreigners or stateless persons, were victims of Nazi persecution and were detained in, or were obliged to flee from, and were subsequently returned to, one of those countries as a result of enemy action, or of war circumstances, and have not yet been firmly resettled therein.

4. The term "refugee" also applies to unaccompanied children who are war orphans or whose parents have disappeared, and who are outside their countries of origin. Such children, 16 years of age or under, shall be given all possible priority assistance, including, normally, assistance in repatriation in the case of those whose nationality can be determined.'

22 Ibid. '1. In the case of all the above categories (...) persons will become the concern of the Organisation [...] if they have definitely, (...) expressed valid objections to returning to those countries.

(*a*) The following shall be considered as valid objections:

(i) Persecution, or fear, based on reasonable grounds of persecution because of race, religion, nationality or political opinions, provided these opinions are not in conflict with the principles of the United Nations, as laid down in the Preamble of the Charter of the United Nations; (...)

(iii) In the case of persons falling within the category mentioned in section A, paragraphs 1 (*a*) and 1 (*c*) compelling family reasons arising out of previous persecution, or compelling reasons of infirmity or illness.'

personal aspect of refugeehood by pointing to the importance of personal circumstances of refugees. The development of a new approach to the definition of a refugee coincided with the emergence of the notion of persecution in international treaties,[23] which shifted the focus from existing categories of people onto the harm faced by each individual, independently from their community.

1.1.2 The emergence of the notion of persecution as a pivotal concept in the refugee definition

By defining who is a refugee through the designation of certain groups of individuals, the pre-1951 definitions were meant to provide temporary protection, until these designated groups had found durable solutions. However, by the end of World War II states realised that the refugee problem was rather pervasive in Europe and that more categories of individuals required assistance. As such, it was decided that a permanent solution was needed.[24] A new refugee agency, the UNHCR, was created in order to 'provide protection (…) for the problem of refugees'. States also decided to draft an international treaty for the protection of displaced people in Europe. For this purpose, the Secretary General of the newly formed United Nations proposed to agree on a new convention that would organise the assistance of 'all persons without international protection'.[25] The focus was therefore more explicitly placed on the protection of individuals in need rather than on the right of states to grant asylum. In spite of this seemingly neutral approach, this proposal was rejected for being too inclusive, in particular

23 Jose Fischel H. De Andrade, '*On the Development of the Concept of "Persecution" in International Refugee Law*' [2008] 2 Anuario Brasileiro de direito internacional 114, 120. Fischel observed that, the definitional provisions of the IRO 'represented a two-fold innovation' by individualising the term 'refugee'. Daniel J. Steinbock, '*Interpreting the Refugee Definition*' [1998] 45 UCLA Law Review 733, DOI: http://df7sm3xp4s.search.serialssolutions.com/?V=1.0&N=100&L=DF7SM3XP4S&S=AC_T_M&C=UCLA Law Review, 806. According to Steinbock '(b)efore 1938, international protection was usually given to groups of displaced or stateless persons described simply by national or ethnic origin, in other words, by category. In 1938, for the first time in the twentieth century, persons driven from their homelands to be given international aid were described in individual rather than categorical or group terms'. Steinbock also noted that under the ICR, UNRRA and IRO regimes, refugees started being defined on the basis of their own experiences, rather than based on their membership to a particular collectivity.

24 Robinson Nehemiah, '*Convention Relating to the Status of Refugees: Its History, Significance and Contents*' [1952] New York: Institute of Jewish Affairs 6. Nehemiah stated that the Convention was the 'expression of a conviction by the comity of nations that refugees are not a temporary phenomenon, which can be dealt with either by half measures or piece-meal, but is one requiring a concerted effort by all states concerned'. See also Rieko Karatani, '*How History Separated Refugee and Migrant Regimes: In Search of Their Institutional Origins*' [2005] 17 International Journal of Refugee Law 517, DOI: https://doi.org/10.1093/ijrl/eei019, 531.

25 James C. Hathaway, '*A Reconsideration of the Underlying Premise of Refugee Law*' [1990] 31 Harvard International Law Journal 129, 144.

by the Soviet Union and its allies who eventually refused to take part in the creation of a new instrument.[26]

Hathaway observed that, as a result, the states that ended up drafting the Convention were 'predominantly Western'[27] and, represented a relatively homogenous ideological bloc. This had considerable consequences for how the new refugee definition was conceptualised. The drafters of the Convention decided to define refugees as individuals who, as a result of the events occurring in Europe before 1951, were outside their country of origin, had a well-founded fear of being persecuted based on a Convention reason and were not able to avail themselves of the protection of their state of origin. In this context, although the notion of persecution allowed the drafters to introduce a generic definition, broader than the category-based definitions from the previous periods, it nonetheless restricted the number of people entitled to protection. It was noted that the notion of persecution was particularly convenient for referring to past experiences of displaced people in Europe who had been victims of the crimes perpetrated by the Nazi or Soviet regimes.[28] McAdam in particular contended that, in this period, there was an implicit understanding of what persecution meant, namely violations of political and civil rights from oppressive regimes.[29] This approach excluded from the new protection regime persons denied other basic rights such as 'food, health care, or education (i.e. the socio-economic rights, where the Western states [had] a poor record)'[30] as well as individuals 'forced to flee because of personal vendettas and private feuds, (…) or internal civil tur-

26 Ibid. 145.
27 Ibid. 146.
28 See Hathaway (n 25) 146; Shacknove was also of the view that the Convention was a mere response to the 'European totalitarian experience [where] refugees were primarily [seen as] the persecuted victims of highly organized predatory states' in Andrew E. Shacknove, '*Who Is a Refugee?*' [1985] 95 Ethics 274, 276, DOI: https://www.jstor.org/stable/2380340; Jacqueline Bhabha, '*Internationalist Gatekeepers? The Tension between Asylum Advocacy and Human Rights*' [2002] 15 Harvard Human Rights Journal 155, 172. For Bhabha, persecution 'was imported from the preceding international refugee regime as a familiar term and a useful Western tool, flexible enough to cover the circumstances of both victims of Nazism, and Soviet and other Eastern dissidents'.
29 Jane McAdam, '*Rethinking the origins of persecution*' [2014] 25 International Journal of Refugee Law 667, 671. DOI: https://doi.org/10.1093/ijrl/eet048. Jane McAdam highlights the fact that persecution was implicit in the refugee concept through the analysis of the drafting record of the international instruments in that period dealing with the protection of refugees.
30 Hathaway (n 25) 150. See also p. 148: 'In the end, it was agreed to restrict the scope of protection in much the same way as UNRRA had done: only persons who feared "persecution" in the sense of being denied basic civil and political rights would fall within the international mandate. (Persecution as an attempt to restrict the scope of individuals protected.) First, the persecution standard was a known quantity, having already been employed to embrace Soviet bloc dissidents under the IRO regime'. See also Karatani who considered that the definition of a refugee was established in order to protect people who fled the Eastern bloc in Karatani (n 24).

moil'[31] as these forms of harm were more common in countries with a failure of economic structures. As a result, concern was raised that 'the adoption of persecution as the central characteristic of the refugee was made to fit a Western interpretation as asylum seekers'.[32]

It appears indeed that the current refugee definition is the direct result of events occurring in Europe and neighbouring countries in the first half of the 20th century. Although the definition progressively changed from a category-oriented definition to a more generic one by introducing the notion of persecution as a pivotal element, the definition of a refugee appeared to be marred by some inherent limitations. This new definition was embedded in a particular regional, historical and cultural context and thus was more convenient to designate individuals who had faced only certain forms of harm (or were at risk to face) such as individual violations of civil and political rights.[33]

Not only did the definition of a refugee appear politically biased, but criticism was also made that it had a male-centric character. A semantic analysis of the text of the 1951 Convention indeed reveals that it was drafted in terms that fit men's experiences as the pronouns 'his' or 'himself' were exclusively used in the text of the Convention.[34] No occurrences of the pronouns 'her' or 'herself' are to be found in the whole document. To Johnsson, 'that (...) is not entirely surprising. The concept of political persecution is much more relevant to the fact of a man in a male-oriented society.'[35] After World War II, the forms of persecution that were in the minds of the plenipotentiaries were indeed mainly occurring in the public sphere, thus mainly affecting men. This did not prevent women from being recognised refugees, but in practice it was the case only for a minority who would conform to a typical male's experiences at the time, namely occurring in the public sphere or for women as part of a family unit. The idea that females could have individual circumstances that are different than males was not part of the debates leading up to the adoption of the 1951 Convention. This probably was in part the case because none of the drafters of the Convention was female.[36] Additionally,

31 Bhabha (n 28) 167.

32 Gil Loescher, *Beyond Charity: International Cooperation and the Global Refugee Crisis* (Oxford University Press 1993) 57, DOI: https://doi.org/10.1177%2F004711789401200205. Mirko Bagaric and Penny Dimopoulos, '*Refugee law - time for a fundamental rethink: need as the criterion for assistance*' [2003] 9 Canterbury Law Review 268, DOI: https://doi.org/10.1017/CBO9781139168670.019. Bagaric and Dimopoulos further noted that 'despite its universal overtones, the 1951 Convention was limited by the fact that it protected mainly Europeans fleeing after the War'.

33 On this see also Michael Parrish, '*Redefining the Refugee: The Universal Declaration of Human Rights as a Basis for Refugee Protection*' [2000] 22 Cardozo Law Review 223, 228.

34 See articles 1 and 33 of the 1951 Convention.

35 Anders B. Johnsson, '*The International Protection of Women Refugees: A Summary of Principal Problems and Issues*', [1989] 1 International Journal of Refugee Law 221, 222, DOI: https://doi.org/10.1093/ijrl/1.2.221.

36 Ibid.

the definition of a refugee was developed in a context where the condition of women was not a major concern of the reigning powers at the time. As a result, the definition of a refugee ended up corresponding to the typical profiles of western men in Europe, whose experiences tended to take place in the public political sphere, more than women's experiences at the time. The relatively narrow nature of the refugee definition was, however, in tension with its progressive universalisation, leading to its application in different geopolitical contexts and new forms of claim brought forward by women, in particular after the end of the Cold War. The ability of the notion of persecution to adapt to these new situations became therefore questionable.

1.1.3 Universalisation of the 1951 Convention

Although the 1951 Convention was not meant to provide protection to all people in need of international assistance over the world, some authors pointed out that its content had a universal character and could be used as a model for establishing a global system of protection.[37] This view aligned with the recommendation of the Final Act of the conference of the plenipotentiaries, expressing the desire that the Convention be applied more extensively, depending on the will of member states. Indeed, the Final Act stated that the 1951 Convention should 'have value as an example exceeding its contractual scope'.[38] The Act further expressed the hope that 'all nations will be guided by it in granting so far as possible to persons in their territory as refugees and who would not be covered by the terms of the Convention, the treatment for which it provides'.[39] This recommendation encouraged states to rely on the Convention for extending their assistance to a larger number people in need, thus emphasising the protection purpose of the 1951 Convention. This indeed suggested that there was a hope that the 1951 Convention could serve as a basis for developing an expanded system of protection. Goodwin-Gill noted that, until 1967, in practice, many states relied on the Final Act recommendation for providing assistance to individuals who had been forcibly displaced during some major world crisis, even after 1951.[40] It was, however, unclear whether this recommendation was meant to cover only individuals who met the criteria of the refugee definition after lifting the geographical and temporal

37 Nehemiah indeed highlighted the inherent universal character of the Convention as he pointed out that whilst 'all preceding Conventions referred to European refugees only', 'the present Convention can be applied to refugees from any part of the world' in Nehemiah (n 24) 8.

38 Final Act of the United Nations Conference of Plenipotentiaries on the Status of Refugees and Stateless Persons by the UN General Assembly, 25 July 1951 available at: http://www.unhcr.org/protection/travaux/40a8a7394/final-act-united-nations-conference-plenipotentiaries-status-refugees-stateless.html.

39 Ibid.

40 Guy Goodwin-Gill and Jane McAdam, *The Refugee in International Law* (3rd edn, Oxford University Press 2011) 36. See also Davies (n 2) 703. According to Davies the need to provide a broader protection to refugee was already clear in the 1950s.

limitations, or larger groups of people.[41] Whilst this point remains uncertain, the recommendation of the Final Act nonetheless indicates that the refugee definition could also adapt to circumstances different than the pre-1951 events.

A few years after the end of World War II, the persistence and the emergence of new refugee crises[42] led states to reconsider the scope of the Convention. In this sense, it was observed that, in the post-war period, the UNHCR had 'grown increasingly frustrated with its limited mandate, with growing refugee problems in Europe and Africa that were beyond the technical reach of the Convention, and with a lower than expected number of accessions to the Convention, particularly amongst recently decolonised states'.[43] It was becoming clearer at this time, that the refugee problem was pervasive, extending beyond the confines of Europe. In light of this situation, Juss noted that 'for the Refugee Convention to remain relevant and apply as a universal treaty, it had to change its Eurocentric orientation'.[44] As a result, states adopted a protocol in 1967 that lifted the geographical and temporal limitations of the refugee definition,[45] and made the 1951 Convention a universally applicable treaty.

The 1967 Protocol, however, did not revise any of the other provisions of the Convention. Given these minimal changes, Hathaway considered that the Protocol failed to substantively reform the Convention. Hathaway observed that even if the Protocol universalised the refugee definition, 'only persons whose migration [was] prompted by a fear of persecution in relation to civil and political rights come within the scope of Convention-based refugee protection'.[46] This meant 'that most Third World refugees [would] remain de facto excluded, as their flight is more often prompted by natural disaster, war, or broadly-based political and economic turmoil than by "persecution", at least as that term is understood in the European context'.[47] Due to that, Hathaway called the

41 Goodwin-Gill and McAdam (n 40) 36 at footnote 110.
42 Astri Suhrke, '*A Crisis Diminished: Refugees in the Developing World*' [1993] 48 International Journal, No 2 (Migrants and Refugees) 215, 217, DOI: 10.2307/40202879. 'The narrowly European orientation of the international refugee regime established in the immediate aftermath of World War II was not seriously challenged until the early 1960s. Then, suddenly, Africa moved to the fore with many nearly simultaneous outflows of population which arose from decolonisation struggles in Algeria (1959ff), Zaire (1960), Rwanda (1963), and Portuguese Africa (circa 1961) as well as the increasingly violent confrontation between north and south in Sudan (circa 1963)'.
43 Davies (n 2) 703.
44 Juss (n 3) 187.
45 UN General Assembly, Protocol Relating to the Status of Refugees, 4 October 1967, No.8791 UNTS 606, 267: Article 1(2) Protocol Relating to the Status of Refugees: '2. For the purpose of the present Protocol, the term "refugee" shall, except as regards the application of paragraph 3 of this article, mean any person within the definition of Article I of the Convention as if the words "As a result of events occurring before 1 January 1951 and..." and the words "...as a result of such events", in article 1 A (2) were omitted'.
46 Hathaway (n 25) 162.
47 Ibid.

reform operated by the 1967 Protocol a 'pyrrhic victory for the less developed world'.[48] For him, the Protocol had not been able to correct the strong Western-centric bias of the Convention and to make it relevant to the evolution of forced migration patterns.[49] It should be added that by maintaining the political character of the definition of a refugee, the Protocol also did not correct the gender bias of the Convention. The type of reform carried out by the 1967 Protocol therefore raised major concerns regarding the fate of the 1951 Convention. Indeed, the failure to provide substantive reform to the refugee definition in turn questioned the capacity of the 1951 Convention to tackle the problem of refugees in the post-cold war world. As such, 'one of the perennial questions of modern-day refugee law is whether the 1951 UN Convention remains applicable to today's global migration crisis'.[50]

The above concerns highlighted, in particular, the restrictive scope of the notion of persecution, assuming that this notion was only intended to correspond to the typical experiences of men in the European post world war context. However, it should be noted that there is nothing in the 1951 Convention indicating that the signatory states chose the notion of persecution in order to restrict their engagement to such situations only. They seemed to refer to the only situations that they were familiar with at the time, but the choice of a vague and broad notion to define refugees leaves the interpretation of persecution quite open and therefore, appears to confer some flexibility to the 1951 Convention. The next section will analyse the developing trends of displacement in order to understand in which context the definition of a refugee needs to be interpreted today.

1.2 A changing geopolitical context

1.2.1 Interpreting the notion of persecution during the cold war polarity: a political understanding of the refugee definition

It seems that the interpretation of the definition of a refugee, and more particularly of the notion of persecution, did not cause particular difficulty until the end of the cold war. Indeed, at that period, refugees escaping from a state belonging to the opposite bloc were automatically granted asylum because the definition of a refugee was mainly used as a political tool against enemy states. As a result, the understanding of the concept of persecution depended simply on the political views of the asylum country. For instance, Widol de Wenden mentioned the practice of the USA, where victims of the Cambodian, Vietnamese or Laotian Communist regimes were systematically granted asylum in the 1970s, simply because those countries were affiliated to the Soviet bloc. Similarly, Cuban

48 Ibid.

49 See discussion on this, in Davies (n 2) 708. Davies expressed the same concerns. More particularly, she noted that the 1967 Protocol did not lift the condition of 'political persecution' which was, according to her, a major impediment for providing protection to 'larger numbers of people fleeing generalised situations of violence and abuse'.

50 Juss (n 3) 197.

refugees were automatically granted asylum by the USA through an open-door policy as an expression of a political stance against Fidel Castro's regime.[51] In this context, American judges did not have any incentive to assess whether the forms of harm claimed by the asylum seekers amounted to persecution.[52]

Other scholars supported the view that, at that time, refugee flows were mainly perceived through the cold war polarity. In this sense, Kennedy stated that persons eligible for international protection were defined 'with political considerations in mind'.[53] Suhrke also highlighted the political nature of forced displacements by stating that, during this period, refugees represented 'a propaganda victory for the other side, which could claim, [...] that these people were voting with their feet'.[54] This mindset prevailed throughout the cold war. In 1980, a debate was launched at the United Nations on the root causes of displacements and unfortunately states again adopted a politically biased view of the situation. Western states generally claimed that the 'mass outflows were caused by totalitarian regimes in the countries of origin which violated human rights' while 'socialist and many developing countries responded by citing colonialism, global economic inequality, and apartheid as the underlying causes of social conflict and related migrant outflows'[55] thus, perpetuating the ideological dichotomy in this period.

Given the strong political use of refugee law during the cold war, the interpretation of the notion of persecution did not raise particular debate amongst jurisdictions. As stated by Hathaway, 'Western states, which initially saw the admission of refugees to be consistent with their more general political goals, found the persecution-based definition to be quite capable of embracing virtually all emigrants from the socialist states of Europe'.[56] Additionally, the types of harms brought forward in refugee claims at that time were relatively similar to the political persecution faced by European refugees when the 1951 Convention was being drafted, thus easily fitting the refugee definition. This situation eventually changed in the 1990s, when the system of political bipolarity collapsed. In a new emerging world governed by multilateralism, political affiliations started having a lesser, or at least a different, impact on the nature of protection afforded to refugees. Moreover, refugee claims started to change in national jurisdictions, bringing to the fore some types of harms that had been disregarded until then, and seeing more women lodging asylum on their own right.

51 Larry Nackerud, Alyson Springer, Christopher Larrison and Alicia Issac, '*The End of the Cuban Contradiction in U.S. Refugee Policy*' [1999] 33 The International Migration Review 176, DOI: 10.2307/2547327.

52 Catherine Withol de Wenden, *La Question Migratoire au XXIe Siècle: Migrants, Réfugiés et Relations Internationales* (2nd edn: Science Po Les Presses, Paris, 2013) 143.

53 David W. Kennedy, '*International Refugee Protection*' [1984] 8 Human Rights Quarterly 1, 3, DOI: http://nrs.harvard.edu/urn-3:HUL.InstRepos:16082842.

54 Suhrke (n 42) 223.

55 Ibid. 219.

56 Hathaway (n 25) 169.

1.2.2 Emerging trends of displacements in the 20th century

Interpreting the notion of persecution in refugee situations that are different than the typical political persecution faced by individuals, and mostly men, in Europe before 1951, progressively became a challenge in the 1990s. Indeed, refugee claims changed with the evolution of international relations at the end of the cold war. The demise of an old world sparked new conflicts in different countries and created new displacement patterns.[57] For instance, Suhrke observed that, in this period, old protracted refugee crises in Asia and Latin America slowly came to an end as 'new flows emerged'.[58] He noted more specifically, that new forms of violence emerged in central Asia and the Caucasus[59] and various conflicts erupted in Africa, such as for instance Somalia.[60] These crises created different types of refugee flows, as larger groups of individuals seemed to be escaping general situations affecting large swaths of population, rather than individual persecution. Further, the extent of these movements was wider than before. Instead of remaining in their own region, as was mostly the case during the cold war,[61] refugees started travelling longer distances due to the 'liberalisation of the economies at the global level, increasing interdependence among nations [and] new infrastructures of transportation'.[62] In that period, 'flows of refugees [...] intensified as their composition [...] diversified and their dynamics [became] more complex'.[63] In particular, the UNHCR observed that globalisation progressively created the 'cultural and technical conditions' for the mobility of refugees.[64] Following the emergence of these new trends, the number of asylum applications surged in developed countries in the early 1990s.[65]

The intensification of refugee movements was also accompanied by a diversification of the nature and causes of displacements. As highlighted by the UNHCR,

57 Alexander Betts and Gil Loescher (eds), *Refugees in International Relations* (Oxford University Press 2011) 32.
58 Suhrke (n 42) 215.
59 Ibid. 216.
60 Ibid. 215.
61 Betts and Loescher (n 57) 48: 'During the Cold War, the proxy conflicts of the 1970s, in which the superpower rivalry between the United States and the USSR was played out in the developing world, led to massive displacement in the Horn of Africa, Southern Africa, Indochina, South Asia, and Central America'.
62 Cedric Audebert and Mohamed Kamel Dorai (eds), *Migration in a Globalised World, New Research Issues and Prospects* (Amsterdam University Press 2010) 7.
63 Ibid. 8.
64 UNHCR, '*The State of the World's Refugees 2006, Human Displacement in the New Millennium*' (Geneva, 2006) 12: https://www.unhcr.org/en-my/publications/sowr/4a4dc1a89/state-worlds-refugees-2006-human-displacement-new-millennium.html.
65 Eduardo Arboleda and Ian Hoy, '*The Convention Refugee Definition in the West: Disharmony of Interpretation and Application*' [1993] 5 International Journal of Refugee Law 66, 67, DOI: https://doi.org/10.1093/ijrl/5.1.66; Andrew I. Schoenholtz, '*The New Refugees and the Old Treaty: Persecutors and Persecuted in the Twenty-First Century*' [2015] 16 Chicago Journal of International Law 81, 86–85 and 88, DOI: https://chicagounbound.uchicago.edu/cjil/vol16/iss1/5; Betts and Loescher (n 57) 42.

recent 'issues which the original delegates [...] never even considered'[66] emerged on the international scene, such as natural disasters, climate change, as well as mixed flows of persons leaving their country.[67] Authors also pointed to the fact that a growing number of individuals were leaving their country for endemic reasons affecting large parts of the population, namely breakdown of economic structures[68] or indiscriminate criminality.[69]

One of the most notable evolutions of refugee claims in the past decades concerns forms of harm perpetrated by non-state actors. Violence perpetrated by non-state agents was traditionally considered to fall within the private sphere and had rarely been considered a basis for asylum prior to this period. However, it became a growing part of the claims of refugees after the end of the cold war.[70] In this context, it was noted that the proportion of women lodging asylum claims due to a fear of harm on account of their gender considerably increased.[71] Women had always been part of displacement flows but little focus was shed on their specific needs and own reasons for departure prior to this period. No statistics could be

66 UNHCR, 'The Refugee Convention at 50', Editorials (Geneva 2001), available at: http://www.unhcr.org/news/editorial/2001/7/3b4c06f0d/refugee-convention-50.html. See also on this, the comments made by Messina, in Claire Messina, '*Refugee Definitions in the Countries of the Commonwealth of Independent States*' in Frances Nicholson and Patrick Twomey (eds) *Refugee Rights and Realities: Evolving International Concepts and Regimes* (Cambridge University Press 1999) 136–150, 136: 'The collapse of the Soviet Union resulted in population displacements of an unprecedented scale and complexity. [...]. The complexity [of refugee flows] is a result of a unique intermingling of pre-existing internal flows turned international [repatriation, labour migration]; of new flows, whose typology is well known to the international community [refugee flows, flows of internally displaced persons, illegal migration, ecological migration, return of demobilised troops]; and of new flows on which little or no international experience exists [return of formerly deported peoples].

67 Erika Feller, 'The Refugee Convention at 60: Still Fit for Its Purpose? Protection Tools for Protection Needs' in Susan Kneebone, Dallal Stevens, Loretta Baldassar (eds) *Refugee Protection and the Role of Law: Conflicting Identities* (Routledge Research in Asylum, Migration and Refugee Law 2015).

68 Alexander Betts, *Survival Migration: Failed Governance and the Crisis of Displacement* (Cornell University Press 2013) 15.

69 UNHCR, 'Guidance Note on Refugee Claims Relating to Victims of Organized Gangs', 31 March 2010, https://www.refworld.org/docid/4bb21fa02.html.

70 Walter Kalin, '*Non-State Agents of Persecution and the Inability of the State to Protect*' [2001] 15 Georgetown Immigration Law Journal 415. According to Kalin: 'the nature of persecution is changing [...]. Although statistics are not available, it is highly likely that the majority of today's refugees are fleeing dangers emanating from non-state agents'.

71 Audebert and Dorai (n 62) 77. Florian Francois Hoepfner, *L'Evolution de la Notion de Réfugié*, Publication de la Fondation Marangopoulos pour les Droits de l'Homme, (Série 18, Paris Pedone, 2014) 314. Hoepfner observed that new types of asylum applications based on sexual orientation started being progressively lodged in European jurisdictions in the mid 1980–90s and became even more significant in recent decades. See also pp. 265–312: Hoepfner noted the emergence of new claims related to harmful traditional practices; 314–332 to domestic violence; and at 333–365 to sexual violence.

found concerning the number of women and girls in the aftermaths of the World War I, as the idea of collecting disaggregated data based on the Age Gender Diversity concept[72] was not even considered at that time. Currently, such exercise is more frequent and women are commonly reported to amount to half of the refugee population,[73] leading authors to speak of a 'feminisation' of migration.[74]

It should however be noted that, even if the number of displaced women globally has increased, this does not mean that it has dramatically changed from the 1960s.[75] The phenomenon of feminisation of migration, including forced displacement, does not in fact only indicate the existence of a larger proportion of women amongst displaced people but it also reflects the changing nature of the claims lodged by women. Indeed, the proportion of women in refugee camps has traditionally been larger than the number of women seeking asylum in urban contexts but this trend is now shifting. In particular, Nilsson explained that:

> The global picture seems to be that women are left behind in refugee camps, while men fight, are imprisoned, killed or flee to the West. (…) According to the United Nations Population Fund (UNFPA) globalization has brought with it a 'feminization of migration', including an increase in the numbers of women seeking asylum independently of their families.

Additionally, there is a change in the approach that the international community has to the refugee women. In particular, it is now acknowledged that women are often placed in situations where they are exposed to gender-related forms of harm either in their country of origin or in the context of displacements, both within their family or alone. Women 'separated from their family members or traditional support mechanisms, or isolated from their communities' have emerged as a new category of individuals who required a particular attention in the delivery aid. For instance, they constitute a specific group deemed to have potential resettlement needs according to UNHCR.[76] The increased awareness of the situation of women and girls led the UN States to dedicate to them a special section of the Global Compact on Refugees, stating that measures should be taken to ensure the empowerment of women and girls in the context of displacements.[77]

72 UN High Commissioner for Refugees (UNHCR), *Age, Gender and Diversity Policy*, 8 June 2011, available at: https://www.refworld.org/docid/4def34f6887.html.

73 UNHCR statistics available on UNHCR webpage: https://www.unhcr.org/en-my/women.html.

74 Eva Nilsson, '*Persecution on Account of One's Gender: Refugee Status or Status Quo?*' [2012] feminists@law, *2*(10) https://journals.kent.ac.uk/index.php/feministsatlaw/article/view/56.

75 Ibid. 2, fn 7.

76 UN High Commissioner for Refugees (UNHCR), *UNHCR Resettlement Handbook, 2011*, July 2011, available at: https://www.refworld.org/docid/4ecb973c2.html.

77 This is showed especially by the presence of women in the recent Global Compact on Refugees, see General Assembly, Official Records, Seventy-third Session, Supplement No. 12 (A/73/12 (Part II)), Report of the United Nations High Commissioner for Refugees, Part II, Global compact on refugees, New York, [2018]75–76 at: https://

In addition to the development of new displacement trends, it should be noted that growing attention to existing forms of harm that were not traditionally considered a reason for asylum took place in a global society, where human rights progressively became a central concern of geopolitical relations.[78] Individuals have started developing a larger sense of rights entitlement, leading to a growing popular discontent in the globalised world and a lesser tolerance to forms of harm that were considered traditional or simply engrained in the society prior to this. According to Streeck, this movement announced the 'return of the repressed'.[79] This larger sense of rights entitlement can be perceived in turn as further contributing to the increasing diversity of refugee claims and the larger focus on refugee women. Whilst the forms of persecution brought forward in asylum applications are not necessarily new per se, they appear to have gained more currency in recent years and to reflect new concerns on the international scene. In this sense, Streeck considered that the world is currently facing an 'interregnum'[80] period, namely 'a period of uncertain duration in which an old order is dying but a new one cannot yet be born'.[81] The old refugee order, based on typical male experiences and when individuals were fleeing repressive state policies on account of their race, religion or political opinion seems to have been gradually replaced by a new order where forced displacements occur at a larger scale, for a broader variety of reasons with a lesser acceptance of harms that were not considered until now a matter of public intervention. More voices are raised to denounce injustice, discriminations, and in particular different forms

www.unhcr.org/gcr/GCR_English.pdf. See also *The World's Biggest Minority? Refugee Women and Girls in the Global Compact on Refugees*. The Forced Migration Research Network, University of New South Wales (Australia), https://www.unhcr.org/59e5bcb77.pdf; 'One way to get a sense of the emphasis on gender in each of the compacts is to look at counts of words or phrases appearing in the texts. At a surface level, women received five mentions in the Migration Compact zero draft and seventeen in the final draft, and in the Refugee Compact women received only thirteen mentions in the zero draft and by the final draft were mentioned twenty-seven times. This indicates that in both domains women were identified specifically, and that attention to their specific experiences and needs grew considerably as a result of the interventions during negotiations'. The authors however lamented that there is no gender analysis of the root causes of the reasons for departure, in Jenna L. Hennebry and Allison J. Petrozziello, *Closing the Gap? Gender and the Global Compacts for Migration and Refugees* [2019] Wiley Online Library: https://doi.org/10.1111/imig.12640.

78 Scott Sheeran and Sir Nigel Rodley, *Routledge Handbook of International Human Rights Law* (Taylor and Francis 2014) 18: 'Over time, human rights have become a recognised code of conduct, making their way into a majority of contemporary constitutions and providing a standard for relations between the state and the citizen. In the 1990s, human rights were advancing to the centre of international relations'.

79 Wolfgang Streeck, '*The Return of the Repressed*', [2017] 104 New Left Review 5, DOI: https://newleftreview.org/issues/II104/articles/wolfgang-streeck-the-return-of-the-repressed.

80 As per the words of Gramsci in Streeck, ibid.

81 Ibid. 20.

of violence exercised against women who are constituting a larger and more visible part of the refugee population. The needs and priorities of refugees are, therefore changing and new vulnerabilities that were not anticipated by the drafters of the Convention are being now brought to light. This situation questions considerably the extent to which the notion of persecution could adapt to the new priorities of refugees and in particular to refugee women.

1.3 Interpretive challenges

1.3.1 The notion of persecution: a malleable notion?

The increased variety of refugee claims, including amongst other major concerns, the 'feminisation' of displacements and the changing context of the application of the 1951 Convention raise concerns as to whether or not the definition of a refugee can adapt to the new circumstances of refugees. In order to understand whether the notion of persecution could be considered a malleable notion, it should first be pointed out that the plenipotentiaries have not provided any explicit limitations to this notion. Not only is there no definition of persecution in the 1951 Convention, but there is also barely any guidance in the *travaux preparatoires* of the Convention.[82] Different views have been expressed as to the reasons for this lack of guidance.[83] In particular, McAdam argued that the political dimension of the notion of persecution was so clear to the plenipotentiaries that they did not feel the need to introduce a definition.[84] Her view aligned with Betts who stated that the drafters of the 1951 Convention 'did not anticipate that its obligations would be spread to the rest of the world'.[85] Although Betts acknowledged that the refugee definition was meant to have a certain flexibility, he believes that the plenipotentiaries did not foresee extensive interpretations of the Convention outside the European context, let alone the male dominated context. For him, their choice of persecution as a central element of the definition has, in fact, been a bar to extensive applications of the 1951 Convention.[86] In contrast with these authors, other commentators considered that, from the outset, even though the plenipotentiaries had a certain meaning in mind, they were aware of their inability to anticipate the diverse forms that persecution might take in the future and, therefore, they wanted to make persecution a flexible notion that could evolve depending on the changing conditions and priorities of refugees.

82 Steinbock (n 23) 809. See also Paul Weis, *The Refugee Convention, 1951. The Travaux Préparatoires Analysed with a Commentary by the Late Dr Paul Weis* (Cambridge University Press 1995) 8.
83 UNHCR, '*Note on The International Protection of Refugees: Interpreting Article 1 of the 1951 Convention Relating to the Status of Refugees*' [2001] 20 Refugee Survey Quarterly 1, 16: https://www.refworld.org/docid/3b20a3914.html.
84 McAdam (n 29).
85 Alexander Betts, *Survival Migration* (Cornell University Press, 2013) 13.
86 Ibid.

For instance, Grahl-Madsen argued that the drafters of the Convention did not define persecution because they wanted ‘to introduce a flexible concept which might be applied to circumstances as they might arise’. For him, it looked like the plenipotentiaries had ‘capitulated before the inventiveness of humanity to think up new ways of persecuting fellow men’.[87] Of note however, is that he referred again to the generic term ‘men’, rather than a more gender-neutral terminology. In any event, his views on the malleability of the notion of persecution were also shared by Chimni who stated that the plenipotentiaries ‘deliberately left the meaning of persecution undefined as it was an impossible task to enumerate in advance the myriad forms it might assume’.[88] Similarly, Chetail considered that the plenipotentiaries wanted to introduce a ‘concept flexible enough to encapsulate any possible future forms of mistreatment’.[89] Chetail further argued that the drafters of the Convention simply wanted to relinquish the meaning of persecution ‘to the subsequent interpretation of each state party’.[90] Hathaway's position on this issue is a little bit more ambiguous. He contended in 1990 that the notion of persecution had a strong political imprint in the mind of the plenipotentiaries and did not detect any intention on their part to develop a flexible concept. However, he adopted a more nuanced view in his seminal book, *The Law of Refugee Status* (LORS) in 1991 (and subsequent editions), as he explicitly stated that the drafters did not define persecution because they considered that it was impossible to enumerate ‘in advance all of the forms of maltreatment that might legitimately entitle persons to benefit from international protection’.[91] Whilst this does not directly contradict his earlier contention, it nonetheless puts a greater emphasis on the flexible character of the notion as opposed to its political character.

In an attempt to reconcile different views, the UNHCR drafted a note on the interpretation of Article 1 of the 1951 Convention, observing that ‘whatever the reasons, the fact that the Convention does not legally define persecution is a strong indication that, on the basis of the experience of the past, the drafters intended that all future types of persecution should be encompassed by the

87 Atle Grahl-Madsen, *The Status of Refugees in International Law* (Leyden, A. W. Sijthoff, vol. I, 1966) 193.

88 B. S. Chimni, *International Refugee Law: a Reader* (2nd edn, Sage Publication 2002) 4.

89 Vincent Chetail, ‘*Are Refugee Rights Human Rights? An Unorthodox Questioning of the Relations between Refugee Law and Human Rights Law*’ in Ruth Rubio-Marín (eds), *Human Rights and Immigration*, (Oxford University Press 2014) 19–72, 26. On the notion of flexibility, Lambert also considered that the ‘drafters of the Refugee Convention opted for an open-ended and flexible approach to the concept of persecution’ in Helene Lambert, ‘*The conceptualisation of “persecution” by the House of Lords: Horvath v. Secretary of State for the Home Department*’ [2001] 13 International Journal of Refugee Law 16, 18, DOI: https://papers.ssrn.com/sol3/papers.cfm?abstract_id=1335237.

90 Ibid. 26.

91 James Hathaway and Michelle Foster, *The Law of Refugee Status* (2nd edn; Cambridge University Press 2014) 82.

term'.[92] Whether these types of persecution were meant to relate to forms of harm perpetrated by oppressive states is unclear. In any case, the different positions on the reasons for the absence of a definition are both reconcilable with the fact that such omission allows for the term to be interpreted in an evolutionary manner. This view appears now to be the dominant one in national courts.[93] Authors also concurred with this approach as for instance, McAdam argued that the 1951 Convention proved to have an 'enduring relevance'.[94] To Sztucki, although the Convention was a 'cold war product',[95] 'in the course of time it has lost its primarily cold war and Eurocentric character'.[96] He considered that even though the notion of persecution emerged in a specific context, it remains open to 'a wide range of interpretation'.[97] Supporting this view, Carlier observed that the 'Convention does not suffer from any legal or conceptual weakness'[98] per se and can adapt to various circumstances. He believed that the major obstacle to an evolutionary understanding of the Convention is the political reluctance of interpretive agents rather than the refugee definition itself.[99] In line with these views, Durieux noted that the refugee definition has conferred a certain dynamism to the 1951 Convention, which explains the 'remarkable resilience of a norm that was adopted over 60 years ago'.[100] More specifically, Zetter considered that the malleability of the refugee definition has been due, in part, to the element of persecution which proved to be an evolutionary notion.[101] This view rejoins the one of Shoenholtz who also pointed out that the refugee definition 'has proven adaptable to the

92 UNHCR (n 83).

93 *Ram v. Minister for Immigration and Ethnic Affairs and the Refugee Review Tribunal*, (1995) 130 ALR 314 FCA (27 June 1995) at [7]: 'It seems to me that those who framed the provision wisely chose broad expressions, which it is not the court's task to constrict'. A similar view is expressed in: *Hassan Adan and Others v. Secretary of State for the Home Department*, [1997] 2All ER 723, CA, United Kingdom: Court of Appeal (England and Wales), 13 February 1997; *Sepet v Secretary of State for the Home Department*, UKHL 15 [2003] 1 WLR 856 United Kingdom: House of Lords, 20 March 2003.

94 Jane McAdam, '*The Enduring Relevance of the 1951 Refugee Convention*' [2017] 29 International Journal of Refugee Law 1, DOI: https://doi.org/10.1093/ijrl/eex017.

95 Jerzy Sztucki, '*"Who is a Refugee?" The Convention Definition: Universal or Obsolete?*' in Frances Nicholson and Patrick Twomey (eds) *Refugee Rights and Realities: Evolving International Concepts and Regimes* (Cambridge University Press 1999) 55–84, 56.

96 Ibid.

97 Ibid. 58.

98 Jean-Yves Carlier, '*The Geneva refugee definition and the "theory of the three scales"*' in Frances Nicholson and Patrick Twomey (eds) *Refugee Rights and Realities: Evolving International Concepts and Regimes* (Cambridge University Press 1999) 37–54 40.

99 Carlier, ibid. 40.

100 Durieux (n 1) 149.

101 Roger Zetter, '*Labelling Refugees: Forming and Transforming a Bureaucratic Identity*' [1991] 4 Journal of Refugee Studies 39, 40, DOI: https://doi.org/10.1093/jrs/4.1.39: 'there are severe conceptual difficulties in establishing a normative meaning to a label which is as malleable and dynamic as refugee. It is contingent upon notions of persecution, and sovereignty about which there is little consensus'.

changing nature of persecution' nowadays.[102] Hathaway finally stated in a more recent paper, that the refugee definition has been 'wonderfully flexible, identifying new groups of fundamentally disenfranchised persons unable to benefit from human rights protection in their own countries'.[103] He noted that, amongst other term, the persecution limb was particularly malleable.

It is true that, overall, the refugee definition and more particularly the notion of persecution have proven to be rather open to interpretation. Considering that the plenipotentiaries did not define persecution in the hope that it could be used in a flexible manner, rather than because the meaning of persecution was uncontroversial, seems to be more in line with the Final Act's recommendation that the Convention should be interpreted beyond the confines of its initial limitations. As such, a few decades after the entry into force of the 1967 Protocol, a relatively positive assessment can be made in contrast with the pessimistic views initially expressed by early authors on the biased nature of the refugee definition and the notion of persecution. It appears, indeed, that the 1951 Convention has retained a certain relevance nowadays and that the notion of persecution could be applied in an evolutionary manner, adapting itself, to a certain extent, to various circumstances of refugees. The extent to which this is the case remains however uncertain.

1.3.2 A need for consistent interpretations of the notion of persecution?

The extent to which the notion of persecution is flexible and can adapt to the various types of claims as they arise in the 21st century is indeed unclear. For Durieux, and as per the words used by Shacknove, it is not 'easy to capture what is "essential and universal about refugeehood"'[104] due to the indeterminacy of its elements. As a result, a risk of inconsistent approaches is significant. In this context, major disparities exist as to the way the notion of persecution is applied globally. Indeed, some countries have adopted very restrictive interpretations of the refugee definition[105] whilst others have relied on more extensive views, thus creating major disparities in the asylum systems.[106] Such differences are problematic as it could be assumed that the notion of persecution, although flexible, was also intended to be interpreted in a fairly consistent manner by state parties.

As previously noted, the notion of asylum was considered for a long period of time, to constitute a right of states, thus allowing for inconsistent approaches, depending on states' political interests. However, the development of a generic definition of a refugee in an international treaty, binding on all the signatory parties, indicates the necessity of applying the protection standards enshrined in this

102 Schoenholtz (n 65) 84.
103 James C. Hathaway, '*A global solution to a global refugee crisis*', Open Democracy, 29 February 2016, available at https://www.opendemocracy.net/openglobalrights/james-c-hathaway/global-solution-to-global-refugee-crisis.
104 Shacknove quoted in Durieux (n 1) 149.
105 Schoenholtz (n 65) 88.
106 Ibid. 121.

instrument in a more uniform manner. The fact that states treated displacement as a regional and later as an international issue indicated a shift in the understanding of the concept of asylum. Rather than a national prerogative, asylum had to become a tool of cooperation amongst recipient countries.[107] Additionally, the introduction of a malleable notion without any guidance of interpretation suggests that the signatory parties had intended to create an effective regime of protection for individuals facing persecution, rather than only restricting their political engagement based on their national priorities. If this was the case, assumption could be made that a narrower term or definition would have been introduced to avoid extended applications of the Convention. As a result, it can be considered that important inconsistencies would undermine the general system of protection put in place in 1951. This could create legal uncertainty for asylum seekers, and therefore provide incentives for 'asylum shopping'.[108] Furthermore, it bears the risk of directing refugee flows to the most protective countries, which could further encourage a 'race to the bottom'[109] whereby receiving states would end up competing with each other to apply restrictive standards of interpretation and to limit their engagement. As a result, this situation would create a largely imbalanced regime of assistance at the global level and further undermine the ability of some states to receive refugees. State parties to the 1951 Convention should therefore implement its provisions in a rather consistent manner, based on global standards of interpretation. As noted above, the notion of persecution is however not defined in international refugee law. As an alternative, national courts have at times relied on dictionary definitions but these approaches have generally been rejected for being too diverse depending on the language of the definition.[110] It is therefore necessary to search for guidance in other places.

1.3.3 Basis of definition

i. Persecution akin to the non-refoulement principle?

The non-refoulement principle defined in Article 33 of the 1951 Convention has been advanced as a starting point for defining persecution. In particular, some

107 As explicitly formulated in recital 4 of the 1951 Convention. On this see also Claire Inder, '*The Origins of "Burden Sharing" in the Contemporary Refugee Protection Regime*' [2017] 29 International Journal of Refugee Law 523, DOI: https://doi.org/10.1093/ijrl/eex047. Inder argued that the function of a preamble, although not binding, is to highlight the aim and purpose of the treaty, thus contending that the 1951 Convention has a cooperative purpose.

108 UNHCR, 'The State of the World's Refugees', 1996, available at: http://www.unhcr.org/3eb7ba414.pdf, 8.

109 Naomi Hart, '*Complementary Protection and Transjudicial Dialogue: Global Best Practice or Race to the Bottom?*' [2016] 28 International Journal of Refugee Law 171, DOI: https://doi.org/10.1093/ijrl/eew032.

110 Hugo Storey, 'Persecution: Towards a Working Definition' in Vincent Chetail and Celine Bauloz (eds), *Research Handbook on Migration and International Law* (Edward Elgar Publishing 2013) 459, Carlier (n 98) 44.

authors have proposed to search for the definition of persecution within the provisions of the 1951 Convention.[111] As such, reference was made to the dispositions of article 33 of the Convention pointing to the principle of non-refoulement of refugees. This article states that 'no contracting state shall expel or return ("*refouler*") a refugee in any manner whatsoever to the frontiers of territories where his life or freedom would be threatened on account of his race, religion, nationality, membership of a particular social group or political opinion.' As such, persecution has been understood by authors as a 'threat to life or freedom.'[112] These approaches have been called 'hermeneutical' or systematic.[113] Seemingly encouraging this view, a number of conclusions of the Executive Committee (Excom) of the UNHCR also assimilate the principle of non-refoulement with the concept of persecution.[114] These views, however, raise questions as to the extent of the notion of persecution and whether it should only be interpreted as a threat to life and freedom. As noted by Storey, should a 'threat to life and freedom' be understood more narrowly than the notion of persecution, then there would be a certain anomaly to the 1951 Convention, namely that some refugees could be deported to countries where they are at risk of persecution other than a threat to life and freedom.[115] Given these concerns, the dominant opinion is that the concept of 'threat to life and freedom' can be used as a departure point for interpreting persecution, but it would be too restrictive to confine the notion to Article 33. Some authors considered that the provisions of this article constitute 'core elements' of persecution,[116] stating however that persecution had a broader meaning than this. In the words of Goodwin-Gill, persecution is ultimately a matter of 'degree and proportion'.[117] Similarly, Hathaway argued that persecution is premised on the more general notion of 'serious harm' and was not meant to be confined to 'consequences of life or death proportions'.[118] Furthermore confining persecution to threats to life and freedom would necessarily restrict the notion of persecution to violations of civil and political rights and disregard important aspects of harms that have been raised in national jurisdictions in the recent years as above noted. It would render the refugee definition obsolete and inadequate to the current geopolitical context, which is in tension with what a number of

111 Storey (n 110) 464.
112 Ibid.
113 Ibid.
114 Excom Conclusion No. 6 (XXVIII) – 1977: 'The Executive Committee [...] (c) Reaffirms the fundamental importance of the observance of the principle of non-refoulement—both at the border and within the territory of a State of persons who may be subjected to persecution if returned to their country of origin irrespective of whether or not they have been formally recognized as refugees'. Excom Conclusion No. 15 (XXX)—1979: '(b) Action whereby a refugee is obliged to return or is sent to a country where he has reason to fear persecution constitutes a grave violation of the recognized principle of non-refoulement'.
115 Storey (n 110) 465.
116 McAdam (n 29) 683; Goodwin-Gill and McAdam (n 40) 92.
117 Goodwin-Gill and McAdam, ibid. 92.
118 Hathaway and Foster (n 91) 183.

authors have argued, namely that persecution should be understood as a malleable and evolutionary notion.

This approach is in line with the UNHCR Handbook, which stated that a threat to life and freedom on account of a Convention ground is always persecution but that persecution should be more than that. In addition to the principles of Article 33, the UNHCR Handbook goes on to enumerate other forms of restrictions that could warrant refugee status. In a later document, the UNHCR also observed that according to the *travaux preparatoires*, the principle of non-refoulement was meant to be different than the criteria laid down by the refugee definition. According to the Refugee Agency:

> the words 'where his life or freedom would be threatened [...]' were not intended to lay down a stricter criterion than the words 'well-founded fear of' persecution figuring in the definition of the term 'refugee' in Article 1 A (2). The different wording was introduced for another reason, namely to make it clear that the principle of non-refoulement applies not only in respect of the country of origin but to any country where a person has reason to fear persecution.[119]

It appears indeed that the dispositions of Article 33 concern procedural issues rather than eligibility criteria to refugee status. Whilst, as stated by the UNHCR, these terms can indeed be considered relevant to designate forms of harm that amount to persecution, the notion of persecution ought to be interpreted in a manner that goes beyond Article 33.

ii. The definition of persecution in international criminal law

The notion of persecution has also been widely discussed in the jurisprudence of various international tribunals[120] in the context of the commission of war crimes. An authoritative definition of persecution was eventually codified in the 1998 Statute of the International Criminal Court.[121] According to this statute, persecution consists in 'the intentional and severe deprivation of fundamental rights contrary to international law by reason of the identity of the group or collectivity'.[122] However, in this definition, an act of persecution has to be perpetrated in connection with a crime against humanity, which appears to constitute a rather

119 UNHCR, '*Note on Non-Refoulement*' (Submitted by the High Commissioner) EC/SCP/2, 23 August 1977, available at: http://www.unhcr.org/excom/scip/3ae68ccd10/note-non-refoulement-submitted-high-commissioner.html.

120 Inter alia, *Prosecutor v. Timohir Blaskic* Case IT-95–14-A, 29 Jul. 2004, Appeals Chamber, para. 131–5; *Prosecutor v. Dario Kordic and Mario Cerkez*, Case IT-95–14/2-A, 17. Dec 2004, Appeals Chamber paras. 105–9; mentioned in Goodwin-Gill and McAdam (n 40) 85.

121 UN General Assembly, Rome Statute of the International Criminal Court (last amended 2010), 17 July 1998, ISBN No. 92-9227-227-6 (Rome Statute).

122 Article 7 (g) of the Rome Statute.

strict approach.[123] Indeed, the definition of persecution in the context of the Rome Statute is meant to apply to the prosecution of individuals responsible for international crimes only. As such, it contrasts with the protection purpose of the 1951 Convention. On this point, Goodwin-Gill noted that the value of this definition is 'necessarily limited by its criminal context'[124] and therefore, transposing this definition into refugee law might not be adequate. This observation is in line with Foster's contention that 'since different aims and policy objectives inform different areas of the law, there is a danger in transplanting approaches developed in an area with one set of objectives into a field that has quite different policy aims'.[125] In this sense, particular tensions between the criminal law and refugee law can be highlighted as the notion of persecution in both fields does not 'denote the same meaning'.[126] The particularity of refugee law is that the victims should not 'be required to prove their persecutor's intent in order to establish refugee status.'[127] This element is starkly opposed to the requirement of a criminal intent in international criminal law and, therefore, makes persecution in international refugee law a discrete concept.

However, some authors stressed the fact that victims of persecution under the Rome Statute could qualify as refugees under the 1951 Convention, in particular in view of the severity of the harm suffered. As such, they suggested the Rome Statute be used as a departure point to define persecution in international refugee law. They noted that 'it is possible to deduce from the various crimes contained in the statute the conclusion that their victims are often refugees, which would indicate the breadth of the notion of persecution in the refugee law context'.[128] It can be concluded that whilst the Rome Statute might provide an indication of what types of harm amount to persecution in the context of the refugee definition, it should not be used to restrict the notion. This view has not been disputed, and, in general, the Rome Statute has not been extensively relied upon in domestic jurisdictions to interpret the notion of persecution for the purpose of examining eligibility to refugee status.

In light of the foregoing, no comprehensive guidance can be found in international law for interpreting the notion of persecution, although some insight can be drawn from Article 33 of the 1951 Convention and Article 7 of the Rome Statute. However, both the literature and the UNHCR tend to converge on this point, by considering that persecution has a wider ambit than the above definitions.

123 Goodwin-Gill and McAdam (n 40) 96.
124 Ibid. 95.
125 Michelle Foster, *International Refugee Law and Socio-Economic Rights: Refuge from Deprivation*(Cambridge University Press 2007) 57.
126 Lyal S. Sunga, *The Emerging System of International Criminal Law* (Kluwer Law International 1997) 149.
127 Karen Musalo, '*Irreconcilable Differences? Divorcing Refugee Protections from Human Rights Norms*' [1994] 15 Michigan Journal of International Law 1179, 1200, DOI: https://repository.law.umich.edu/mjil/vol15/iss4/3.
128 UNHCR, '*Refugee Protection in International Law*' edited by Erika Feller, Volker Türk and Frances Nicholson, 1 January 2003, 38, available at http://www.unhcr.org/419c73174.html.

Without clear definition in international law, interpreting the notion of persecution in the 21st century therefore raises more ambiguity than in the politically polarised world of the cold war. A transition from a political application of the notion of persecution towards a more judicialised interpretation in a changing geopolitical context is therefore needed. This transition has gradually taken place thanks to the development of jurisprudential trends that have provided some relevant guidance to define persecution and that have been encouraged by the work of scholars in this field. Nonetheless, in light of new issues that have now become major problems at the global level, interpreting the notion of persecution has remained increasingly contentious.

1.4 Concluding remarks

The present chapter has demonstrated that the notion of persecution emerged in a specific historical and geopolitical context and was meant to meet the needs of individuals who had initially fled repressive regimes in Europe. Additionally, it was mostly based on a model that essential fit men's experiences. In spite of this political imprint and gender bias, the absence of a definition has conferred a flexible character to the notion, making the 1951 Convention adaptable to new circumstances of refugees as they arise and open to different interpretations. During the cold war period, the interpretation of persecution raised little concern in domestic jurisdictions but, after the collapse of the Soviet Union and the end of the global polarity between two opposing blocs, the new geopolitical dynamics brought inexorable changes on to the international scene. In particular, refugee movements started to diversify, and new trends of displacements gradually started to emerge and shed more light on the situation of refugee women, and question the traditional understanding of the notion of persecution. As a result, a significant risk of inconsistent and inadequate interpretations of the notion emerged with a risk to provide limited protection to women seeking asylum. Therefore, an approach that is sufficiently flexible but also relatively consistent amongst states is now needed and some guidance is necessary in order to avoid inconsistent and restrictive understandings of the 1951 Convention.

The extent to which the notion of persecution can adapt to new forms of harm, including harm perpetrated by non-state agents, remains unclear and has been debated in the literature. To solve these issues, scholars have proposed interpretive models. The dominant one calls for an approach specifically based on basic human rights, arguing that this would foster more consistency amongst and within jurisdictions and allow for an evolutionary approach that is more suitable to the current needs and priorities of refugees, including women refugees. The potentials and limitations of this model will be evaluated in the following chapter.

2 Developing an interpretive framework for interpreting the notion of persecution: an assessment of the basic human rights interpretive model

Given the lack of definition of persecution in international refugee law, a principled approach for interpreting the notion seems needed. According to the dominant view, the notion of persecution should be interpreted in light of basic human rights. One of the major proponents of the basic human rights approach is James Hathaway[1] who developed his proposal in the *Law of Refugee Status* (LORS). Given that his approach has gained major traction in the literature and the jurisprudence, particular attention will be paid to it in this chapter. It will be wondered whether the basic human rights narrative is an adequate one, both in terms of its legitimacy and utility and whether it can fit the experiences of refugee women.

The present chapter will first evaluate the legal justifications for using basic human rights as interpretive benchmarks and whether such justifications allow for an evolutionary understanding of the notion of persecution as hoped by numerous authors (Section 2.1). Further to this, the modalities of the basic human rights framework will be closely analysed in order to assess its practical scope. These modalities include the quantitative and qualitative aspects of the notion of persecution (Section 2.2) as well as the role of the surrogacy principle in interpreting the notion (Section 2.3). In Section 2.4), the application of this model in the jurisprudence of some selected countries will be evaluated. It will be argued that a basic human rights framework does not solve the problem of inconsistent approaches and creates the risk of encouraging rather restrictive interpretations of the notion of persecution, depending on the different parameters relied upon by decision makers.

2.1 Legal and theoretical justifications for referring to human rights as interpretive benchmarks

The nature of the 1951 Convention has been debated amongst authors. Hathaway and the proponents of the human rights approach consider that refugee law and international human rights are closely linked and that refugee law should be

1 James Hathaway and Michelle Foster, *The Law of Refugee Status* (2nd edn; Cambridge University Press 2014). The first edition of the book, drafted by Hathaway himself, dates back to 1991.

interpreted in light of human rights (2.1.1). In contrast with these views, some commentators have contended that refugee law and human rights law are disconnected and that refugee law should be understood as establishing a self-contained regime (2.1.2). Others have pointed out that neither perspective is valid, but that the notion of persecution should nonetheless be interpreted in light of human rights because it simply has become the orthodoxy in refugee law (2.1.3). These different positions will be assessed hereunder in order to determine whether human rights should have a role to play in interpreting the Convention and to what extent.

2.1.1 Teleological approach to refugee law: the 1951 Convention as a human rights instrument?

According to Hathaway, objective principles need to be relied upon in order to interpret the notion of persecution in a clear, consistent and predictable manner. For him, interpretive guidance should be sought in the rules of treaty interpretation set out in the 1969 Vienna Convention on the Law of Treaties (VCLT).[2] In particular, he noted that, according to Article 31 (a) of the VCLT, treaties should be interpreted in good faith, taking into account the context, object and purpose of the treaty. To this end, he referred to the Preamble to the 1951 Convention[3] and pointed out that the first two paragraphs clearly mention the UN Charter, the Universal Declaration of Human Rights (UDHR), and the concept of 'fundamental rights and freedoms'.[4] This led him to conclude that the Preamble grounds the 1951 Convention on a human rights context, making the Convention a tool for human rights protection. As such, he believes that human rights standards should be used as benchmarks for interpreting the notion of persecution.

The view that human rights constitute the 'background'[5] against which persecution should be interpreted is not new. After the drafting of the 1951 Convention,[6] some authors had expressed the idea that international human rights were valuable references for informing the purpose of the 1951 Convention. For instance, in 1953, Vernant highlighted the necessity of interpreting the notion of persecution in the most objective manner possible, through the human rights principles existing at that time in the UDHR. He defined the notion of persecution as 'severe measures and sanctions of an arbitrary nature, incompatible with the principles set forth in the "Universal Declaration of Human Rights"'.[7] Although Vernant considered that human rights standards could constitute interpretive benchmarks, he barely gave any doctrinal justification for this and did not

2 United Nations, *Vienna Convention on the Law of Treaties*, 23 May 1969, UNTS, vol. 1155, p. 331. See also Hathaway and Foster (n 1) 5–6. Footnote 23: According to Hathaway, the rules of treaty interpretation set out in the VCLT codify customary law and therefore are applicable to previous treaties.
3 Hathaway and Foster (n 1) 193.
4 Ibid. 193–194.
5 Ibid. 193.
6 The first edition of the LORS dated from 1991.
7 Jacques Vernant, *The Refugee in the Post-War World* (Yale University Press 1953) 8.

further elaborate on the exact role of human rights in informing the meaning of persecution. For him, the UDHR simply constituted 'a code of honor'[8] that could provide normative guidance. He also considered that there were limitations to this framework because the UDHR standards were drafted in general terms.[9] Therefore, he contended that more specific principles were needed to guide the interpretation of the notion of persecution but he did not provide more insight as to the nature of such guidance.

In 1983, Goodwin-Gill also proposed to rely on human rights principles in order to interpret the notion of persecution.[10] However, like Vernant, he did not extensively explain the theoretical roots for choosing this mode of interpretation. It was only in 1991 that Hathaway filled this doctrinal gap when he 'systematised'[11] the existence of an interpretive human rights framework by reference to the rules of treaty interpretations and the major role of the Preamble in setting the object and purpose of the Convention. Similar to his approach, other authors referred to the VCLT to argue that the interpretation of the refugee definition should be consistent with the object and purpose of the Convention for which guidance is to be found in the human rights language of the Preamble.[12] For instance, Foster considered that the Convention was imbued with 'the developing body of international human rights law',[13] which reinforced the conclusion that human rights constituted relevant referential standards for interpreting the refugee definition. This view was further shared by Carlier who stated that the refugee definition should be interpreted 'teleologically'[14] in light of the principle that 'human beings shall enjoy fundamental rights and freedoms without discrimination'[15] as enshrined in the first recital of the Preamble.[16] Parrish also contended that, according to the Preamble, the 1951 Convention was established with 'primary consideration of the UDHR'. For him, these references were justified by the fact that the UDHR had 'been almost universally accepted and repeatedly affirmed' and that 'no state can legitimately argue that its provisions are not valid as, at the very least, aspirations and ideals for its own citizens'.[17]

8 Ibid.
9 Ibid.
10 Guy S. Goodwin-Gill, *The Refugee in International Law* (Oxford University Press 1983) 38–46.
11 Vincent Chetail, '*Are Refugee Rights Human Rights? An Unorthodox Questioning of the Relations between Refugee Law and Human Rights Law*' in Ruth Rubio-Marín (eds), *Human Rights and Immigration*, (Oxford University Press 2014) 26.
12 Michelle Foster, *International Refugee Law and Socio-Economic Rights: Refuge from Deprivation*(Cambridge University Press 2007) 42.
13 Ibid. 49.
14 Jean-Yves Carlier, '*The Geneva refugee definition and the "theory of the three scales"*' in Frances Nicholson and Patrick Twomey (eds) *Refugee Rights and Realities: Evolving International Concepts and Regimes* (Cambridge University Press 1999) 38.
15 Ibid.
16 Ibid. 39.
17 M. J. Parrish, '*Redefining the Refugee: The Universal Declaration of Human Rights as a Basis for Refugee Protection*' [2000] 22 Cardozo Law Review 223, 258. At p. 259, Parrish even proposed a definition of a refugee based on the UDHR: For him refugees

For many of these authors, the view that the notion of persecution should be informed by the body of international human rights also justified the fact that the Convention should be understood in an evolutionary manner, taking into account all the subsequent human rights treaties that have been adopted since 1951 to complement the Refugee Convention.[18] Indeed, international human rights treaties have multiplied after World War I, thus bringing to the fore new types of rights and extending the realm of individual entitlements. Interpreting the 1951 Convention, and more particularly the notion of persecution in references to such norms, implies that an evolutionary understanding of this term, in line with the development of human rights law, should be adopted. International human rights have proved to be an evolving field of law, which confers significant flexibility to the notion of persecution, which in turn is consistent with the view that the plenipotentiaries wanted to introduce a concept that was capable of adapting to the circumstances of refugees.

As the human rights framework of interpretation gained more traction among scholars, some authors in fact considered that there were more than mere teleological links between refugee and human rights protection. They argued that refugee law was a subset of international human rights law, or in other words, an 'early human right treaty'.[19] The 1951 Convention has even been deemed a 'specialist human rights treaty',[20] acting as a form of '*lex specialis*'.[21]

Whilst a human rights narrative appears to provide tangible benchmarks for interpreting the notion of persecution, it should be noted that the above authors referred to different types of human rights standards, thus demonstrating a lack of consensus on which particular human rights norms should be referred to. Some scholars simply refer to the UDHR, others talk about 'fundamental rights and freedoms' and some others mention human rights, more generally as a concept. To clarify exactly which human rights norms are the most relevant for interpreting the 1951 Convention, different proposals have been made by scholars. Before analysing more thoroughly these views, the position of other authors, opposing the primacy of human rights in interpreting the Convention, will be considered below in order to define more precisely the contours of the interpretive debate.

are individuals who have left their country 'because of persecution or a well-founded fear of persecution on account of a violation of the principles embodied in the Universal Declaration of Human Rights'. Deborah E. Anker, '*Refugee Law, Gender, and the Human Rights Paradigm*' [2002] 15 Harvard Human Rights Journal 133, 134. DOI: http://nrs.harvard.edu/urn-3:HUL.InstRepos:11357476, Anker supported the view that refugee law and human rights were closely linked as she noted that 'refugee law grants protection to a subset of persons who have fled human rights abuses' and it should be therefore interpreted in human rights terms.

18 Tom Clark and François Crépeau, '*Mainstreaming Refugees. The 1951 Convention and International Human Rights Law*' [1999] 17 Netherlands Quarterly of Human Rights 389, 391, DOI: https://papers.ssrn.com/sol3/papers.cfm?abstract_id=1586498.

19 Ibid. 392.

20 Jane McAdam, *Complementary Protection in International Refugee Law* (2nd edn, Oxford University Press, 2011) 209.

21 Ibid. 209

2.1.2 International refugee law as a self-contained regime?

The view that the 1951 Convention has a human rights background has not been shared by all authors. Some commentators considered that refugee law and human rights law are actually disconnected and that the 1951 Convention has established a self-contained regime.[22] As such its object and purpose should not be understood in light of its preamble, but through direct reference to the plain text. For instance, Steinbock rejected the human rights interpretive method by contending that according to the VCLT, the notion of persecution should not be interpreted in light of basic human rights. For him, 'the objects and purposes [of a treaty] must be grounded in the terms of the treaty itself'.[23] He stated that the 1951 Convention does not have the same purpose as other human rights treaties because it provides for a limited regime of protection. He pointed out that, according to the refugee definition, only individuals facing persecution for some specific reasons should be protected, which contrasts with the broader philosophy of human rights. As a result, Steinbock considered that interpreting persecution in light of human rights would contravene the meaning of the text and, in particular disregard the limitations established by the five Convention grounds.[24] He contended that a more restrictive approach should be applied, and that only a minimal set of rights should be referred to.[25] Some other authors concurred with this view, rejecting the human rights character of the 1951 Convention.[26] It was for instance contended that human rights simply do not align with the inherent limitations of refugee law whereby sovereign states are able to impose limitations on entry and on the rights afforded to refugees within their territory. In the words of one author, refugee protection is 'instigated more by issues of state security than humanitarian concerns.'[27]

Recently, Cantor also argued that nothing in the preamble of the 1951 Convention suggests that the purpose and object of the Convention are consistent with international human rights law. For him, the Preamble 'offers a meagre basis on which to ground a human rights-based interpretation of Article 1A(2)'.[28] He

22 Patricia Tuitt, '*Human rights and refugees*' [1997] 1 The International Journal of Human Rights 66, 69, DOI: https://doi.org/10.1080/13642989708406667, Tuitt highlighted the 'refugee law's reluctance to embrace human rights norms'. She did not address the legal grounds for rejecting the human rights narrative but she rather emphasised the practical concerns raised by this narrative to conclude that it did not constitute an adequate mode of interpretation.

23 Daniel J. Steinbock, '*Interpreting the Refugee Definition*' [1998] 45 UCLA Law Review 733, 772.

24 Ibid. 780.

25 Ibid. 783.

26 Tuitt (n 22); Emma Haddad, '*Refugee protection: a clash of values*' [2003] 1 The International Journal of Human Rights 1, DOI: https://doi.org/10.1080/13642980310001726106.

27 Haddad, ibid. 14.

28 James Cantor, '*Defining Refugees: Persecution, Surrogacy and the Human Rights Paradigm*' in Human Rights and the Refugee Definition Comparative Legal Practice and Theory (Brill Nijhoff 2016) 349–395, 374.

noted that, apart from the first two paragraphs, the Preamble does not adopt a strong human rights narrative.[29] Therefore, he questioned the weight that has been given to the first two paragraphs while the rest of the Preamble seems to have been disregarded as he considered that the first two paragraphs have in fact a 'backward-looking' orientation, 'speaking to the past concerns of the UN'.[30] In contrast, the three remaining paragraphs are forward-looking, and, as such, Cantor contended that they carry more normative weight. According to him, they present the refugee problem as a 'social and humanitarian problem'[31] instead of a human rights problem. He concluded that the plenipotentiaries, in fact, aimed at creating a regime 'afresh on its own intrinsic terms rather than via [at the time] novel UN human rights concepts'.[32] He did not dispute the relevance of human rights standards in informing the meaning of the notion of persecution but he considered that they should be used as 'illustrative rather than determinative of the concept of persecution'.[33] He however provided little guidance as to how human rights should inform the meaning of persecution.

For the above authors, the 1951 Convention established an independent legal regime, distinct from human rights law. Even though some of them considered that human rights standards are not entirely irrelevant in interpreting the Convention, they considered that they should have a minimal role in providing interpretive guidance.[34] In line with the above views, it is true that the historical background to the 1951 Convention gave little consideration to human rights principles. In particular, no human rights standards were mentioned in the pre-war instruments for refugee protection as these instruments pre-dated the emergence of a human rights movement on the international scene. The *travaux preparatoires* also barely refer to human rights. As such, it appears that the elaboration of the 1951 Convention is anchored to a legal movement different from the development of international human rights law. This has been demonstrated by early authors[35] who have highlighted that the 1951 Convention was drafted as a compromise between the interests of states and the humanitarian needs of individuals, and that it was imbued with a particular political orientation as noted in Chapter 1. This theoretical and political background, therefore, departs from the human rights purpose strongly advocated by Hathaway and his proponents. However, the historical and legal background of the Convention is not the only aspect that needs to be taken into consideration for interpreting its term as

29 Ibid.
30 Ibid. 374.
31 Ibid. 375.
32 Ibid.
33 Ibid. 393.
34 In Steinbock (n 23) 783, the author noted that human rights rules of customary law could be relevant interpretive benchmarks. Cantor, (n 28) 395, did not reject entirely the relationship between human rights and refugee law but he considered that the role that human rights should play in interpreting refugee law notions should be more 'modest'.
35 See Section 1.1.

nothing indicates that it informs the 'object and purpose' of a treaty as stipulated in the VCLT. In fact, in order to justify references to human rights, in addition to Article 31 (1) of the VCLT mentioned by Hathaway, reference could also be made to Article 31 (3) (b) and (c). These articles provide an even stronger basis for a human rights model of interpretation as they highlight the importance of the evolving legal context of a Convention.

2.1.3 The compromise: human rights as the orthodoxy?

These divergent views on the nature of the 1951 Convention could be reconciled by a careful reading of Article 31 (3) (b) and (c) of the Vienna Convention:

> 3. There shall be taken into account, together with the context:
> (*b*) any subsequent practice in the application of the treaty which establishes the agreement of the parties regarding its interpretation;
> (*c*) any relevant rules of international law applicable in the relations between the parties.

Article 31(3)(b) emphasises the importance of an interpretive practice embedded in the evolving legal context of the Convention. Closer attention should, therefore, be given to the way the definition of a refugee has been understood by the parties to the 1951 Convention since its adoption. A brief overview of the jurisprudence demonstrates that international human rights have been largely referred to when interpreting the 1951 Convention,[36] making human rights law 'the new orthodoxy of refugee law.'[37] In the words of one author, conflating human rights law and refugee law has become 'contemporary practice'[38] and has been widely endorsed by decision makers.[39] As such, only 'legal purists'[40] would reject the importance of human rights in informing the meaning of the Convention. In particular, the evolution of human rights on the international scene can be perceived as reflecting to a certain extent the concerns of the international community, which can be seen as an incentive by asylum judges to refer regularly to human rights norms in their decisions. As such, disconnecting human rights law and refugee law seems to disregard the evolution of modern societies which in turn would contravene the arguable intention of plenipotentiaries to provide for a tool of protection that could adapt to the evolving circumstances of refugees.

36 See below Section 2.4.
37 Chetail (n 11) 71. To Chetail: 'in a normative environment largely dominated by human rights, all observers are now convinced of the human rights nature of the Geneva Convention.'
38 Vera Gowlland-Debbas, *The Problem of Refugees in The Light of Contemporary International Law Issues* (Series of Papers, Gowlland-Debbas ed., Martinus Nijhoff Publishers, 1994) 3.
39 Ibid.
40 Ibid.

This view is also consistent with Article 31(3)(c) stipulating that relevant rules of international law amongst state parties should be referred to for interpreting the provisions of the Convention. In particular, it should be pointed that numerous human rights treaties developed after World War II have been signed and ratified by the same states that signed the 1951 Convention and, thus they appear to constitute relevant standards of interpretation. Taking this aspect into consideration, Ghrainne recalled that although there is no clear position in the scholarship on whether human rights should only influence the interpretation of the Convention or should entirely define its parameters, human rights should 'at the very least'[41] inform the meaning of the refugee definition.

2.1.4 Concluding remarks

In light of the above, various positions regarding the relationship between international refugee law and international human rights law have been expressed. Some commentators argued that, given the close teleological links between human rights law and refugee law, human rights should closely influence the interpretation of the refugee definition. Others go as far as to affirm that the Convention is, in itself, a human rights treaty, thus implying that human rights have a pivotal importance in informing the application of the Convention. Different authors warned that caution should be exerted when using human rights standards as interpretive benchmarks because this could contravene the initial purpose of the Convention. For others, the initial purpose of the Convention should be understood in light of the context in which it is interpreted, leading to the conclusion that a human rights interpretation of the notion of persecution has now become the new orthodoxy.

These divergent views show that the intent of the plenipotentiaries as to the role of human rights standards remains unclear. In any event, human rights law and international refugee law should not be entirely disconnected, as pointed out above. As already noted, questions then emerged, such as, which human rights ought to be relied upon for determining what forms of harm constitute persecution, and to what extent should this be the case? How should human rights inform the meaning of the notion of persecution? The interpretive exercise has to respect at least the protective purpose of the refugee definition and has to be sufficiently adaptable to the evolving circumstances of refugees, keeping in mind that the notion of persecution confers an individual dimension to the harm feared.[42]

In order to answer the above questions, different views have been advanced on the modalities of a human rights narrative for interpreting persecution. Hathaway has proposed the most detailed study on this element and developed an interpretive framework that relies on basic human rights as relevant benchmarks.

41 Brid Ni Ghrainne, '*The Internal Protection Alternative Inquiry and Human Rights Considerations -Irrelevant or Indispensable*' [2015] 27 International Journal of Refugee Law 29, 34.

42 As demonstrated in Chapter 1.

According to him, persecution should be understood as the 'sustained or systemic violation of basic human rights demonstrative of a failure of state protection'.[43] Through this formulation, Hathaway considered that persecution is composed of serious harm plus failure of state protection. His framework will be assessed below and evaluated against the proposals of other authors to determine whether it is sufficiently adapted to the modern circumstances of refugees.

2.2 The quantitative and qualitative aspects of persecution

The notion of persecution has a bi-faceted nature through its quantitative and qualitative aspect.[44] Hathaway has subsumed these two elements into a sub-test of 'serious harm' to which he added an extra requirement of lack of state protection to evaluate persecution. This section will analyse both the quantitative and qualitative aspects of 'serious harm' as defined by Hathaway, but, a greater focus will be put on the qualitative aspect of persecution (2.2.1), because it is the part that has been the most widely debated within the literature and the jurisprudence. In contrast, the quantitative test proposed by Hathaway has been more consensually rejected (2.2.2).

2.2.1 Qualitative aspect of persecution: basic human rights used as interpretive benchmarks

In order to assess what amounts to persecution, Hathaway argued that the nature of the harm needs to be evaluated in light of specific human rights norms, namely 'basic' human rights. The meaning of basic human rights requires further analysis.

Serious harm: which human rights should be used as benchmarks?

In the first edition of his book in 1991, Hathaway stated that basic human rights are the norms set out in the International Bill of Rights, namely the UDHR, and the two international covenants, the International Covenant on Civil and Political Rights (ICCPR) and the International Covenant on Economic, Social and Cultural Rights (ICESCR).[45] In the last edition of the LORS, he expanded the array of human rights standards that he believed should be considered 'basic human rights' as he added that reference should also be made to certain specialised treaties.[46] He did not consider that all specialised treaties entail basic human rights as he stated that only the ones that have been widely endorsed by states enjoy 'normative legitimacy'.[47] According to him, if the interest at stake is not:

43 Hathaway and Foster (n 1) 183.
44 Carlier (n 14) 45; Hathaway and Foster (n 1).
45 Hathaway and Foster (n 1) 193.
46 Ibid. 200–201.
47 Ibid. 194.

> within the ambit of a human rights norm as defined by a widely ratified international human rights treaty [...] it is unlikely to constitute serious harm in refugee law, since for the human rights fairly to be considered a generally agreed interpretive benchmark for the 'being persecuted' inquiry, one should expect to see the norm having been ratified by a supermajority of states across a politically and geographically diverse range of states.[48]

For Hathaway, basic human rights standards are, therefore, only to be found in treaties that have reached some form of consensus on the international scene. Foster also provided extensive argument to support the contention that basic human rights enshrined in widely endorsed treaties can constitute relevant standards of interpretation.[49] She further added that reference could also be made to customary law, as well as the work of treaty bodies.[50] In addition to this, she mentioned new sources of basic human rights, namely normative standards developed in soft law instruments.[51] According to her, soft law norms should also be referred to for interpreting the notion of persecution because they 'explicate or amplify existing obligations'.[52] Whilst her view on the value of customary law and the normative production of treaty bodies was endorsed in the 2014 edition of the LORS—which she co-edited—her position on the value of soft law sources has not been retained. To define basic human rights, Hathaway only referred to treaties but remained silent on the role of soft law instruments. In fact, in a different piece of writing, he had specifically rejected the argument that soft law instruments could constitute appropriate references for assessing the notion of persecution because, for him, soft law 'does not bespeak a sufficient normative consensus'.[53] In his view, these standards 'should not [...] be treated as authoritative in and of themselves'.[54]

The basic human rights framework as proposed by Hathaway has been accepted by many commentators as adequate guidance for interpretation.[55] For instance, Haines enumerated a series of widely endorsed international treaties to define

48 Ibid. 205.
49 Foster (n 12) 59.
50 Ibid.
51 Ibid. 70.
52 Ibid. 72. She noted, however, that 'basic human rights' enshrined in international treaty norms should prevail, 79.
53 James C. Hathaway, '*The Relationship between Human Rights and Refugee Law: What Refugee Judges Can Contribute*' in *International Association of Refugee Law Judges, The Realities of Refugee Determination on the Eve of a New Millennium: The Role of the Judiciary* (Haarlem, The Netherlands: International Association of Refugee Law Judges, 1999) 86.
54 Ibid.
55 See UNHCR, Division of International Protection, '*Gender-Related Persecution: An Analysis of Recent Trend*' (1997) 9 International Journal of Refugee Law 79, 82, DOI: https://doi.org/10.1093/reflaw/9.Special_Issue.79. Also, Mark Symes, '*Case-law on the Refugee Convention: The United Kingdom's Interpretation in the Light of the International Authorities*' (London: Refugee Legal Centre 2000) 70. Cited in Foster (n 12) 31.

'core' human rights relevant, according to him, for interpreting persecution.[56] This view has been also shared by Goodwin-Gill who suggested developing an interpretive narrative that relies on basic human rights[57] 'embodied in international Conventions'.[58] Similarly, Carlier proposed to rely on 'basic human rights', which he believes are the rights formulated in treaties, to assess the qualitative aspect of persecution.[59]

The proposition that basic human rights are only human rights that are enshrined in treaties has the advantage of encouraging conceptual clarity by referring to written norms that are clearly referenced. As such, this interpretive framework seems to have a certain potential for fostering consistency amongst decision makers. Additionally, by referring to a uniform set of norms, the basic human rights approach could theoretically ensure more legal certainty in the decision-making process. It provides clear and relatively undisputed benchmarks for assessing refugee claims, thus enjoying some form of legitimacy. In light of the above benefits, it cannot be denied that international human rights standards should have a major role to play in informing the meaning of the notion of persecution. However, confining the interpretation of this notion to violations of human rights codified in widely accepted instruments raises a number of interpretive challenges that will be assessed below.

Basic human rights approach: a framework that is too broad?

For the opponents of a basic human rights approach to interpreting the 1951 Convention, the norms enshrined in human rights treaties constitute an interpretive framework that is too broad. They in fact do not believe that the 1951 Convention should be interpreted in a flexible manner, consistently with the development of the international human rights law corpus. For instance, Steinbock argued that one of the deficiencies of the basic human rights narrative is that it separates the notion of persecution from the Convention grounds. For him, this interpretation is simply too large[60] as it bears the risk of making 'millions of people potential refugees in today's world'.[61] He and other authors considered that the positivist approach to the human rights framework of interpretation does not set clear boundaries to who should be a refugee because it refers to a normative system that is ambiguous.[62] Additionally, Steinbock noted that there is not any

56 Rodger Haines, *Gender-Related Persecution* in *Refugee Protection in International Law: UNHCR's Global Consultations on International Protection* (Erika Feller, Volker Turk and Frances Nicholson eds, Cambridge University Press 2003) 327–328.
57 Guy S. Goodwin-Gill and Jane McAdams, *The Refugee in International Law* (Oxford University Press 2011) 91.
58 Ibid. 93.
59 Jean-Yves Carlier, '*The Geneva refugee definition and the "theory of the three scales"*' in Frances Nicholson and Patrick Twomey (eds) *Refugee Rights and Realities: Evolving International Concepts and Regimes* (Cambridge University Press 1999) 37, 45–46.
60 Steinbock (n 23) 780 and 738.
61 Ibid. 782.
62 Ibid. 782. See also Haddad (n 26).

clear reference to the UDHR in the refugee definition. According to him, if the refugee definition was meant to be interpreted in light of the principles enshrined in human rights instruments such as the UDHR, this would have been, simply, mentioned in the definition. Thinking otherwise would amount to considering that the 'wording of the refugee definition was [...] illustrative'[63] which does not seem to be a reasonable approach. He, however, acknowledged that human rights law and refugee law overlap in the sense that refugee law protects only violations of certain subsets of human rights. However, he stated that human rights law and refugee law have different purposes and, therefore refugee law should be more narrowly understood than human rights law. For the opponents of the basic human rights approach,[64] certain human rights remain nonetheless relevant for interpreting the notion of persecution, namely only the 'most basic human rights involving the most serious harms, such as those recognized as customary international law'.[65]

The proposal to only rely on norms of customary law for interpreting the notion of persecution seems, however, quite severe as it would confine refugee law to the most egregious forms of hardship, which correspond to the norms that usually reach a very large consensus on the international scene and gain the status of customary law, or *jus cogens*. This would only refer to a very limit set of norms. Additionally, customary law allows for little flexibility in the interpretation of legal norms. It fixes an existing practice, which takes time to define. Therefore, making it a benchmark for interpretation does not easily align with the argued purpose of the Convention, namely to ensure an evolutionary approach of the definition of a refugee. This also does not appear to be consistent with the possible intention of plenipotentiaries who had left the definition of persecution open.[66] Generally, the proposal that only customary law norms should be used as benchmarks has not been widely adopted in the jurisprudence, nor in the literature.

However, in line with the concerns raised by the opponents of the basic human rights approach, it could be noted that international standards enshrined in treaties do not always constitute clear and defined norms as they tend to be formulated in an ambiguous manner. This in turn questions their ability to always provide for solid benchmarks of interpretation and to encourage consistent interpretations in national jurisdictions. Rather than providing for too broad a framework, they could in fact encourage rigid interpretations of the notion of persecution as the section below will demonstrate.

63 Steinbock (n 23) 785.
64 Ibid. See also Matthew Price, *Rethinking Asylum: History, Purpose, and Limits* (Cambridge University Press 2009).
65 Steinbock (n 23) 787.
66 See Chapter 1.

Basic human rights: vague notions?

(A) SHIFTING THE INTERPRETIVE EXERCISE TO AN EQUALLY VAGUE 'DISCURSIVE TERRAIN'?[67]

It could indeed be argued that exclusively relying on basic human rights does not adequately solve the problem of inconsistent interpretations of the refugee definition and the notion of persecution as hoped by Hathaway. The imprecise character of basic human rights could in fact lead to more fragmentary applications of the refugee definition in state parties, which could in turn undermine the overall coherence of the protection regime of the 1951 Convention. This view has been shared by many commentators who have pointed to the vague and general character of codified human rights and demonstrated that they can be applied in very different ways.

Vernant, who was one of the first scholars to propose that the notion of persecution should be interpreted in light of human rights standards, also warned against the difficulties that could arise from this interpretive approach as he stated that human rights codified in the UDHR were 'couched in very general terms'.[68] He specifically highlighted concerns with regard to certain rights, which he believed could pose serious challenges of interpretation such as the 'right to work, to free choice of employment, to just and favourable conditions of work'.[69] He concluded that 'some lack of precision is [...] inevitable'[70] when using a human rights approach for interpreting persecution. According to him, reference to external standards enshrined in the international legal order was necessary to guide the interpretation of the notion of persecution but the norms of the UDHR were not sufficient to constitute a proper analytical framework. As such, Vernant seemed to hope for the development of more precise human rights notions that would complement the abstract concepts of the UDHR.

In line with his wishes, international human rights treaties developed at a rapid pace in the second half of the 20th century but in spite of this multiplication of new norms, human rights codified in all sorts of treaties have remained general and still raise interpretive challenges.[71] The way human rights are being formulated in international treaties is often the result of a long and rigid process for elaborating these instruments. All international human rights treaties are multilateral treaties that involves a large number of parties. Furthermore, they all tend to be elaborated in various phases including

67 Cantor (n 28) 386.
68 Vernant (n 7) 15, 8.
69 Ibid.
70 Ibid.
71 Ibid. 4. Also see John Tobin, '*Seeking to Persuade: A Constructive Approach to Human Rights Treaty Interpretation*' [2010] 23 Harvard Law Journal 1, https://ssrn.com/abstract=2030005. For him 'human rights are invariably vague and ambiguous', and as such, he stated that interpreting these standards constitutes 'a dilemma'. He observed that there is a 'vast range of potential meanings' for every human right, and general rules of treaty interpretation are of minimal help to elucidate what the meaning of a right is.

negotiations, drafting sessions and conferences until an agreement by consensus from all the parties is reached. The intervention of multiple actors in this formal process naturally has an impact on the way human rights norms are formulated. In order to reach a common understanding amongst a large panel of different parties, the plenipotentiaries generally expressed human rights notions in quite general terms. For example, economic, social and cultural rights that are formulated in a particularly vague manner, such as the right to family[72] or the right to health which was qualified by an author as a 'nebulous right'.[73] It in indeed unclear what is encompassed under these rights and they can be interpreted in very divergent manners, depending on the interpretive agent. As a result, the impreciseness of human rights can lead to different outcomes in interpreting the notion of persecution and it can also encourage narrow interpretations. This lack of conceptual clarity was highlighted by several authors. For instance Tobin stated that human rights are not 'self-defining'.[74] For him, they are so general that they do not help to determine whether some specific laws (he provided the example of Islamic dress) are persecutory in nature.[75] Similarly, Cantor contended that the language of human rights treaties is particularly unclear and, therefore, relying on a human rights approach for interpreting the notion of persecution simply shifts 'the interpretative exercise from the terms of the Refugee Convention to a new discursive terrain'.[76] He mentioned another example which is the prohibition of 'torture or inhuman and degrading treatment'. For him, this is as equally vague a concept as the concept of persecution.

In line with the foregoing, some human rights scholars, such as Ignatieff and Donnelly, have demonstrated that international human rights law constitutes a limited normative field by nature, and that it provides for a minimal set of standards. Ignatieff deemed international human rights a 'thin theory'[77] because, according to him, human rights values are applicable in any culture and traditions due to their minimal aspect. He stated that the role of human rights 'is not in defining the content of culture but in trying to enfranchise all agents so that they can freely shape that content'.[78] As such, he highlighted

72 Universal Declaration of Human Rights (adopted 10 December 1948 UNGA Res 217 A(III)
(UDHR), Art 16.

73 Tobin (n 71). Tobin makes reference to the work of Jennifer Prah Ruger, '*Toward a Theory of a Right to Health: Capability and Incompletely Theorized Agreements*' [2006] 18 Yale Journal of Law and the Humanities 273.

74 Tobin (n 71) 122: 'Human rights themselves are not self-defining but require interpretation in light of underlying principles; and human rights often conflict, requiring a decision-maker to rely on a theory that explains why some rights should be prioritized over others'.

75 Ibid.

76 Cantor (n 28) 386.

77 Michael Ignatieff, *Human Rights as Politics and Idolatry* (Gutman ed. Princeton University Press 2001) 56.

78 Ibid. 73.

the fact that human rights do not 'prescribe the "positive" range of good lives that human beings can lead'[79] and do not constitute a comprehensive answer to all the complex needs of individuals. On a similar note, Donnelly considered that human rights are broad concepts[80] that can be relativised depending on the way they are interpreted or implemented. According to him, human rights 'permit a wide range of particular practices'.[81] In their respective analyses, Ignatieff and Donnelly pointed to the general character of basic human rights and demonstrated that human rights norms can be variably interpreted depending on the context in which they are applied. These observations, however, contrast with the initial contention made by the proponents of the basic human rights model, namely that interpretive guidance based on codified human rights constitute an objective basis for interpreting the 1951 Convention in a consistent manner.

As such, indexing an interpretive approach exclusively on basic human rights enshrined in international treaties raises the risk of constructing a vague framework that can create more confusion and lead to inconsistent applications of the 1951 Convention.

(B) HUMAN RIGHTS JURISPRUDENCE: A SOLUTION TO PROVIDE PRECISE INTERPRETIVE GUIDANCE?

When difficulties of interpretation arise, notably due to the vagueness or unclear meaning of a right, it is possible to rely on the work of treaty bodies[82] as they provide guidance of interpretation for these rights. Indeed, these bodies have been established to monitor the application of their treaty of reference and to recommend authoritative interpretation of certain human rights provisions.[83] Whether the interpretation of treaty bodies should be used for interpreting the notion of persecution is however questionable as this could raise additional difficulties. Indeed, the jurisprudence of treaty bodies has been criticised for being inadequate, and at times, controversial.

In particular, Edwards has pointed to many concerns regarding the work of treaty bodies. Firstly, she observed that women are underrepresented in the decision-making process, thus raising issues as to the equal representation of their interests when human rights are interpreted.[84] She provided an example of such gender bias as she stated that domestic violence is rarely qualified as torture by

79 Ibid. 73.
80 Jack Donnelly, '*The Relative Universality of Human Rights*' [2007] 29 Human Rights Quarterly 281, 299: https://www.jstor.org/stable/20072800.
81 Ibid. 300.
82 Hathaway (n 1) 195.
83 On this, see Nadia Bernaz, '*Continuing evolution of the United Nations treaty bodies system*' in *Routledge Handbook of International Law* edited by Scott Shiran and Sir Nigel Rodley (Routledge 2013) 707.
84 Alice Edwards, *Violence against Women under International Human Rights Law* (Oxford University Press 2010) 124.

treaty bodies.[85] This is particularly concerning given that in the past decades, an increasing number of women refugees have lodged asylum claims based on gender-related forms of violence.[86]

In addition, Edwards demonstrated that the work of treaty bodies does not necessarily solve the problem of indeterminacy of human rights standards. For instance, in the case of individual communications, she argued that the legal process is generally consensual and, therefore, can 'lead to compromise to the lowest common denominator'.[87] Further to this, she observed that treaty bodies often follow an unclear methodology of interpretation, which regularly results in inadequate decisions. According to her, many General Comments simply remain broad 'statements as to the meaning of particular terms of rights without explaining fully the background to, or reasons for, such an interpretation'.[88] Finally, Edwards also observed that 'deciding the subject matter for a General Comment is largely ad hoc and is not based on any long-term strategy'.[89] In this sense, she highlighted the fact that the overall jurisprudence of treaty bodies lacks a coherent vision. The lack of an overall principled approach has also been pointed out by Mechlem, who noted that committee members of treaty bodies often made 'contradictory remarks',[90] thus undermining the coherence of the system. Similarly, Komanovics pointed to the inconsistent interpretations of the treaty bodies on certain human rights terms.[91] More specifically, Goodwin-Gill demonstrated that the decision of treaty bodies, and in particular of the Human Rights Committee (HRC) can be ambiguous and mislead the interpretation of the terms of the 1951 Convention[92] as was the case in claims relating to conscientious objection to military service.

85 Ibid. 129.
86 On this see Section 1.2.
87 In Edwards (n 84) 123, the author however acknowledged the increase of dissenting opinions in the past years.
88 Ibid. 116. Similar remarks are noted by Mechlem, noting that the treaty bodies follow a precise methodology as they often neglect the rules of treaty interpretation, in Kerstin Mechlem, '*Treaty Bodies and the Interpretation of Human Rights*' [2009] 42 Vanderbilt Journal of Transnational Law 905, 908.
89 Edwards (n 84) 116.
90 Mechlem (n 88) 908.
91 Adrienne Komanovics, '*Strengthening the Human Rights Treaty Bodies: A Modest but Important Step Forward*' [2014] 29 Pecs Journal of International and European Law 7, 13: http://epa.oszk.hu/02600/02691/00001/pdf/EPA02691_pjiel_2014_1.pdf
92 Goodwin-Gill more specifically pointed to the ambiguous nature of the work of the HRC. He analysed the decisions of the HRC in the context of claims arising out of objections to compulsory military service and criticised the controversial decisions of the HRC majority in these cases. In particular, he regretted the overreliance of the UNHCR on the HRC's position in the guidelines on international protection on asylum claims related to military service and warned that extra diligence should be exercised when referring to the work of treaty bodies. Goodwin-Gill demonstrated here that the decision of the majority of the HRC can be at times controversial and simplistic. See Guy S. Goodwin-Gill, '*The Dynamic of International Refugee Law*' [2013] 25 International Journal of Refugee Law 651, 657–661, https://doi.org/10.1093/ijrl/eeu003.

Additionally, another problem with the activity of treaty bodies is that it seems to foster the emergence of some discrete rights that are only entailed in widely accepted human rights instruments. For instance, the HRC has developed the meaning and scope of only certain civil and political rights based on the normative standards of the ICCPR, such as the right to conscientious objection[93] or Lesbian Gay Bisexual Transsexual Intersex (LGBTI) rights.[94] The same reasoning is applicable to any treaty body that only interprets the rights of their treaty of reference. As a result, human rights jurisprudence has left untouched numerous other forms of harm such as collective rights of societies, as for example the right to development, that have not been set out in any treaty but nonetheless reflect contemporary concerns of individuals.

In light of the foregoing, it can be argued that there are inherent deficiencies in the work of treaty bodies. Whilst treaty bodies provide authoritative interpretations of human rights provisions, uncritical acceptance of their work appears, however, controversial. As such, there is no clear evidence that the normative activity of treaty bodies could encourage more consistency in the interpretation of the notion of persecution.

Basic human rights approach: a restrictive framework?

The positivist approach for interpreting persecution in reference to norms that have been codified in international treaties could also be questioned in light of the developments of new normative sources. It could indeed be argued that the different protection needs of individuals have not been covered by all the rights enshrined in international treaties and as such, these treaties do not reflect the complexity of refugees' experiences.[95] Therefore, restricting the interpretation of persecution to such norms could encourage a rather rigid and too narrow

93 See extensive reliance on the jurisprudence of the HCR in the UNHCR Guidelines on International Protection No. 10: *Claims to Refugee Status related to Military Service within the context of Article 1A (2) of the 1951 Convention and/or the 1967 Protocol relating to the Status of Refugees*, 3 December 2013, HCR/GIP/13/10/Corr.1, 3, https://www.unhcr.org/en-my/publications/legal/529efd2e9/guidelines-international-protection-10-claims-refugee-status-related-military.html.

94 On the work of the HRC on LGBTI rights, see Paula Gerber and Joel Gory '*The UN Human Rights Committee and LGBT Rights: What is it Doing? What Could it be Doing?*' [2014] 14 Human Rights Law Review 403, https://doi.org/10.1093/hrlr/ngu019.

95 Alice Edwards, '*Age and gender dimensions in international refugee law*' in Erika Feller, Volker Turk, Frances Nicholson (eds), *Refugee Protection in International Law: UNHCR's Global Consultations on International Protection* (Cambridge University Press 2003) 50. According to Edwards: 'it is possible that all forms of persecution have not yet been identified or codified in international human rights law.' See also Kate Jastram, '*Economic Harm as a Basis for Refugee Status and the Application of Human Rights Law to the Interpretation of Economic Persecution*' in James C. Simeon (ed) *Critical Issues in International Refugee Law: Strategies Towards Interpretative Harmony* (Cambridge University Press 2010) 143–173. Jastram stated that 'human rights law can also be under-inclusive. If a judge cannot locate specific textual support

application of the 1951 Convention. Even though new human rights standards have been developed in treaties in the past decades, there is no guarantee that these standards will be sufficient to respond to the rapidly evolving circumstances of refugees. For instance, Edwards mentioned the case of gender-based violence. She explained that before women's rights were codified in international treaties, gender-based violence was, nonetheless, an existing form of persecution. She also mentioned that the principle of the best interest of the child, as derived from the recognition of specific children's rights in international instruments, was an existing principle before the adoption of the Convention on the Rights of the Child (CRC).[96] According to her, this does not mean that human rights should be ignored. In fact, she considered that human rights law has a role to play in elucidating the meaning of certain forms of persecution, but she stated that the interpretation of persecution should not be restricted to a rigid human rights framework and should take into account broader circumstances of refugees.[97]

Indeed, due to the rigidity of the process for adopting international treaties, non-binding normative sources, such as Resolutions, Recommendations, Guidelines, Guidance Notes etc. … have multiplied on the international scene in the recent years. They constitute a relevant alternative to regulate systems at the international level. In the words of Juss, 'a new generation of international lawyers is now beginning to argue that one must abandon formal mechanisms to determine the pedigree of rules'[98] as the 'majority of international normative activity takes place outside the ambit of traditional international law'.[99] For instance, Betts noted that the protection of Internally Displaced Persons (IDPs) has been ensured through the development of soft law instruments such as guidelines, rather than through codified human rights.[100] In line with the above views, Lambert argued that with the disaggregation of state power,[101] transnational actors and networks

in human rights law relevant to his or her understanding of the harm at issue, the persecution analysis may be cut short', p. 165.

96 Edwards, in ibid. 51.

97 See for instance, *Matter of Pierre*, 15 I&N 2433 (Board of Immigration Appeals 1975) at [4610]. This case was adjudicated before the adoption of the CEDAW. The Board concluded that the domestic violence faced by the Applicant was a private issue and therefore, fell outside the ambit of the refugee definition.

98 Satvinder Juss, '*The UNHCR Handbook and the Interface Between "Soft Law" and "Hard Law" in International Refugee Law*' in Satvinder Juss and Colin Harvey (eds), *Contemporary Issues in Refugee Law* (Edward Elgar, Cheltenham 2013) 31–67, 39.

99 Juss ibid. 39. See also Corinne Lewis, '*UNHCR's Contribution to the Development of International Refugee Law: Its Foundations and Evolution*' [2005] 17 International Journal of Refugee Law 67, 78, https://doi.org/10.1093/ijrl/eei004. Lewis believed that there is an 'ongoing need to further elaborate new standards and to develop international refugee law even if these new standards are not codified in international treaties.'

100 Alexander Betts, '*Towards a "Soft Law" Framework for the Protection of Vulnerable Irregular Migrants*' [2010] 22 International Journal of Refugee Law 209, https://doi.org/10.1093/ijrl/eeq018.

101 Helene Lambert, '*International refugee law: dominant and emerging approaches*', in *Routledge Handbook of International Law* (2009 Routledge, London) 344–354, 349.

have contributed to the 'international normative activity and to a changing conception of the world less dominated by a vertical notion of international law and domestic law'.[102] She considered that, in this context, the human rights approach to refugee law is less 'useful in capturing the complexities of the process of law formation and law developments'.[103] Indeed, the rigidity of the normative system of treaties allows for little flexibility in adapting to the changing geopolitical context. The catalogue of treaty-codified human rights norms appears quite restricted nowadays as the needs and priorities of refugees are changing rapidly. As such, the basic human rights approach might not adequately reflect the most recent evolutions of refugee situations. The promise that it could constitute an evolutionary approach to the notion of persecution is therefore questionable.

Overall, it appears that using basic human rights enshrined in international treaties as normative guidance for interpreting persecution constitutes a restrictive interpretive scheme as it confines the experiences of refugees to a limited set of rights through a rather formalist approach. As such, the interpretive exercise encouraged by the basic human rights framework creates the risk of disregarding important aspects of refugees' circumstances in today's world and of contributing to the criticisms that the 1951 Convention is an inadequate instrument.

2.2.2 Quantitative aspect of persecution

Sustained and systemic approach: a restrictive threshold?

In addition to the qualitative aspect analysed above, the level of harm required to amount to persecution is also questionable. This raises questions as to what the threshold necessary for a certain form of harm to amount to persecution is. Hathaway proposed that only the most egregious forms of human rights violations should warrant refugee status, namely violations that are 'sustained' or 'systemic'. However, this approach has been widely criticised for being too strict as his formulation indicates that, in most cases, a single violation of a basic human right would not be enough to amount to persecution. In opposition to Hathaway, Storey argued that the requirement of a sustained or systemic violation of human rights sets an unduly high threshold for interpreting the notion of persecution and 'is plainly too restrictive'.[104] The condition of persistency seemed also to have been rejected by other scholars. For instance, Goodwin-Gill did not retain this criterion when he analysed the concept of persecution. For him, 'persecution within the Convention [...] comprehends measures, taken on the basis of one or more of the stated grounds, which threaten' a series of rights that he

Lambert also makes reference to Slaughter who argued that in an age of global governance, states are disaggregating and new types of actors progressively emerge.

102 Ibid. 345.

103 Ibid. 353.

104 Hugo Storey, '*What Constitutes Persecution? Towards a Working Definition*' [2014] 26 International Journal of Refugee Law 272, 279, https://doi.org/10.1093/ijrl/eeu017.

enumerates.[105] He further stated that the 'nature and severity of the restriction'[106] should be taken into consideration when assessing what harms amount to persecution. Through such formulations, he omitted to explicitly mention the element of persistency, thus seemingly waiving it. In contrast, he stated that persecution should be a matter of 'degree and proportion',[107] and, therefore, he adopted a more moderate position.

Although Carlier is a proponent of Hathaway's basic human rights approach, he also did not maintain the criteria of persistency. Instead, he proposed a different threshold for assessing persecution as he considered that, in principle, the requirement of severity of harm must be high, but it should be 'relaxed' in certain situations.[108] He developed a test based on a sliding scale of proportionality depending on the nature of the rights violated.[109] Similarly, Foster barely discussed the test of 'sustained and systemic violations' of human rights[110] in her book. Although she agreed that violations of basic human rights can amount to persecution, she seemed to depart from the strict approach proposed by Hathaway as she did not propose any specific test for assessing the threshold of persecution. She simply argued that, ultimately, the assessment of whether some forms of harm amount to persecution should be relinquished to decision makers. For her, human rights simply provide a form of guidance that should not be understood in a rigid manner,[111] which is in contrast to the persistency criteria of Hathaway.

Given the overwhelming criticisms against the restrictiveness of his test, Hathaway refined his position in 2014. He stated that his definition of persecution could in fact entail instances of a single harm. For him, the term 'sustained' refers to an ongoing form of harm such as 'death or severe torture' and the term 'systemic' refers to a form of harm that is 'endemic in a social or political system'.[112]

Even if Hathaway admitted that a single harm could rise to the level of persecution, the threshold that he sets appears to be, nonetheless, particularly severe. Indeed, the 'ongoing' nature of harm, remains a relatively vague notion and could result in applying an excessively strict test. For instance, he refers to 'severe torture', which implies the existence of different degrees in the infliction of torture. This could lead to the conclusion that a 'simple' act of torture, not severe enough, would not amount to persecution, which seems rather restrictive. Additionally, Hathaway did not explain to what extent he considers that a harm should be endemic in the society. This could in turn suggest that certain forms of harm that are not widespread enough in some communities, but that nonetheless affect some individuals, would not amount to persecution. As such, his test remains unduly severe.

105 Goodwin-Gill and McAdams (n 57) 93.
106 Ibid. 92.
107 Ibid. 92.
108 Carlier (n 14) 50.
109 Ibid. 45.
110 Foster (n 12).
111 Ibid. 79.
112 Hathaway and Foster (n 1) 195.

The basic human rights approach: a formalist and uniform threshold

In addition to the above, it should be pointed out that the basic human rights approach relies on a formalist view of what persecution is by considering that individuals ought to enjoy only certain types of entitlements listed in international treaties. This approach could in turn lead to a rather compartmentalised understanding of persecution as it encourages us to consider different aspects of harms in an abstract manner and to posit that one single threshold is applicable to everybody. Foster had pointed to this caveat in the context of claims based on social and economic deprivation, as she noted that the 'problem with any approach that is based on categorical distinctions is that it can lead to a rigid analysis, which fails to take into account the reality of the particular circumstances of the individual applicant and the interconnectedness of levels of rights'.[113] Storey also warned that a human rights approach for interpreting persecution should not obviate contextual considerations of the personal circumstances of individuals. According to him, persecution has to be 'person-specific' so that 'not every violation of human rights will have equally serious consequences for different individuals'.[114] Both authors cautioned against a formalist understanding of the threshold of persecution, detached from the context of its application. Indeed, the level of severity of a harm can be experienced differently depending on the context or the individual concerned as well as the possible existence (or not) of certain vulnerabilities. As such, an element of subjectivity should be taken into consideration in assessing the level of harm required in order to amount to persecution. The impact that certain human rights violations have on certain individuals can change from one case to another, depending on the circumstances and personal experiences of each individual. Age, gender, medical condition, mental health are elements that need to be taken into account as they could possibly amplify the effects of certain human rights violations. As such, the threshold of harm required to amount to persecution is bound to vary and a rigid understanding of this element is likely to disregard important aspects of the life of refugees. Therefore, caution should be exerted when relying on an interpretive framework that only refers to external normative standards for interpreting a notion that touches upon personal aspects of refugee claims.

2.3 The surrogacy principle as part of the persecution test?

Another important modality of Hathaway's test is the notion of state protection. Through his formulation, Hathaway argued that the harm perpetrated on an individual should be 'demonstrative of a failure of state protection'. Hathaway here affirms the principle of surrogacy, by emphasising that international protection is warranted only when the state of origin does not provide adequate

113 Foster (n 12) 147.

114 Hugo Storey, '*Persecution: Towards a Working Definition*' in Vincent Chetail and Celine Bauloz (eds), *Research Handbook on International Law and Migration* (Edward Elgar, 2014) 459–518, 476.

protection to victims of human rights violations. It will be demonstrated that his view on surrogate protection has been wrongly equated with the test of persecution for it adds an extra burden of proof on claimants (2.3.1). Additionally, it will be pointed out that his approach to the relationship between Internal Flight Alternative (IFA), surrogacy principle and persecution provides for a convoluted framework. Other views on how the notion of IFA and persecution could be better articulated will be considered below (2.3.2) to conclude that persecution, the principle of surrogacy and IFA should remain separate concepts.

2.3.1 The notion of state protection wrongly equated with the test of persecution?

For Hathaway, refugee law is a form of 'substitute protection'[115] and is meant to 'interpose the protection of the international community [...] in situations where there is no reasonable expectation that national protection of human rights will be forthcoming'.[116] As a result, he makes the notion of persecution conditional upon the absence of state protection. However, it should be noted that this view can appear quite ambiguous given that a similar principle was already mentioned in the refugee definition of the 1951 Convention in a separate limb relating to the lack of national protection in one's country.[117] As such, Hathaway's definition of persecution further emphasises the surrogate character of asylum and provides a different understanding of the additional element of state protection mentioned in the definition. Goodwin-Gill's view on this point diverged from Hathaway's as he considered that there is a clear distinction between the 'well-founded fear of being persecuted' and the lack of state protection concepts. He observed that 'the Convention definition begins with the refugee as someone with a well-founded fear of persecution, and only secondly, as someone who is unable or unwilling, by reason of such fear, to use or take advantage of the protection of their government'.[118] He therefore contended that 'the point of reference is the individual particularly as a right-holder, rather than the system of government and its efficacy or intention in relation to protection'.[119]

Cantor also pointed out that subsuming the test of state protection under the persecution limb 'unsatisfactorily ignores the plain text of the definition'.[120] He lamented that Hathaway had 'little to say about the element of the Convention refugee definition that refers specifically to state protection' ('unwilling or, owing to such fear, is unable to avail himself of [state] protection')[121] as he rather subsumed this element under the persecution test. Cantor developed a different paradigm to define the concept of surrogacy. He observed that the overall text of

115 Hathaway and Foster (n 1) 292.
116 Ibid. 292.
117 According to the refugee definition, a refugee is someone who is 'unable, or owing to such fear, is unwilling to avail himself of the protection of that country'.
118 Goodwin-Gill and McAdams (n 57) 10.
119 Ibid.
120 Cantor (n 28) 360.
121 Ibid.

the 1951 Convention defines surrogate protection in relation to protection standards attached to effective nationality. He noted that the 1951 Convention sets protection standards for refugees in the host countries that are not predicated upon human rights law. The external surrogate protection as he theorised it, is not premised on the human rights paradigm but rather on protection standards in the context of alienage or diplomatic protection. This observation led him to conclude that 'human rights law struggles to adequately describe the nature of national protection by the country of origin [...] or the quality of protection afforded by refugee status'.[122] Therefore, he argued that the absence of state protection should be understood in broader terms, including the protection afforded to the nationality holders (in the context of alienage). He further observed that persecution is a separate concept and that 'ultimately the persecution element is simply not capable of exhaustively describing the form of surrogate protection provided by refugee law'.[123] Cantor here demonstrated that persecution and surrogate protection are distinct, and that persecution cannot be considered the 'root'[124] of surrogate protection. For him, this observation is all the more valid since surrogate protection should not be read in human rights terms as argued by Hathaway.

Indeed, there is nothing in the text of the Convention indicating that persecution should encompass a lack of state protection. It has been demonstrated above that the notion of persecution has both a qualitative and a quantitative aspect and adding another limb to the concept seems to constitute an extra burden for asylum seekers as the section below will argue:

2.3.2 Persecution: a bifurcated approach to the Internal Flight Alternative (IFA) test?

Whilst Cantor was right to point out that Hathaway dealt with the notion of 'lack of state protection' under the persecution limb of the Convention, his observation that Hathaway had little to say on the phrase 'unable, or owing to such fear, is unwilling to avail himself of the protection of that country' appears quite severe. In fact, Hathaway elaborated on this portion of the refugee definition in a separate chapter dedicated to the internal protection alternative[125] (also considered IFA as per the UNHCR's official formulation).[126] He observed that according to the refugee definition, when someone can 'avail himself of the protection of [the home] country',[127] refugee status is not warranted. In order to explore this element, Hathaway suggested applying an IFA test, by enquiring whether state

122 Ibid.
123 Ibid. 363.
124 Ibid.
125 Hathaway and Foster (n 1) 332.
126 Guidelines on International Protection No. 4: '*Internal Flight or Relocation Alternative Within the Context of Article 1A(2) of the 1951 Convention and/or Protocol Relating to the Stats of Refugees*', HCR/GIP/03/04, 23 July 2003, https://www.refworld.org/docid/3f2791a44.html.
127 Hathaway and Foster (n 1) 332.

protection is available in another area of the home country. If state protection is available in a different place than the place of origin of an applicant, then the applicant does not meet the eligibility criteria for refugee status. Hathaway seemed to disconnect the IFA test from the persecution enquiry, thus applying a convoluted understanding of the notion of surrogate protection that is subsumed into two different elements (one is inherent to the notion of persecution and one is external). To add to the complexity of his framework, Hathaway suggested departing from the human rights narrative initially proposed for the notion of persecution. Instead, he considered that IFA should be interpreted in light of 'the provision of legal entitlements and rights of the kind set by the Convention'.[128] According to him, the legal entitlements of refugees under the Convention constitute the only benchmarks against which the level of state protection expected for an IFA enquiry should be assessed. He therefore developed two different paradigms for different aspects of the same refugee definition, thus creating a confusing interpretive scheme.[129]

In an attempt to provide a more coherent approach, the UNHCR has developed an entirely different paradigm for interpreting the notion of IFA, by considering that IFA and state protection are part of a holistic assessment attached to the overall refugee definition and not specifically related to one of his elements.[130] The UNHCR therefore made clear that the IFA test and the notion of internal state protection is not an inherent component of the concept of persecution. In the guidelines on IFA, the UNHCR considered that the IFA test is an additional two-pronged test requiring that it should be both 'relevant' and 'reasonable'[131] for an applicant to relocate to another area of the home country. In order to assess whether a relocation is reasonable, the UNHCR suggested that a claimant should not experience 'undue hardship' in the proposed area. The Refugee Agency also proposed that this notion could be interpreted in light of international human rights.[132] With the reasonableness criteria added to the IFA requirement, the UNHCR established a threshold that is much lower than the one proposed by Hathaway. The refugee agency developed in fact a discrete narrative, entirely disconnected from the persecution analysis.

The foregoing has demonstrated that ample disagreement was raised regarding the relation between the tests of persecution, state protection and IFA. According to Hathaway's interpretive framework, the notion of internal state protection should always be part of the persecution limb, whilst the possibility of IFA is

128 Ibid. 355.

129 Hugo Storey, '*The Internal Flight Alternative Test: The Jurisprudence Re-examined*' [1998] 10 International Journal of Refugee Law 499, 529. This deficiency has been highlighted by Storey who claimed that 'not to apply a human rights approach to the IFA test has increasingly apparent disadvantages. It is difficult to square with the growing consensus in contemporary case law that the concepts of persecution and protection require a human rights reformulation'.

130 UNHCR (n 126) 3.

131 Ibid.

132 Ibid. at [24].

separated and interpreted through a different paradigm, thus lacking conceptual clarity. In order to develop clearer approaches, some authors have proposed to entirely separate the surrogacy and IFA elements from the interpretation of the notion of persecution. In particular, the proposal made by the UNHCR[133] that the existence of IFA should be linked to the overall sentence 'well-founded fear of being persecuted' appears valuable as it could lift any confusion. It alleviates the burden of proof on claimants and appears more in line with the plain meaning of the refugee definition.

2.4 Inconsistent applications of the basic human rights framework in national jurisdictions

The previous sections have highlighted the theoretical deficiencies of the basic human rights framework for interpreting persecution, noting that this paradigm bears the risk of encouraging inconsistent and inadequate interpretations of the notion of persecution through a rigid understanding of this notion. One could, however, wonder how this framework has been implemented in practice by decision makers? The basic human rights framework of interpretation has been largely adopted in the jurisprudence of countries that have developed RSD systems but variable interpretations have been noted. A brief overview of the jurisprudence of some of the countries that have the most advanced asylum jurisprudence such as New Zealand, Australia, Canada and the USA demonstrates that there is a significant level of inconsistency in interpreting what forms of harm amount to persecution. This tendency is noticeable, not only between national jurisdictions but also within them. The jurisprudence of some countries of the European Union that have adopted an alternative definition of the notion will be analysed in the following chapter.

The Refugee Status Appeal Authority (RSAA) in New Zealand started regularly referring to basic human rights for interpreting the notion of persecution in the early 1990s[134] after the human rights framework was developed by Hathaway. New Zealand judges, however, did not consistently apply the modalities of this basic human rights model. Although judges in New Zealand have retained the idea that basic human rights were valuable benchmarks for interpreting

133 Ibid. at [3].

134 Rodger Haines, '*Gender-Based Persecution: New Zealand Jurisprudence*' [1997] 9 International Journal of Refugee Law 129, 138, https://doi.org/10.1093/reflaw/9.Special_Issue.129. Haines noted that, in this period, the interpretation of persecution in the jurisprudence was following that of James Hathaway. See also numerous cases referring to various human rights to interpret the notion of persecution quoted in *Refugee Appeal No 2039/93 Re MN, RSAA* (12 February 1996); *Refugee Appeal No. 10/91 Re CPY* (27 August 1991); *Refugee Appeal No. 14/91 Re JS* (5 September 1991) (derogation); *Refugee Appeal No. 29/91 Re SK* (17 February 1992); *Refugee Appeal No. 150/92 Re SS* (9 December 1992) 9; *Refugee Appeal No. 135/92 Re RS* (18 June 1993) 23; *Refugee Appeal No. 265/92 Re SA* (29 June 1994) 12; *Refugee Appeal No. 732/92 Re CZZ* (5 August 1994) 13–17; *Refugee Appeal No. 1222/93 Re KN* (5 August 1994).

persecution,[135] they have used different parameters of interpretation to factor in their human rights analysis. They have tended to combine the human rights approach with a more pragmatic methodology by assessing various forms of human rights restrictions and by applying ad hoc thresholds. Judges still explicitly mention Hathaway's model as a reference in their decisions but in practice they actually rather rely on the notion of 'serious harm'.[136] For instance, in *Refugee Appeal No. 76015* (4 November 2007), the RSAA mentioned that for a violation of the ICESCR to amount to persecution, '[t]he breach must go to the core of the right and must occasion *serious harm*. A breach at the margins of a right or one that does not bring about *serious harm*, will not reach the being persecuted threshold'.[137] In fact, this approach developed in the jurisprudence proved to be more protective of the rights of refugees and more transparent, as judges seemed to be encouraged to assess a larger variety of factors in order to assess the level of 'seriousness' of the harm. However, it bears the risk of again causing inconsistent approaches due to the vague character of the concept of 'seriousness'. Overall, in New Zealand, the assessment of whether a harm constitutes persecution is assessed on a case-by-case basis with the human rights narrative mostly used as a guiding framework, but not confined to it.

Similarly to the evolution observed in New Zealand, Australian Courts progressively acknowledged the importance of human rights in interpreting the refugee definition.[138] Human rights became increasingly referred to in the 1990s.[139]

135 Bruce Burson, 'Give way to the Right: The Evolving Use of Human Rights in New Zealand Refugee *Status Determination*', in Bruce Burson and David James Cantor (eds) *Human Rights and the Refugee Definition, Comparative Legal Practice and Theory* (Brill Nijhoff 2016) 25–48, 34. See also *Refugee Appeal Nos. 76226 and 76227* RSAA (12 January 2009), at [88] and [102] the RSAA refers to the CEDAW and at [111] to the CRC. *Refugee Appeal No. 75221 and 75225* RSAA (23 September 2005).

136 *Q (Pakistan) 800675* NZIPT (29 April 2015) at [35]; *BN (Fiji) 800688* NZIPT (20 April 2012) at [29]. *AC (Lebanon) 800688* NZIPT (5 March 2015) at [31]. In these cases, the test of persecution according to Hathaway's formulation is supplemented with the test of 'serious harm'. *AB (Slovakia), AF (Czech Republic)* [2015] NZIPT 800734–738, 29 June 2015.

137 *Refugee Appeal No. 76015* RSAA (4 Nov. 2007) para. 37 quoted in James C. Simeon (ed), *Critical Issues in International Refugee Law: Strategies Towards Interpretative Harmony* (Cambridge University Press 2010) 153.

138 Alex de Costa, '*Assessing the Cause and Effect of Persecution in Australian Refugee Law: Sarrazola, Khawar and the Migration Legislation Amendment Act*' [2001] 30 Federal Law Review 535, 558. De Costa pointed out that 'the reference to the Universal Declaration of Human Rights 1948 ("the Universal Declaration") in the Convention's preamble marks it as an instrument for the protection and realization of human rights has been acknowledged in Australian refugee jurisprudence'.

139 *Case No. N93–02362* RRTA 369 (27 February 1995) at 3; *Case No. N93–02050* RRTA 484 (10 March 1995) at 3; *Wang v. Minister for Immigration and Multicultural Affairs*, FCA 1599 (10 November 2000); *NACM of 2002 v Minister for Immigration and Multicultural and Indigenous Affairs* FCA 1554 (22 December 2003) at [54]; *Minister for Immigration and Multicultural and Indigenous Affairs v Sarrazola* FCA 263 (21 March 2001) at [31].

Although Hathaway's definition was not always expressly quoted and uncertainty remained as to which human rights were relevant, a certain influence of Hathaway's paradigm on Australian judges has been noticeable.[140] However, Kirk observed that, in the early 2000s, some judges dissociated themselves with Hathaway's narrative in order to adopt a more expansive interpretation of persecution.[141] In view of these jurisprudential developments (amongst other reasons), the Australian Parliament decided to narrow down the definition of a refugee in order to avoid too generous an approach to the 1951 Convention. As a result, in 2001, the Parliament passed a new law, introducing a statutory definition of the notion of persecution, which entailed a threefold analysis, moving away from the basic human rights narrative.[142] This new definition was meant to clearly limit the interpretational activity of the judges and to provide a restrictive understanding of the definition of a refugee in the 1951 Convention. In spite of these changes, Kirk noted that the legislation in fact 'received limited attention from Australian Courts',[143] which continued interpreting the notion of persecution quite broadly and, in practice, with some sporadic references to international human rights standards through ad hoc interpretive schemes.[144] Due to the absence of concrete changes in the jurisprudence and the internally inconsistent approaches adopted by Australian judges, the Parliament passed a second amendment to the Migration Act in 2014, amending the onshore protection visa regime of individuals coming to Australia. The amendment removed references to the 1951 Convention in the Migration Act in an attempt to create a 'new independent and self-contained statutory framework',[145] thus isolating Australian Courts from the influence of other international jurisprudences and from

140 *Applicant A v Minister for Immigration and Ethnic Affairs* HCA 190 CLR 225 (24 February 1997) at 232, mentioned in Mirko Bagaric, Kim Boyd, Penny Dimopoulos, John Vrachnas (eds), *Migration and Refugee Law: Principles and Practice in Australia* (Cambridge University Press 2005) 223. *Kord v. Minister for Immigration and Multicultural* Affairs, FCA 1163 (24 August 2001) para 15.

141 Ibid. in *Kord*, Judge Hely considered that the definition of Hathaway was too restrictive and that 'unjustifiable and discriminatory conduct, officially tolerated, directed at an applicant by reason of his race [constituted] persecution unless the impact of that conduct on the applicant [was] trivial or insignificant'. Linda Kirk, '*Island Nation: The Impact of International Human Rights Law on Australian Refugee Law*', in Bruce Burson and David James Cantor (eds), *Human Rights and the Refugee Definition, Comparative Legal Practice and Theory* (Brill Nijhoff 2016) 49–85, 64.

142 Migration Legislation Amendment Act (No 6.) 2001 Section 91R(1).

143 Kirk (n 141) 68.

144 For instance, see Judge Kirby who specifically referred to Hathaway's definition of persecution in *Applicant NABD of 2002 v Minister for Immigration and Multicultural and Indigenous Affairs* HCA 29 S70/2004 (26 May 2005) para 111. However, in *Case No.0903537*, RRTA 851 (30 July 2009) a more circumstantial approach based on the concept of discrimination was relied upon. See also, Bagaric et al. (n 140) 225.

145 Explanatory Memorandum to the Migration and Maritime Powers Legislation (Resolving the Legacy Caseload) Bill 2014, 168 at [1153]. Available at http://www.austlii.edu.au/au/legis/cth/bill_em/mamplatalcb2014832/memo_0.html.

international human rights law. Since then, references to international human rights are less common, with ad hoc approaches rather being adopted.[146] Very broad decisions are also rare.[147] However, in some cases, Australian judges have continued adopting quite expansive interpretations of persecution, and more rarely, have continued to refer to human rights norms. In particular, Kirk mentioned two recent cases, *SZTEQ v Minister for Border Protection*[148] and *Minister for Immigration and Border Protection v WZAPN*,[149] whereby the courts recently reiterated that the refugee definition should be applied consistently with international standards. In *SZTEQ v Minister for Border Protection*, the court referred to human rights law and human rights contained in the International Bill of Rights in order to analyse the notion of persecution. The court further expanded the human rights framework by adding that this interpretive scheme should be applied as part of a holistic analysis.[150] In this case, the judges considered that the assessment of a violation of a human right should be compounded by other considerations relating to the personal circumstances of the asylum seeker. The court relied on a loose human rights narrative as part of the analysis of what constitutes persecution and complemented it with other considerations based on circumstantial elements, thus adopting a more pragmatic approach.[151] Overall, Kneebone noted that the methodology used by decision makers in Australia is in general 'both pragmatic and confused',[152] thus raising legal uncertainty for individuals who seek asylum there.

In the 1990s, the influence of the basic human rights approach on Canadian jurisprudence also became quite significant. At that time, domestic judges started to rely increasingly on basic human rights standards in order to interpret the 1951 Convention and, more particularly, the notion of persecution.[153] In subsequent cases, in spite of the express recognition of the importance of basic human rights in the legislation, Canadian judges only sporadically relied on international human rights norms for interpreting the notion of persecution. Through a comprehensive study of the Canadian jurisprudence, Meili noted that references to human rights

146 Inter alia: *Case No. 1420100*, AATA 4383 (6 September 2016); *Case No. 1501978* AATA 3621 (9 November 2015); Case *No. 1605812*, [2017] AATA 158 (16 January 2017). None of these cases relied on a human rights approach.

147 See for instance: *Case No.1503327, AATA 4341 (24 August 2016)*, *Case No. 1502343*, AATA 4053 (6 July 2016): the applicant's claim was rejected after circumstantial analysis of her claim rather than a human rights approach.

148 *SZTEQ v Minister for Border Protection*, FCAFC 39 (11 February 2015), cited in Linda J. Kirk (n 141) 69.

149 *Minister for Immigration and Border Protection v WZAPN*, HCA 22 (17 June 2015), cited in Linda J. Kirk (n 141) 69.

150 *SZTEQ v Minister for Border Protection* (n 148) at [92].

151 Similar methodology can also be found for instance in *Case No.1419893* AATA 4338 (19 August 2016) at [43].

152 Susan Kneebone, '*Refugees as objects of surrogate protection: shifting identities*' in Susan Kneebone, Dallal Stevens, Loretta Baldassar (eds) *Refugee Protection and the Role of Law: Conflicting Identities* (Routledge Research in Asylum, Migration and Refugee Law, 2014) 98–121, 112.

153 *Canada (Attorney General) v. Ward*, [1993] 2 S.C.R. 689, Canada: Supreme Court.

treaties in the Canadian case law started declining at the end of the 1990s.[154] According to him, 'only 11.3 per cent of published RPD [Refugee Protection Division] and Federal Court decisions since 1990 contained either direct or indirect references' to one of the six major international human rights treaties considered in the study.[155] He calls this phenomenon the 'Canadian contradiction'[156] and attributes it to diverse factors such as the fact that lawyers are not necessarily human rights experts,[157] that judges seem to suffer from a form of human rights fatigue,[158] and that human rights standards are so widely accepted in the legal system of the country that judges do not feel the need to express direct references to international treaties.[159] Given the overall lack of a principled approach in the Canadian jurisprudence, it is difficult to define a clear practice as to the interpretation of the notion of persecution, although it appears that human rights have to a certain extent underpinned the development of the jurisprudence. It seems, however, that cases are generally adjudicated more on an ad hoc basis, with a risk of inconsistent interpretations.

In the USA, asylum judges have more rarely referred to basic human rights standards in their decisions. They instead adopted a case-by-case approach to the notion of persecution, based on the subjective evaluation of the judge. According to Hathaway, the American jurisprudence represents 'the zenith of a fundamentally subjective approach to the identification of persecutory harm',[160] leading to very inconsistent decisions. For instance, in *Nagoulko v INS*, the court adopted a very subjective view of what amounts to persecution by stating that it consists in 'the infliction of suffering or harm upon those who differ (in race, religion or political opinion) in a way regarded as offensive'.[161] In some other decisions, adjudicators followed a similar line of analysis as they assessed persecution from their own standpoint rather than in consideration of the particular circumstances of the applicant. In particular, in *Begzatowski v INS*, the court considered that persecution amounted to acts 'that this country does not recognize as legitimate'.[162] In another case, the judges used a different methodology by characterising persecution as meaning 'more than plain harassment and may arise from actions such as detention, arrest, interrogation, prosecution, imprisonment, illegal searches, confiscation of property, surveillance, beatings, or torture'.[163] In *Matter of M-F-W*, the BIA gave yet another definition of persecution by stating that

154 Stephen Meili, '*When Do Human Rights Treaties Help Asylum Seekers? A Study of Theory and Practice in Canadian Jurisprudence Since 1990*' [2014] 51 Osgoode Hall Law Journal 627, 630, http://digitalcommons.osgoode.yorku.ca/ohlj/vol51/iss2/7.
155 Ibid. 647.
156 Ibid. 636.
157 Ibid. 648.
158 Ibid. 650.
159 Ibid. 651.
160 Hathaway and Foster (n 1) 187.
161 Foster (n 12) 37.
162 *Begzatowski v Immigration and Naturalization Service*, No 01–2225 (United States Court of Appeals for the Seventh Circuit 2002).
163 *Tesfu v Ashcroft*, 322 F.3d 477, 481 (7th Circuit Court 2003).

'persecution involves significant suffering or harm because of a protected ground in the Act' and should not cause 'merely harassment or discomfort'.[164] Not only did the above proposed definitions differ in nature, but they are also quite imprecise. As such, in the absence of a coherent framework, the approaches adopted by US judges have tended to vary. Vittor and Anker considered that this lack of a principled approach led decision makers to be, at times, 'cautious and conservative'.[165] However, the authors pointed out that international human rights have, to a certain extent, influenced the evolution of the US jurisprudence, thus providing some form of guidance to define what sorts of harm amounted to persecution. For instance, they observed that human rights have become a central and integral part of the training of decision makers.[166] Indeed, the official training manual for the officers of the Asylum Office provides basic courses in human rights and encourages the officers to consider human rights violations when they determine what forms of harm amount to persecution.[167] For instance, Anker explained that through the human rights advocacy of different stakeholders, gender-based forms of violence have been increasingly accepted by decision makers.[168] Without the clear use of a defined framework for interpreting the notion, there remains a certain risk of uncertainty and lack of transparency in the adjudication of asylum claims lodged in the US. Indeed, a 2007 study of the jurisprudence conducted by Schoenholtz and colleagues confirmed this view by demonstrating that there were significant disparities between the different American courts adjudicating cases, which led them to call the asylum system in the US, a 'refugee roulette'.[169]

In countries that have referred often and explicitly to human rights, such as New Zealand and Australia, it does not appear that this narrative has fostered more consistency in the jurisprudence. Although a certain influence of the model developed by Hathaway is noticeable, decision makers seemed to have variably applied the parameters of his framework. In the words of Cantor, the human rights paradigm has proven to be 'not cohesive' but has rather reflected 'a number of divergent understandings of the role of human rights in the interpretive

164 *Matter of M-F-W- & L-G-*, 24 I&N Dec 633 (Board of Immigration Appeal 2008).

165 Deborah Anker and Josh Vittor, '*International Human Rights and US Refugee Law: Synergies and Contradictions*' in Bruce Burson and David James Cantor (eds), *Human Rights and the Refugee Definition, Comparative Legal Practice and Theory* (Brill Nijhoff 2016) 109–137, 121.

166 Ibid. 110.

167 Ibid. 116.

168 Deborah Anker, '*Legal change from the bottom up: The development of gender asylum jurisprudence in the United States*', Chapter 2 in Efrat Arbel, Catherin Dauvergne and Jenni Millbank (eds) *Gender in Refugee Law- from the Margins to the Centre* (Routledge 2014) 46–72, 48.

169 Andrew I. Schoenholtz, Jaya Ramji-Nogales and Philip G. Schrag '*Refugee Roulette: Disparities in Asylum Adjudication*' [2007] 60 Stanford Law Review 295, 379, https://scholarship.law.georgetown.edu/facpub/1902. For these authors, the lack of statutory definition for the notion of persecution is not necessarily the cause of discrepant interpretations. They impute it instead to other circumstantial factors in refugee procedures.

exercise'[170] of various jurisdictions. As such, the human rights approach based on objective standards of interpretation has not really fulfilled its promise of encouraging more coherence in the application of the 1951 Convention in a manner that adapts to the needs of refugees in the 21st century. Other countries, such as Canada and the USA have followed their own evolution with a certain influence of human rights law but there are still divergent views on how to assess the notion of persecution in the jurisprudence of these jurisdictions, thus raising significant legal uncertainty for asylum seekers in the 21st century.

2.5 Conclusion

Extensive literature has been produced on the interpretation of the refugee definition and, particularly on the notion of persecution through the basic human rights framework developed by Hathaway. This model has been largely commented on and, in recent years, arguments have been voiced to demonstrate that it does not always provide an adequate answer for the changing protection needs of refugees. Firstly, the vague and general character of basic human rights does not seem adequate to solve the problem of inconsistent applications of the 1951 Convention. Secondly, using basic human rights codified in international treaties as interpretive benchmarks raises a number of difficulties because they cover a minimal range of individuals' experiences. Additionally, Hathaway's test to assess the severity of the harm required has been deemed unduly strict and has been generally rejected by scholars. Lastly, his approach to surrogate protection and IFA has also been debated. It has been demonstrated that considering state protection as an inherent part of the test of persecution could lead to rather restrictive interpretations of the notion of persecution that are not consistent with the protective purpose of the Convention.

Overall, this chapter has attempted to demonstrate that the dominant perception that refugee protection equates with surrogate human rights protection raises conceptual difficulties. Different opinions on the role that human rights should play in interpreting the notion have been expressed and authors do not seem to agree on the various modalities of a human rights interpretive framework. As Cantor puts it, 'the sheer variety of human rights-based approaches to Article 1A (2) that are currently discernible in refugee law practice and scholarship calls into question the existence of a single interpretive paradigm'.[171] This in turn questions the validity and utility of the basic human rights narrative. Whilst the necessity of a principled approach has been widely accepted by commentators, one might wonder whether this approach should maintain basic human rights as interpretive benchmarks or whether a new paradigm is desirable.

It should not be concluded from the above criticisms that human rights law is irrelevant for interpreting the refugee definition today. It can indeed provide, in certain cases, normative references for assessing what forms of harm amount to

170 Cantor (n 28) 379.
171 Cantor (n 28) 392.

persecution and constitute an objective guidance that has reached a certain consensus on the international scene. However, as Toufayan put it, treaty interpretation 'far from being the accounting of raw interpretive data or the prioritisation of certain interpretive means over others [,] is in reality a holistic construct'.[172] In order to develop this holistic construct, other legal tools are needed. For this purpose, alternative approaches for interpreting the notion of persecution have been proposed and will be analysed in the following chapter.

172 Mark Toufayan, '*Human Rights Treaty Interpretation: A Postmodern Account of its Claim to "Speciality"*' (Center for Human Rights. & Global Justice, Working Paper No. 2, 2005), quoted by John Tobin (n 71) 10.

3 Alternative proposals to the basic human rights approach for interpreting the notion of persecution

The preceding chapter demonstrated that the basic human rights framework for interpreting constitutes a coherent and principled approach but, at the same time, it suffers from inherent limitations. In particular, it encourages a formalist methodology that does not appear to sufficiently take into account the various circumstances of refugees and does not solve the problem of inconsistent interpretations of the Convention due to its inherently vague character. It might, therefore, be wondered whether an alternative paradigm for interpreting persecution should be developed in order to overcome these deficiencies.

The present chapter will explore alternative models that have been proposed for interpreting persecution. The first part of this chapter will analyse the development of alternative narratives for interpreting persecution based on models that have built upon but expanded the basic human rights paradigm (Section 3.1), such as the definition developed by the Qualification Directive (QD) of the European Union and the framework proposed by Storey. However, it will be contended that none of these models are found adequate in order to meet the needs of refugees in the 21st century. A second part will then consider alternative models that adopted a more subjective or circumstantial analysis of the situation of refugees by emphasising other aspects of persecution (Section 3.2). It will be eventually argued that a holistic approach, taking into consideration the basic protection needs and the personal circumstances of refugees, might be desirable to assess the level of harm that individuals are likely to face upon return to their country in a more accurate and transparent manner. This view does not imply that external benchmarks, such as basic human rights norms, should be disregarded. They can indeed be factored into the assessment of what amounts to persecution, but they should not be used as primary and unique elements for analysing persecution because relying on abstract concepts risks obviating some protection needs of refugees.

3.1 A severe violation approach: an expanded basic human rights model?

As demonstrated in the previous chapter, the basic human rights model bears the risk of being too formalistic or restrictive. Therefore, European law has developed an alternative approach by expanding this human rights framework in order to take into account different forms of restrictions and encourage a more holistic analysis of the notion of persecution. The parameters of the European framework will be evaluated below together with a detailed analysis of the jurisprudence that this model has generated, both from CJEU and some national courts (3.1.1). Storey's proposal to expand the QD narrative in order to include any relevant norm of international law as interpretive benchmarks[1] will be also considered (3.1.2).

3.1.1 The Qualification Directive of the European Union: first treaty to provide a definition of persecution in refugee law

A severe violation approach

EU countries agreed in 1999, at the Tempere Summit, to create a Common European Asylum System (CEAS), in order to set minimum standards for harmonising asylum systems in Europe.[2] One of the major instruments of the CEAS is the QD that established eligibility criteria for determining who is entitled to receive international protection in countries of the European Union.[3] The QD, however, did not establish a self-contained regime separate from international refugee law. In fact, the directive drew extensively upon the provisions of the 1951 Convention to develop a European system of protection in line with international standards.[4]

1 Hugo Storey, '*Persecution: Towards a Working Definition*' in V. Chetail and C. Bauloz (eds), *Research Handbook on International Law and Migration* (Edward Elgar 2014) 459–518.

2 Directive 2013/32/EU of the European Parliament and of the Council of 26 June 2013 on common procedures for granting and withdrawing international protection; Directive 2003/09/EC of the European Parliament and of the Council of 27 January 2003 laying down minimum standards for the reception of asylum seekers; Recast Directive 2011/95/EU of the European Parliament and of the Council of 13 December 2011 on standards for the qualification of third-country nationals or stateless persons as beneficiaries of international protection, for a uniform status for refugees or for persons eligible for subsidiary protection, and for the content of the protection granted; Regulation (EU) No 604/2013 of the European Parliament and of the Council of 26 June 2013 establishing the criteria and mechanisms for determining the Member State responsible for examining an application for international protection lodged in one of the Member States by a third-country national or a stateless person; Regulation (EU) No 603/2013 of the European Parliament and of the Council of 26 June 2013 on the establishment of 'Eurodac' for the comparison of fingerprints.

3 Jane McAdam, '*The Qualification Directive: An Overview*', in Karin Zwaan (eds), *The Qualification Directive: Central Themes, Problem Issues, and Implementation in Selected Member States* (Nijmegen: Wolf Legal Publishers 2007) 8–30, 8. McAdam noted that, for the first time in Europe, the QD elaborated 'a distinct status for extra-Convention refugees'.

4 Hélène Lambert, '*The EU Asylum Qualification Directive, Its Impact on the Jurisprudence of the United Kingdom and International Law*' [2006] 55 International and Comparative Law Quarterly 161, DOI: https://doi.org/10.1093/iclq/lei070.

One of the most significant innovations of the QD is the development of a binding definition of the notion of persecution. Article 9 of the Directive states that persecution consists either in a 'severe violation of basic human rights', or in various measures that would have the same effect. Article 9(1) stated that '[a]cts of persecution … must':

> (a) be sufficiently serious by their nature or repetition as to constitute a severe violation of basic human rights, in particular the rights from which derogation cannot be made under Article 15(2) of the European Convention for the Protection of Human Rights and Fundamental Freedoms; or
> (b) be an accumulation of various measures, including violations of human rights which is sufficiently severe as to affect an individual in a similar manner as mentioned in (a).

Further to this, Article 9(2) goes on to enumerate, in a non-exhaustive manner, different types of harms that could be considered persecutory. By establishing a clear list of harms that could fall within the ambit of the notion of persecution, the QD provides specific and concrete guidance for decision makers. The UNHCR welcomed these examples as positive clarifications of certain grey areas of refugee law.[5]

Through Article 9, the QD is the first international instrument that officially endorsed the basic human rights narrative.[6] The modalities of this interpretive framework are, however, quite different to the ones suggested by Hathaway in the 1990s. The QD abandoned the persistency criteria of harm and referred to 'severe violations' rather than 'sustained or systemic' violations. In addition to this, the QD expanded the definition of Hathaway by adopting a broader view that takes into consideration various forms of predicaments, also amounting to a severe violation of a basic human right. By considering the consequences that various other measures can have on an individual, the QD seemed to adopt a more pragmatic approach and encouraged decision makers to take into consideration a larger number of restrictions to assess the gravity of various restrictions in an individual's life. This approach is, however, limited by the reference to external benchmarks, as the QD stated that, in order to amount to persecution, such restrictions should affect an individual in a manner similar to 'severe violations of basic human rights'. By setting a fixed threshold based

For Lambert, the QD is an instrument that directly 'goes to the heart of the 1951 Convention Relating to the Status of Refugees' and, as such, constitutes 'the most important instrument in the new legal order in European asylum'.

5 UNHCR, 'UNHCR Annotated Comments on the EC Council Directive 2004/83/EC of 29 April 2004 on Minimum Standards for the Qualification and Status of Third Country Nationals or Stateless Persons as Refugees or as Persons Who Otherwise Need International Protection and the Content of the Protection Granted' (OJ L 304/12 of 30.9.2004) (January 2005) 21.

6 Storey (n 1) 478. See also McAdam (n 3) 11: The Qualification Directive 'reflects very strongly Hathaway's human rights approach to "persecution".'

on basic human rights norms, the QD therefore minimised the subjective approach and made the notion of 'basic human rights' the keystone of the definition of persecution.

The definition proposed by the QD, whilst more flexible than the basic human rights framework developed by Hathaway, raises some other conceptual difficulties. In particular, Lehmann observed that the formulation used in the QD poses questions such as 'what is a "basic" human right and how should severity be determined'?[7] Indeed, the QD relies extensively on the notion of 'basic human rights' to define persecution but there is no authoritative definition of what a 'basic' human right is in international law, thus causing some uncertainty as to which benchmarks should be used for interpreting persecution. Whilst Hathaway suggested that basic human rights are the rights enshrined in widely accepted treaties, there is nothing in the text of the QD that expressly endorses this approach. In fact, the QD provided some different guidance in article 9(1)(a) indicating that non-derogable rights could be considered as basic human rights. More precisely, this article stipulated that, 'in particular', reference could be made to the non-derogable rights of the European Convention for the Protection of Human Rights and Fundamental Freedom (ECHR) in order to identify basic human rights. The term 'in particular' used in the definition seems to imply that these non-derogable rights are merely illustrative and that other benchmarks could be also referred to. However, there is no further explanation as to whether or not other types of human right norms could be considered 'basic human rights'. This ambiguity is concerning as it could allow restrictive interpretations of the notion of persecution. Klug, for instance, noted that the formulation of the QD 'bears the danger of a minimalistic approach, restricted to the rights mentioned in Article 15 para. 2 of the ECHR'.[8] For her, the QD does not encourage 'an interpretation of the term "persecution" from a broader human rights' perspective.[9]

Guidance on the meaning of basic human rights can be found in the jurisprudence of the European Court of Human Rights (ECtHR) referring to rights with a 'non-refoulement' dimension.[10] However, Lehmann noted that such guidance might not be adequate for refugee law purposes. In particular, that this non-refoulement dimension is assessed through a nebulous narrative, notably by referring to the notion of 'flagrant breach' or 'flagrant denial' of core elements of certain rights. Lehmann argued that this framework is rather general and does not provide sufficient indication for assessing the threshold of persecution in refugee law. According to him, the 'flagrant denial' and 'flagrant breach' doctrine

7 Julian M. Lehmann, '*Persecution, Concealment and the Limits of a Human Rights Approach in (European) Asylum Law – The Case of Germany v Y and Z in the Court of Justice of the European Union*' [2014] 26 International Journal of Refugee Law 65, 71, https://doi.org/10.1093/ijrl/eeu006.

8 Anja Klug, '*Harmonization of Asylum in the European Union – Emergence of an EU Refugee System?*' [2004] 47 German Yearbook of International Law 594, 602.

9 Ibid. 62.

10 Lehmann (n 7) 72.

constitutes an 'abstract rationale for a particular seriousness' and provides 'little further guidance'[11] on how to identify what is the 'core' of a right and what a basic human right is. He also pointed out that the jurisprudence of the HRC has provided some guidance in this field but overall it remains unclear.[12]

Whilst the guidance of the ECHR for identifying basic rights appears indeed quite general, it could be further argued that the threshold proposed by the ECHR seems, in any case, inadequate because it is particularly severe. The non-refoulement dimension of certain rights sets a test that is too strict. It significantly limits the array of rights that could be referred to and relies on notions that are quite vague. In this sense, Juss noted that the 'flagrant breach' doctrine sets an 'unrealistically high threshold'.[13] An example of how the non-derogable or non-refoulement rights narrative has unduly limited the application of the 1951 Convention will be assessed below by considering the recent caseload of the Court of Justice of the European Union (CJEU).

Another concern justly pointed out by Lehmann in the definition of Article 9 (1)(a) is that the test that it proposes, namely 'severe violations', is quite ambiguous. Lehmann pointed out that external guidance either in the ECHR or in the HCR, does not provide more precision.[14] One could therefore wonder whether the wording of Article 9(1)(b) could present more indications as to the degree of harm expected. On this point however, Article 9(1)(b) seems to set a rather high threshold again. This portion of the definition refers to certain measures that are 'sufficiently serious by their nature or repetition' as to amount to persecution, but then goes on to refer to 'non-derogable rights'[15] to assess the level of harm required. This might indicate that one violation of a non-derogable right that is not either serious or repeated, would not suffice to constitute persecution. As such, it remains unclear how milder violations of non-basic human rights should be treated or how more subjective aspects will be factored into the analysis of persecution. By stating that certain measures should affect an individual in a similar manner as a severe violation of a basic human right, the QD maintains a rather rigid and vague test. Additional guidance could be found in Article 9(2) but this

11 Ibid. 73.

12 Ibid. 73: The HRC developed the theory that there is a core of each right that needs to be taken into consideration and that, in certain cases, can never been derogated. The question that arises here is whether these non-derogable dispositions could be considered 'basic human rights' in the words of the QD. Lehmann rejected this idea by pointing at the deficiencies of this approach due to the fact that there 'is no agreed-upon and consistent method for identifying the non-derogable cores of rights'. In general, he convincingly concluded that human rights law 'does not provide a conclusive answer to what "basic" human rights are'.

13 Satvinder. S. Juss, *International Migration and Global Justice* (Ashgate, Aldershot, 2006) 204. See also Cathryn Costello, *The Human Rights of Migrants and Refugees in European Law* (Oxford University Press 2015) 197. Costello also pointed to the limited ambit of the 'flagrant breach' theory of the ECHR in refugee law cases. For her, 'refugee law can offer better protection than the ECHR in important aspects'.

14 Lehmann (n 7) 73.

15 Through the formulation: 'in a similar manner as (a)'.

list simply defines the forms that persecution can take and does not really say much about the degree of harm required to amount to persecution.

In contrast to the above criticisms, Labayle argued that Article 9(1)(a) is quite clear and specific. He believes that this article should be interpreted as only covering the non-derogable rights under Article 15 of the ECHR[16] in order to constitute a well-defined framework of interpretation. However, Labayle did not seem to take into consideration the plain text of Article 9. As above mentioned, Article 9 specifically stated that, 'in particular', non-derogable rights should be used as benchmarks. The 'in particular' limb suggests that other human right norms could also be relevant for assessing the notion of persecution. For Cantor, the non-derogable rights of the ECHR mentioned in the QD constitute only a 'minimum threshold' to evaluate what amounts to persecution[17] and implied that a wider array of rights could be also relevant for interpreting the notion. In line with Cantor's position, it appears more reasonable to consider that the non-derogable rights should be viewed as a safety net for applying the refugee definition but not as rigidly delineating the parameters of the interpretive framework. Otherwise, the QD definition would adopt a particularly restrictive approach.

Bearing the above limitations in mind, the UNHCR warned against a strict interpretation of the QD that would only rely on a formalist framework based on codified human rights. In its annotated comments on the text of the QD, the UNHCR stated that:

> while international and regional human rights treaties and the corresponding jurisprudence and decisions of the respective supervisory bodies influence the interpretation of the 1951 Convention, persecution cannot and should not be defined solely on the basis of serious or severe human rights violations.[18]

According the UNHCR, the assessment of persecution under the QD is to be undertaken on a case-by-case basis, in a more holistic manner. The refugee agency recommended that, in general, different factors should be assessed in order to determine whether certain measures 'make life in the country of origin so insecure from many perspectives for the individual concerned, that the only way out of the predicament is to leave the country of origin'.[19] The UNHCR

16 Henri Labayle, '*Le Droit d'Asile devant la Persécution Religieuse: la Cour de Justice ne se Dérobe pas*', Reseau Universitaire Européen Droit de l'Espace de Liberté, Securité et Justice, 9 September 2012 available at: <http://www.gdr-elsj.eu/2012/09/09/asile/le-droitdasile-devant-la-persecution-religieuse-la-cour-de-justice-ne-se-derobe-pas/>.

17 James Cantor, '*Defining Refugees: Persecution, Surrogacy and the Human Rights Paradigm*' in Bruce Burson and Cantor David James (eds), *Human Rights and the Refugee Definition, Comparative Legal Practice and Theory* (Brill Nijhoff 2016) 349–395, 383.

18 UNHCR (n 5) 20.

19 Statement by Ms. Erika Feller, Director, Department of International Protection, UNHCR, SCIFA (Brussels, 6 November 2002) available at: http://www.unhcr.org/admin/dipstatements/42bab1b52/statement-ms-erika-feller-director-department-international-protection.html.

criticised the strict and ambiguous test established by the QD in its definition of persecution and recommended that more emphasis should be put on the impact that various measures, regardless of their nature, have on the daily life of an individual. Whilst the QD focuses mostly on the nature of human rights violations, the UNHCR proposes to shift the paradigm by instead considering the consequences that these various measures have on someone's life. This position was supported by other authors who considered that the QD developed a human rights narrative that is too rigid and disregards the subjective and personal circumstances of refugees.[20]

The restrictive guidance of the CJEU on the notion of persecution

As mentioned above, the definition of the QD remains, to a certain extent, ambiguous. Therefore, after it was adopted, there was a great hope[21] that the CJEU would provide a more detailed guidance[22] in order to harmonise different approaches in member states. Since 2004, the CJEU has issued three main decisions that analysed the notion of persecution in light of Article 9. Unfortunately, in these decisions, the court also adopted a restrictive interpretation of persecution, which departed from the protection purpose of the 1951 Convention.

In *Bundesrepublik Deutschland v. Y and Z*[23] on 5 September 2012, the Federal German Court requested the CJEU to determine to what extent a violation of the right to freedom of religion constituted a persecutory act in the context of an asylum request made by two Pakistani applicants belonging to the Ahmadi religious minority.[24] The court started by rejecting the traditional German doctrine that considered that there was a 'core' to each human right and that such a core was necessary to determine whether certain measures amounted to persecution. The CJEU decided, instead, that all sorts of acts interfering with a basic human right—in the present case, the freedom of religion—needed to be taken into account in order to interpret persecution. In this sense, it adopted a broader approach than in the German courts. The European judges then added that a more pragmatic approach should be adopted for evaluating the gravity of a harm as they considered that both the nature of the restrictions and the consequences

20 Klug (n 8) 603: According to Klug, the joint proposal presented a better alternative by emphasising the importance of the subjective element of persecution.

21 Roland Bank, '*The Potential and Limitations of the Court of Justice of the European Union in Shaping International Refugee Law*' [2015] 27 International Journal of Refugee Law 213, 215.

22 Treaty on the Functioning of the European Union (TFEU), Art 267.

23 *Bundesrepublik Deutschland v Y and Z*, C-71/11, C-99/11 (CJEU 5 September 2012).

24 Bruce and Cantor observed that it was the very first time that a supranational court endorsed the human rights approach for interpreting the notion of persecution: Bruce Burson and David James Cantor, '*Interpreting the Refugee Definition via Human Rights Standards*', Chapter 1 in Bruce Burson and David James Cantor (eds), *Human Rights and the Refugee Definition, Comparative Legal Practice and Theory* (Brill Nijhoff 2016) 1–24, 9.

that they have for an individual should be factored into the assessment of persecution.[25] For the judges, what mattered was the severity of the restriction, not the restriction itself.[26] Whilst European judges seemed to initially develop a broad understanding of the QD by straying away from the 'core' human rights doctrine, they then narrowed down their views by imposing a very high degree to the harm required as they stated that persecution was only characterised if 'an applicant for asylum, as a result of exercising that freedom in his country of origin, runs a genuine risk of, inter alia, being prosecuted or subject to inhuman or degrading treatment or punishment'.[27] Through this formulation, the court equated the notion of persecution with the severity of harm required under the non-refoulement principle of the ECHR and the 1951 Convention and relied on rather vague notions. Commentators criticised the severe threshold used by the court. For instance, Bank considered that the court established an 'exceptionally high standard for an act of persecution'.[28] Other authors also noted that the test established by the court was rather unclear. For instance, Lehmann considered that in 'implicitly relying on the scope of non-refoulement under the ECHR', the court endorsed 'a very narrow, conceptually vague human rights approach to the notion of persecution'[29] and undercut 'the autonomous and wider scope of harm relevant under the Convention's refugee definition'.[30] Araújo also observed that, after the court decision, some 'level of uncertainty' remained as to the threshold that should be applied in cases of religious persecution.[31] Interestingly, in the present case, the European judges had pointed to the circumstantial dimension of persecution as they considered that it was necessary to assess the consequences that certain measures can have for an individual. Although this element could have further encouraged the judges to evaluate, in a holistic manner, the broad impact that certain restrictions have on claimants' lives, the court unfortunately ended up restricting the scope of the QD by setting a very high threshold to the notion of persecution.

25 *Bundesrepublik Deutschland v Y and Z* (n 23) at [65].
26 See Alexandra Maria Rodrigues Araújo,'*The Qualification for Being a Refugee under EU Law: Religion as a Reason for Persecution Court of Justice of the European Union (Grand Chamber), Judgment of 5 September 2012, Joined Cases C-71/11 and C-99/11, Bundesrepublik Deutschland v. Y and Z*' [2014] 16 European Journal of Migration and Law 553, 546, https://doi.org/10.1163/15718166-12342068: 'the Court adopted the following touchstone: it is the severity of the measures and sanctions adopted or the liability to be adopted against the person concerned which will determine whether a violation of religious freedom constitutes persecution (…) the Court established that the acts regarded as constituting persecution must not be judged on the basis of the particular aspect of religious freedom that is being interfered with, but on the basis of the intrinsic severity of the repression inflicted on the individual and the severity of its consequences'.
27 *Bundesrepublik Deutschland v Y and Z* (n 23) at [67].
28 Bank (n 21) 226.
29 Lehmann (n 7) 81.
30 Ibid. 79.
31 Araújo (n 26) 556.

Regrettably, the court confirmed this restrictive approach in *Minister voor Immigratie en Asiel v X, Y and Z* on 7 November 2013.[32] In this case, the court had to examine the claim of two homosexual applicants, hailing from Sierra Leone and Uganda. The European judges found that the violation of the right to private and family life did not in itself amount to persecution because this right was a derogable right.[33] The court concluded from this observation that:

> the mere existence of a legislation criminalising homosexual acts cannot be regarded as an act affecting the applicant(s) in a manner so significant that it reaches the level of seriousness necessary for a finding that it constitutes persecution within the meaning of Article 9(1) of the Directive.[34]

This approach was highly criticised by the International Commission of Jurists (ICJ), pointing out that the non-derogability of a right could not be equated with the concept of severity on which the notion of persecution rested.[35] Although the Court considered that penalisation did not amount to persecution, it stated that implemented penal sanctions, such as imprisonment, could constitute persecution. European judges then proposed to take into consideration 'all the relevant facts concerning that country of origin'[36] in order to assess whether an applicant was at risk of facing persecution. They did not, however, specifically mention what kind of facts should be examined and seemed to propose only to refer to facts relating to the geopolitical circumstances in the country of origin, namely to external facts. Again, by not encouraging a more holistic assessment of the personal experiences of the claimants and affirming that penalisation of homosexuality did not per se amount to persecution, the judges adopted a narrow and rigid view of the refugee definition. The consequences that criminal laws have for the life of homosexuals should have been better highlighted in the judgment. Indeed, such laws can have devastating impacts on homosexuals who live in permanent distress and are not free to express their emotions and their sexual orientation in public as well as to enjoy the possibility of living freely with their partners. Unfortunately, the court overlooked this aspect. The judges adopted a 'compartmentalised'[37] approach by

32 *X, Y, Z v Minister voor Immigratie en Asiel*, C-199/12 – C-201/12 (CJEU 7 November 2013).
33 Ibid. at [54].
34 Ibid. at [55].
35 '*X, Y and Z: a Glass Half Full for Rainbow Refugees?*' The International Commission of Jurists' observations on the judgment of the Court of Justice of the European Union in *X, Y and Z v. Minister voor Immigratie en Asiel*, International Commission of Jurists, 3 June 2014 available at: http://icj.wpengine.netdna-cdn.com/wp-content/uploads/2014/06/CommentaryXYZ-Advocacy-2014.pdf at [49].
36 *X, Y, Z v Minister voor Immigratie en Asiel* (n 32) at [58].
37 ICJ (n 35) at [57]: 'the fact that consensual same-sex sexual orientation and/or acts are criminalized requires a thorough, individualized and holistic assessment—rather than a false and compartmentalized one—of whether these laws affect the lived experience of asylum applicants in their country of origin in such a way as to give rise to a well-founded fear of persecution'.

encouraging a formalist assessment of abstract entitlements rather than adopting a more circumstantial methodology. The position of the court also disregarded the views of the UNHCR which considered that 'even if irregularly, rarely or ever enforced, criminal laws prohibiting same-sex relations could lead to an intolerable predicament for an LGBTI person rising to the level of persecution'.[38] In reaction to this judgment, the ICJ and Amnesty International issued a joint statement criticising the reasoning of the court. The statement affirmed that legislation penalising homosexuality actually fosters social homophobia with the tacit approval of the authorities even when it is not applied in practice.[39] In light of the foregoing, it appears that the court adopted a narrow view of persecution again, and should have encouraged member states to engage in a broader analysis of the situation faced by homosexuals in their country, by considering for instance that the criminalisation of homosexuality, could, depending on the objective country conditions and the personal circumstances of claimants, raise a rebuttable presumption of persecution.

Not only did the cases mentioned above adopt a restrictive approach of the human rights narrative, but they also provided inconsistent guidance on what amounts to persecution, thus demonstrating that human rights law does not always resolve the problem of fragmentary jurisprudence. For instance, Heijer noted that the European judges gave contradictory information in relation to the requirement to conceal certain elements of one's identity in order to avoid persecution. In *Y and Z*, the court indicated that the personal circumstances of an applicant should be taken into consideration in order to assess whether he would engage in public practice of his religion. This indicated that, although it cannot be reasonably expected of someone to abstain from practising her religion in public, she might also act discreetly as per her personal conviction and, as such, persecution might not apply. The language of the court was however different in *X, Y and Z*, as the European judges clearly stated that: 'the fact that (the applicant) could avoid the risk by exercising greater restraint than a heterosexual in expressing his sexual orientation is not to be taken into account'.[40] In this case, the court adopted a more categorical approach in relation to the discreet attitude that one can be expected to have. It indicated that, under no circumstances should the evaluation of persecution be conducted with the eventuality in mind that one could try to avoid the harm feared. To Heijer, these different formulations

38 UNHCR, *Guidelines on International Protection No 9: Claims to Refugee Status based on Sexual Orientation and/or Gender Identity within the context of Article 1A(2) of the 1951 Convention and/or its 1967 Protocol relating to the Status of Refugees*, 23 October 2012, HCR/GIP/12/01, at [27], https://www.refworld.org/docid/50348afc2.html.

39 Amnesty International, '*Observations by Amnesty International and the International Commission of Jurists on the case X, Y and Z v Minister voor Immigratie, Integratie en Asiel*' (C-199/12, C-200/12 and C-201/12) following the Opinion of Advocate General Sharpston of 11 July 2013, 2 October 2013, POL 33/003/2013, https://www.amnesty.org/en/documents/POL33/003/2013/en/.

40 *X, Y, Z v Minister voor Immigratie en Asiel* (n 32) at [75].

demonstrate that 'different tests apply to the persecution reasons of homosexuality and religion'.[41] Heijer highlighted the absurdity of these solutions according to which it will 'never be tolerable for a homosexual to conceal his identity, but it can be tolerable for a religious person to only worship in private'.[42] These inconsistent solutions in fact reflect the variable approaches that can be adopted under the QD, and to a broader extent under the human rights narrative.

In the previous cases, the court essentially dwelled on the interpretation of Article 9(1) but in *Shepherd*[43] it provided some guidance on the interpretation of Article 9(2) when this article was the object of a set of questions referred to the CJEU by the High Administrative Court of Bavaria. The court had to examine the case of a former soldier who served for two years in Iraq as a helicopter maintenance mechanic. He eventually deserted because he considered that the war was illegal and because he believed that war crimes were committed by his army. He argued that because of his desertion, he was at risk of prosecution and social ostracism in his country of origin. According to the QD Article 9(2), prosecution or punishment for refusal to perform military service may amount to persecution only when performing military service would involve the commission of crimes or acts falling under the exclusion clauses.[44] This approach is quite narrow as it overlooks any other personal motivation that a conscientious objector could have for not abiding by national obligations. Not only did the CJEU endorse this position, but it further limited the possibilities of granting asylum based on conscientious objection. The court posited new conditions to the granting of asylum in cases of desertion from the military, namely that the commission of crimes should be 'highly likely', that desertion should be the only way to avoid the commission of such crimes and that an endorsement of the conflict by the international community should be taken into account in assessing the possibility of committing war crimes. Unfortunately, the result of this conclusion was to heighten the burden of proof for asylum seekers.[45] Commentators criticised the position of the court by considering that the judges did not apply a broad human rights approach as required by the QD[46] and as recommended by the UNHCR. For instance, Vicini recently contended that the position of the CJEU in this case was 'incompatible with recent developments within international human rights law, which progressively protect the right to

41 Maarten den Heijer, '*Persecution for reason of sexual orientation: X, Y and Z* [2014] 51 Common Market Law Review 1217, 1231, https://dare.uva.nl/search?identifier=23dcc9a2-29c5-49d2-9e18-270dd37f0c36.

42 Ibid. 1231.

43 *Andre Lawrence Shepherd v Bundesrepublik Deutschland*, Case C-472/13 (CJEU, 26 February 2015).

44 The Qualification Directive, Art 9(2)e.

45 *Andre Lawrence Shepherd v Bundesrepublik Deutschland* (n 43) at [46].

46 Julian M. Lehmann, '*Of Shepherds and Sheepdogs—Andre Lawrence Shepherd v. Bundesrepublik Deutschland before the Court of Justice of the European Union*', 9 March 2015, University of Michigan Law School blog, available at: http://www.reflaw.org/of-shepherds-and-sheepdogs-andre-lawrence-shepherd-v-bundesrepublik-deutschland-before-the-court-of-justice-of-the-european-union/#.

conscientious objection as an essential part of the right to freedom of thought, conscience and religion'.[47] Additionally, the judges did not propose specific guidance as they did not clarify what they believed were the protected activities under human rights law, nor did they explain what infringements and limitations of such activities were admissible. In particular, the court seemed to accept that up to five years of imprisonment was acceptable for deserting the US army but did not justify why this would be so. The judges also did not engage in a holistic appreciation of what would be the exact nature of the harm feared in the country of origin of the applicant.

In light of the foregoing, it appears that the uncertainty raised by Article 9 of the QD regarding the definition of persecution has not so far been lifted by the CJEU. Although the court endorsed the basic human rights approach, it used human rights standards to, in fact, adopt narrow views of the notion of persecution. According to Cantor, in analysing 'subtle questions about the boundaries of persecution', the Court had 'recourse to human rights [...] to serve as a justification for restrictive interpretations of this element'.[48] Indeed, the European judges failed to develop a detailed framework of interpretation in line with broader international norms and with the UNHCR's recommendations. Instead, they made used of the vague wording of the QD to develop restrictive standards of interpretation. As a result, the highly difficult task of interpreting the QD pursuant to the spirit of the 1951 Convention still rests on the member states themselves without effective coordination, which further heightens the risk of inconsistent decisions within the European Union.

Inconsistent practices in Europe after the adoption of the QD

Since the adoption of the QD in 2004, national jurisdictions have been encouraged to use human rights standards for interpreting persecution in order to ensure more harmonisation at the European level.[49] There has been, however, no clear methodology for doing so. An overview of the decisions of a few selected countries with detailed asylum jurisprudence, namely the UK, France and Belgium will demonstrate that inconsistencies remain in Europe.

The modalities of interpretation of the QD have been adopted in the UK.[50] However, a rather formalist methodology seems to have been favoured by British

47 Giuli Vicini, '*Conscientious objection to military service and the notion of persecution in European Union asylum law, the Shepherd Judgment of the Court of Justice of the European Union*' [2015] 13 Journal of International Criminal Justice 845, 859, DOI: 10.1093/jicj/mqv033.
48 Cantor (n 17) 386.
49 See p. XXX above.
50 The UK has opted out from the recast QD but has transposed into national law the Council Directive 2004/83/EC of 29 April 2004 on minimum standards for the qualification and status of third country nationals or stateless persons as refugees or as persons who otherwise need international protection and the content of the protection granted. The UK has however withdrawn from the European Union on 31 January 2020.

judges as they often specifically refer to a limited set of rights, such as the non-derogable standards of the ECHR.[51] This risk of narrow interpretations has been pointed out by various authors who warned against the ambiguous wording of the QD.[52] For instance, in *SH (Palestinian Territories)*,[53] the Court of Appeal interpreted the QD quite strictly by considering that only violations of non-derogable rights in the ECHR could amount to persecution, thus setting a particularly high threshold that disregards the plain text of the directive. In another case involving an accumulation of various predicaments of an economic and social nature, the Upper Tribunal considered that in order to meet the test for persecution, the restrictions faced should necessarily amount to violations of Article 3 of the ECHR (inhuman or degrading treatment or punishment).[54] In this case, the tribunal analysed the claim of an Azerbaijani unmarried mother of Russian ethnicity and Christian religion. She had a child of a mixed origin out of wedlock and, because of that, she was rejected by her family who threatened to kill her. The tribunal accepted that 'women in Azerbaijan are treated as inferior to men and there is, for example, discrimination in the work place',[55] that the 'mixed African/European descent would at best mean that he would stand out from the rest of the population, and at worst that he would be shunned',[56] and that 'corruption is commonplace, and a system of favours may operate when looking for housing or work'.[57] However, the court considered that the treatment the applicant received was not contrary to Article 3 because there was evidence that the claimant could obtain a job and live a fairly decent life. Unfortunately, this decision did not assess how the accumulation of various restrictions could significantly impact the applicant's life in other ways, and thus, lacked comprehensive justification for rejecting this asylum claim. Conversely, the same year in *JA Nigeria*,[58] the Upper Tribunal adopted a broader approach. The tribunal conducted an analysis based on human rights, and also adopted a more circumstantial methodology, including a subjective assessment of the frame of mind of the applicant who, in this case, was a minor. The tribunal then relied on the UNHCR guidelines by considering that

51 *A (Iraq) v Secretary of State for the Home Department* [2017] EWCA Civ. 944, 11 July 2017; *C (Albania) v Secretary of State for the Home Department v. the United Nations High Commissioner for Refugees (Intervener)* [2017] EWCA Civ 351, 9 May 2017; *MST and Others (national service-risk categories) Eritrea CG* [2016] UKUT 00443 (IAC), 11 October 2016.

52 See p. XXX above.

53 *SH (Palestinian Territories) v Secretary of State for the Home Department* [2008] EWCA civ 1150, 22 October 2008. Also quoted in Raza Husain, '*International Human Rights and Refugee Law: The United Kingdom*' in Bruce Burson and Cantor David James (eds), *Human Rights and the Refugee Definition Comparative Legal Practice and Theory* (Brill Nijhoff 2016) 138–155, 152.

54 *SL (Unmarried mother with mixed race child) Azerbaijan CG. Secretary of State for the Home Department* [2012] UKUT 00046 (IAC) 13 February 2013 at [97].

55 Ibid. at [125].

56 Ibid. at [127].

57 Ibid. at [128].

58 *JA (Child - risk of persecution) Nigeria* [2016] UKUT 00560 (IAC) 20 December 2016.

'ill-treatment which may not arise to the level of persecution in the case of an adult, may do so in the case of a child, and the child's youth immaturity, vulnerability, etc. will rightly be related to how that child experiences or fears harm'.[59] It was then concluded that the assessment of persecution depended 'upon the circumstances of [the claimants'] individual positions, their age, no doubt and their background'[60] and in this case, the appeal was allowed.

In the cases mentioned above, different human rights methodologies have been used, yielding different results. In the first two cases, the judges relied on a rather formal human rights approach, which seemed to have led to restrictive interpretations of persecution, whilst in the latter, they combined a human rights assessment of the situation with the circumstantial approach, engaging in a more holistic analysis of the situation. A later decision in *MA (Pakistan) and Secretary for the Home Department*,[61] the judges again departed from this holistic approach and maintained a rather rigid view of what amounts to persecution. Overall British judges have continued to rely on human rights notions for interpreting persecution after the adoption of the QD but they sometimes have done so in a rather inconsistent manner and, at times, have adopted narrow interpretations of the notion of persecution.

Conversely to the UK, in other countries of the European Union, such as France and Belgium, references to human rights norms or other protection standards remain quite rare. Although some references to external human rights have been sporadically made in those jurisdictions after the adoption of the QD, most cases did not assess the notion of persecution in light of objective benchmarks and continue evaluating the notion through a case-by-case analysis.

In general, no clear methodology has been followed by French judges, who only refer to human rights as benchmarks of interpretation on an irregular basis. In fact, in some cases, the court barely provided explanation for considering the absence of persecution.[62] For instance, the Cour Nationale du Droit d'Asile (CNDA) rejected the case[63] of an Armenian man married to an ethnic Azeri woman and fearing hostility and discrimination on this account. In the opinion of the court, the existence of a prejudice and a sentiment of intolerance against minorities in Armenia did not amount to persecution. Unfortunately, the court did not justify this position, thus making a subjective assessment of the situation without evaluating the impact that various forms of social hostility could have on

59 Ibid. at [16].

60 Ibid. at [26]. See also earlier cases where the Upper Tribunal proposed to engage in a holistic assessment of the claimant's circumstances, rather than a formalist human rights approach: in *MS (Coptic Christians) Egypt CG v Secretary of State for the Home Department* [2013] UKUT 00611 (IAC) 3 December 2013.

61 *MA (Pakistan) and Secretary for the Home Department*, AA030622015 [2016] UKAITUR (28 January 2016).

62 CNDA Sections réunies, 16 novembre 2011 *M. B.* n° 10018108 R; CNDA 23 décembre 2013 Décision No. 11024877: no reference to any methodological approach to assess persecution is made.

63 CNDA, ordonnance 10 octobre 2016 *M. B.* n° 16020922 C.

the applicants. In a different case,[64] however, the court assessed more carefully the applicant's profile against the situation in the country of origin. In this case, the applicant was a single Tamil female from Sri Lanka. The court considered various elements, such as the former membership of the applicant's brother in the Liberation Tigers of Tamil Elam (LTTE) organisation, her current isolation and high level of visibility in her locality, compounded by rampant discrimination against women in the north of country and concluded that the predicament that the applicant was likely to face upon return amounted to persecution. No reference to human rights was made, but a general analysis of the applicant's individual circumstances was conducted to evaluate the harm that she might be at risk of enduring upon return. A similar approach was adopted in a Nigerian case, where the Court engaged in a rather holistic analysis of various elements to conclude that an 'accumulation of facts' including discrimination, ostracism from one's family, amounted to persecution.[65] In these two cases, the court adopted a principled and protective approach but, regrettably, such methodology has not been consistently applied in French jurisprudence. For instance, in another case,[66] the court again adopted an unclear interpretation of persecution by rejecting a Sudanese claimant from a Darfuri African tribe on the ground that he had not established a personal experience of harm. In this case, however, the Court did not take into account the overall circumstances of the applicant's profile as a member of an African tribe often associated with rebels, who could be imputed a political opinion on that account. These elements could indeed have indicated the existence of a risk of a persecutory form of harm. The applicant was unfortunately rejected without further analysis and simply granted subsidiary protection on account of the generalised violence. In general, it seems from the recent jurisprudence in France, that asylum judges have continued to interpret persecution on an ad hoc basis,[67] without any clear line of analysis, although some sporadic references to human rights norms are notable.[68]

64 CNDA, grande formation 8 décembre 2016 *Mme K* n° 14027836 C+ at [5].

65 CNDA, 24 mars 2015 *Mlle E.* n° 10012810 C+: In this case, although the court mentioned the definition of the QD, it did not adopt a human rights interpretive framework.

66 CNDA, 3 juillet 2014 *M. S. H.* n° 13024480 C.

67 See other cases where the court adopted variable methodologies for interpreting persecution. In CNDA, 21 mai 2012 *M W.* n° 08019247 C+, the court stated that the repression against a racist man in Namibia from the state authorities did not amount to persecution because it was neither 'systematic, nor discriminatory' nor 'disproportionate' in CNDA 1 septembre 2011 *Mme F ép G et Mlle G n°s10018546 et 10018545 C+*: various acts of discrimination do not amount to persecution without clear explanation as to why they are not considered serious enough. However, in CNDA 18 mars 2016 *M.K* n°15031443: accumulation of stigmatisation, ostracism and discrimination amount to persecution.

68 See for instance case whereby by the rapporteur of the court questioned whether the consideration of a right to a normal private life (absence thereof) could be relevant to assess the notion of persecution in an LGBTI case: CNDA, 8/06/09, 609800/07012945 in Caroline Kobelinsky, '*L'Asile Gay, Jurisprudence de l'Intime à la Cour Nationale du droit d'Asile*' [2012] 82 Droit et Société 583, 592, https://www.cairn.

Belgian case law also rarely relied on human rights standards and seemed to have favoured a broader approach when interpreting persecution by taking into consideration subjective aspects of the harm feared.[69] For instance, in *X v Commissaire général aux réfugiés et aux apatrides*,[70] the Appeal Authority considered that the predicament of a Kurdish woman in Turkey who had faced domestic violence amounted to persecution. In this case, the Appeal Authority argued that 'the assessment of a well-founded fear of persecution should take into account her individual circumstances, including psychological and physical trauma'.[71] The harm that the applicant faced was assessed in light of her profile and cumulated experiences, without reference to human rights standards, eventually yielding a positive result for this applicant.[72] The same interpretive pattern was applied in other cases. For instance, in *Council for Alien Law Litigation, Case No. 101488*, the judges assessed the risk of persecution of a Senegalese applicant who was homosexual. It was considered that the penalisation of homosexuality alone did not amount to a risk of persecution per se, thus seemingly conforming to the guidance of the CJEU. However, in order to reach thisdecision, the judges engaged in a more thorough analysis of the situation in the country, including the level of stigmatisation faced by homosexuals and how such elements could impact the applicant in light of his personal circumstances.[73] For the judges, the level of stigmatisation[74] that the applicant was at risk of facing depended on several factors including 'his personal experiences, the attitude of his family and his entourage, his social and economic situation, his professional profile and cultural background as well as whether or not he lives in an urban area'.[75] Although the judges

info/revue-droit-et-societe1-2012-3-page-583.htm#. In this case however, the court avoided answering this question by displacing the analysis of the refugee definition onto the well-founded fear terrain. See other case with references to human rights by the court: CNDA 4 Janvier 2011 *Mme H.* n° 10000337 C+: this case mostly referred to national human rights. See also: CNDA, 24 mars 2015 *Mlle E* n° 10012810 C+.

69 Belgium: Conseil du Contentieux des Etrangers, 27 October 2016; *Arrêt n° 138 876*, Belgium: Conseil du Contentieux des Etrangers, 19 Février 2015; *Arrêt n° 90 730*, Belgium: Conseil du Contentieux des Etrangers, 30 October 2012: in this case the CCE considered that the accumulation of discriminations faced by the Applicant, compounded by her fragile mental state, amounted to persecution. For instance, see *Arrêt n° 177 178* Belgium: Conseil du Contentieux des Etrangers, 27 Octobre 2016: in this case, the judges took into consideration the applicant's very fragile mental state to assess the notion of persecution and recognised her. See also similar case for a man from Kosovo: *Arrêt n° 138 404*, Belgium: Conseil du Contentieux des Etrangers, 12 Février 2015; *Arrêt 89 927*, Belgium: Conseil du Contentieux des Etrangers, 17 Octobre 2012. No human rights framework was adopted in any of the above cases.

70 *X v Commissaire général aux réfugiés et aux apatrides*, No 177, 178: Conseil du Contentieux des Etrangers, 27 Octobre 2016 [2017] International Journal of Refugee Law 29, 138.

71 Ibid.

72 Ibid. 139.

73 *Arrêt n° 10148824*, Belgium: Conseil du Contentieux des Etrangers Avril 2013 at [5.21].

74 Ibid. 11.

75 Ibid. 10.

mentioned the definition of the QD,[76] they did not in fact assess the notion of persecution in light of fundamental human rights but rather, they proposed to take into consideration the applicant's practical circumstances, eventually rejecting the asylum claim as a number of facts could not be established. In this case, the rejection appeared quite fair and transparent given the comprehensive assessment conducted by the judges. In another similar case, a claimant who was also a homosexual man from Senegal was granted refugee status due to a diverse set of circumstances.[77] Again, an overall assessment of his background and experiences, against the conditions in the country, was conducted to reach this decision.

In light of the above, it can be observed that the adoption of the QD has not yet fulfilled its objective of harmonisation in Europe. Battjes in particular pointed to the persisting variations of interpretation in EU countries which, according to him, are due to the vague and general wording of the QD.[78] In spite of some advances, the QD has not fostered significant consistency since its adoption, nor has it encouraged a more protective approach in countries of the EU.

3.1.2 The Qualification Directive: a 'template for a universal working definition' of persecution?[79]

In spite of the uncertainty surrounding the interpretation of its terms, the QD is the first international instrument that provides a detailed definition of persecution in the context of refugee law. As such, Storey considered that the QD could be used as a model for interpreting the notion of persecution at the global level. Unlike what has been argued above, Storey contended that the human rights narrative in the QD is adequate because it departs from the restrictive framework developed by Hathaway in 1991[80] and provides a more expansive narrative. By removing the restrictive elements of Hathaway's framework such as the persistency criteria, Storey contended that the QD marked one 'very significant improvement'.[81] He also observed that the QD developed a broad scheme, by suggesting that 'other measures' than severe human rights violations could also amount to persecution. He observed that a greater variety of benchmarks could be taken into consideration for interpreting persecution and, therefore, he praised the new approach of the QD as being more flexible.[82] Whilst it is true that the QD proposed a paradigm that is broader than the definition initially developed by

76 Ibid. at [5.17] 11.
77 *Arrêt n° 50967*, Belgium: Conseil du Contentieux des Etrangers, 9 Novembre 2010.
78 Hemme Battjes, '*Piecemeal Engineering: The Recast of the Rules on Qualification for International Protection*' in Vincent Chetail, Philippe De Bruycker and Francesco Maiani (eds) *Reforming the Common European Asylum System: The New European Refugee Law* (Brill Nijhoff 2016) 195–239, 200. DOI: https://doi.org/10.1163/9789004308664_009.
79 Storey (n 1) 478.
80 Ibid. 470.
81 Ibid. 472.
82 Ibid. 471.

Hathaway, the optimistic vision of Storey has, however, been contradicted by the jurisprudence of the CJEU as previously demonstrated. The court has shown that the human rights paradigm adopted by the QD could also lead to very narrow interpretations of persecution, thus failing to provide for the flexible approach that was so greatly expected.

In any event, Storey developed an interesting new interpretive scheme. He considered that the QD could constitute a good departure point for elaborating a universal definition of persecution but he believed that the QD definition was in need of some refinements, in order to make it a global model. According to him, not all aspects of persecution should be translated into human rights terms. He considered that the QD should be better anchored to the overall system of international public law and, for this purpose, he proposed that a larger spectrum of international norms be referred to. For instance, when harms arise in times of conflict, he argued that International Humanitarian Law (IHL) norms should apply instead of human rights. Similarly, when the notion of nationality is involved in the assessment of persecution, rules of nationality law might be needed. According to him, the model of the QD allows for such a large interpretation. To summarise his proposal, he stated that persecution should be understood as the 'severe violations of international law norms, in particular international human rights norms'. He further endorsed the threshold of harm required under the QD.[83] Storey then detailed the modalities of persecution relating to the temporal, material and personal scope of the harm.[84]

Storey advocated a wider approach for interpreting the notion of persecution that appears more protective of refugees than the approach proposed by Hathaway and, to a certain extent, than the approach of the QD. Indeed, he developed a more flexible framework that encompasses numerous parameters in order to better assess the personal impact that certain measures can have on an individual's life as he considered that more norms of international law should be taken into consideration. As a result, his position takes into account a greater variety of situations.

However, one criticism that could be made of him is that his narrative refers to a very large array of norms and standards and, therefore, it appears quite ambiguous. He argued that international law norms could be referred to for interpreting persecution but he did not specify the exact nature of legal norms that he proposed to consider. Although he mentioned that nationality law or IHL could be used as benchmarks, he did not further state what other rules would be relevant for interpreting persecution. It is, for instance, unclear from his framework whether regional norms or soft law norms could be used as referential standards. Further to this, the risk of inconsistent and restrictive approaches to a human rights narrative has been exemplified by the recent case law of the CJEU. This risk seems even greater if we consider any norm of international law in general. Additionally, the threshold that Storey proposes to assess the level of harm, namely

83 Ibid. 517.
84 Ibid. 517–518.

'severe violations of international law norms' remains rather imprecise as argued above in the case of the QD regarding severe violations of basic human rights.

Finally, it should be pointed out that Storey specified that the individual circumstances of refugees should be examined for interpreting the notion of persecution.[85] Whilst this proposal would permit the balancing of different aspects of refugees' protection needs, Storey did not clearly explain how he would combine these different tests. As such, the definition that he proposed seemed to put greater emphasis on formal norms than on the practical protection needs of refugees, which could then lead to a certain confusion. This, therefore, suggests that a different focus might be needed to assess persecution.

3.2 Departing from a human rights narrative: alternative approaches for interpreting the notion of persecution

The foregoing demonstrated that interpretive frameworks, exclusively relying on human rights and international norms, entail the risk of developing a rigid and restrictive methodology by referring to formal norms, without taking into account various aspects of the refugees' circumstances including a subjective element. Some authors have proposed alternative approaches that depart from a human rights and positivist narrative of refugee law and consider other concepts as pivotal for interpreting persecution, such as the concepts of identity, dignity and personhood (3.2.1) or the concept of discrimination (3.2.2). Whilst their proposals have gained less traction in the scholarship than the basic human rights model, they provide valuable insights on different aspects of the notion of persecution. In addition to the proposals of other scholars, the UNHCR has developed its own approach, which relies on the individual circumstances of refugees as a departure point for assessing what forms of harm amount to persecution (3.2.3). These various models will be analysed in turn to argue that UNHCR's model appears the most comprehensive and protective of the situation of refugees.

3.2.1 Persecution, identity, dignity and the concept of personhood

Firth and Mauthe[86] developed a singular narrative that strays away from the formalist human rights framework and proposes to take into consideration a more subjective aspect of the concept of persecution. They proposed to rely on the notion of 'personhood' for determining what forms of harm amount to persecution. In order to do so, they considered how this concept has developed in various legal areas and how the jurisprudence has determined what makes a person a person. In particular, the authors quoted the case of the Delhi High Court, *Naz Foundation v Delhi and Others*[87] that provided some guidance on how 'personhood' should be assessed. In

85 Ibid. 495.

86 Georgina Firth and Barbara Mauthe, '*Refugee Law, Gender and the Concept of Personhood*' [2013] 25 International Journal of Refugee Law 470.

87 *Naz Foundation v Delhi and Others* [2009] 4 LRC 838 at [47] quoted in ibid. 490.

this case, the court stated that 'the holder of rights is (not) an isolated, lonely and abstract figure possessing a disembodied and socially disconnected self, rather people live in their bodies, their communities, their cultures, their places and their times'. In light of this formulation, the authors concluded that the personhood of an individual is shaped by various social, economic, psychological and cultural factors and that these factors should be taken into consideration for interpreting the notion of persecution.[88] This assessment also includes the subjective perception that individuals have of their own identity.[89] Their view echoes the position of Slater who highlighted the major role of the concepts of human dignity and subjectivity in order to understand what persecution is. For her 'human dignity grounds respect individual autonomy and justified claims to basic needs required to have a life of one's own'.[90] Both concepts stress the value of personal agency and presuppose the 'individual as autonomous and, therefore, entitled to respect for this autonomy'.[91]

Firth and Mauthe believed that the notion of personhood is particularly adapted to women as it encourages 'decision makers to consider a more complex construction of the realities of refugee women's myriad experiences'.[92] Their view aligned with those of numerous authors who have pointed to the sheer complexity of women's activities that are not reflected in the current international human rights paradigm.[93] It also overcomes the danger of having a 'single story'[94] about women, as pointed out by the Nigerian activist Chimamanda Ngozi Adichie. The single story about women is based on stereotypes, that are not necessarily wrong, but that obviate various other aspects of women's experiences. In this sense, the concept of 'personhood' highlights the personal dimension of persecution and encourages a consideration of various elements constituting an individual's identity and without mainstreaming people's profiles.

However, as noted by the authors themselves, this concept can appear quite vague and overly subjective as it might 'depend on the view that an individual has on their self, rather than the view of another'.[95] The authors argued that this pitfall could be overcome by using specific criteria for determining personhood but they simply referred to

88 Firth and Mauthe argued that the concept of personhood can be based on the notion of 'autonomy which enables an individual to attain fulfilment, grow in self-esteem, build relationships' and 'fulfil legitimate goals', in Firth and Mauthe (n 86) 490.
89 Ibid. 498–499.
90 Rachel Helen Slater, *A jurisprudential analysis of the interpretation of 'persecution' under the 1951 convention relating to the status of refugees at the domestic level* (Birmingham Law School 2014) 110.
91 Ibid. 116.
92 Firth and Mauthe (n 86) 473.
93 Charlotte Bunch, '*Women's Rights as Human Rights: Toward a Re-Vision of Human Rights*' [1990] 12 Human Rights Quarterly 486, https://www.jstor.org/stable/762496, Celine Romany, '*Women as Aliens: A Feminist Critique of the Public/Private Distinction in International Human Rights Law*' [1993] 6 Harvard Human Rights Journal 87, https://heinonline.org/HOL/LandingPage?handle=hein.journals/hhrj6&div=8&id=&page=; Alice Edwards, *Violence against women under international human rights law* (Cambridge University Press 2010) 305.
94 Chimamanda Ngozi Adichie, Ted Talk, The Danger of a Single Story: https://www.ted.com/talks/chimamanda_ngozi_adichie_the_danger_of_a_single_story.
95 Firth and Mauthe (n 86) 499.

the different approaches developed in the jurisprudence and did not propose any tangible criteria for defining what constitutes personhood.

Whilst the concept of personhood appears valuable for reasserting the inherent subjectivity and complexity of individuals' experiences, as well as evaluating how identity can shape the protection needs of refugees, it remains a rather ambiguous concept. Indeed, as admitted by the authors, it can have very different meanings[96] depending on the context. In particular, the subjective element of personhood, that is, how individuals perceive themselves, can raise difficulties in evaluating the notion of persecution, when major emphasis is placed on it.

Although the concept of personhood adequately emphasises the need to examine various circumstances of refugees, including the subjective aspect of what could constitute persecution, this concept seems to be quite difficult to apply in practice. Even if this approach adopts a more circumstantial paradigm in contrast with the basic human rights approach, it does not constitute a practical model and raises risks of inconsistent interpretations. As such, it has gained very little influence in the literature or in the jurisprudence. More detailed and principled frameworks, also based on the analysis of the personal circumstances of refugees, need therefore to be further considered.

3.2.2 Persecution and the core concept of discrimination

Some commentators have proposed a teleological interpretation of the notion of persecution that strays away from the basic human rights approach. They have suggested relying on the notion of discrimination in defining a refugee rather than focusing on human rights standards. According to these authors, the reason for perpetrating a harmful act is the keystone for understanding persecution. In their view, persecution is primarily an action aimed at the suppression of a difference.[97] As such, they considered that the 'unjustifiable and unacceptable'[98] character of persecution is a major component of the notion. However, there has been some debate as to the scope of this narrative. Whilst some commentators have argued that, for a harmful act to amount to persecution, it should primarily be based on at least one of the five grounds enshrined in the 1951 Convention, others considered that this aspect of persecution was too restrictive, and instead contended that the broader notion of discrimination is sufficient to underpin the interpretation of persecution.

96 Ibid. 488.

97 Jean-Francois Durieux, '*Three asylum Paradigms*' [2013] 20 International Journal on Minority and Group Rights 147, 157, https://doi.org/10.1163/15718115-02002002; Daniel J. Steinbock, '*Interpreting the Refugee Definition*' [1998] 45 UCLA Law Review 733, 804, http://df7sm3xp4s.search.serialssolutions.com/?V=1.0&N=100&L=DF7SM3XP4S&S=AC_T_M&C=UCLA Law Review.

98 Alexander Aleinikoff, '*The Meaning of "Persecution" in United States Asylum Law*' [1991] 3 International Journal of Refugee Law 5, 12, https://doi.org/10.1093/ijrl/3.1.5.

Persecution as an act based on the five Convention grounds: the pivotal role of the Convention nexus in defining persecution

One of the main authors who advocated a teleological interpretation of the notion of persecution is Steinbock. He considered that understanding the 'core purpose of the refugee definition'[99] is a major condition for interpreting persecution. For him, this core purpose is the 'protection against the persecution of difference'.[100] Whilst differences can be varied, Steinbock contended that the Convention had specifically delineated the contours of what could amount to persecution by fleshing out five grounds, which he believed should constitute an inherent and pivotal element of the notion. Steinbock elaborated this view in opposition to the human rights narrative. According to him, not only does this narrative omit to feature the five elements as inherent aspects of persecution, but it provides too wide a catalogue of possible harms, which he believes is not what the plenipotentiaries had in mind.

Steinbock, therefore, considered that only certain forms of infringement of peremptory norms, based on Convention reasons, should be considered persecution. For him, 'the plain meaning of the term "persecution" in the refugee definition, read in light of its history, makes clear that persecution does not exist apart from a prohibited reason for the suffering that it produces'.[101] This view has traditionally been adopted in US jurisprudence as pointed out by Aleinikoff.[102] It seemed to have been also endorsed by the QD in its definition of acts of persecution.[103] It has also been shared, to a certain extent, by Price, who considered that persecution is a harmful act that should be based on 'illegitimate reasons',[104] which he believed should be defined by the five Convention grounds entailed in the refugee definition. He added an exception, as he considered that for certain egregious forms of harm, the Convention reasons should not be considered an essential element of the notion of persecution, given the gravity of such predicaments.[105] However, for the residual harms, Price maintains that the five Convention grounds are a major component of persecution.[106]

To consider the Convention grounds crucial elements of the notion of persecution appears, however, problematic for several reasons. It might lead to restrictive interpretations of the Refugee Convention by suggesting that there should be a persecutory intent behind the act itself. From a formal point of view, this

99 Steinbock (n 97) 804.
100 Ibid. 804.
101 Ibid. 757.
102 Aleinikoff (n 98).
103 Qualification Directive, Art 9(3).
104 Matthew Price, *Rethinking asylum: history, purpose and limits* (Cambridge University Press 2009) 107: for Price, persecution is cumulatively composed of (1) serious harm that is (2) inflicted or tolerated by official agents (3) for illegitimate reasons.
105 Ibid. 110: Price argues for an anti-brutality norm.
106 Ibid. 108: For instance, Price stated that shock therapy perpetrated on mentally ill individuals might not amount to persecution, whilst it could well be considered persecution if it was meant to constitute a treatment of homosexuals.

approach seems to ignore the plain text of the refugee definition, which states that a refugee is someone who has a 'well-founded fear of being persecuted' for one of the five Convention reasons. As such, tying the Convention reasons to the persecution limb of the definition somehow disregards the 'well-founded fear' aspect of the definition. There is indeed nothing to suggest in the 1951 Convention that the five Convention grounds should only be related to the persecution element. Additionally, adopting this view could heighten the burden of proof on claimants. It could be more difficult to demonstrate that a specific harm is based on a Convention ground, than to demonstrate that the overall fear of being persecuted is linked to at least one of these grounds. Whilst an act of persecution in itself might not be motivated by a Convention reason, the risk of harm might be. The approach adopted by the above authors is particularly detrimental in the case of refugee women, who often claim harm from non-state actors. For instance, consider the case of domestic violence where a woman faced severe harm at the hands of her husband based on purely personal reasons. The harm inflicted upon her is not based on a Convention ground. However, it could be argued that she might not be able to seek protection from the state authorities given the rampant discrimination existing against women in her country. As such, it is the lack of state protection that is based on a Convention reason. Whilst authors have argued that the lack of state protection is directly tied to the notion of persecution,[107] as previously noted, this view remains contentious. It could also be considered that the lack of protection is in fact linked to the overall 'well-founded fear of being persecuted' test as it contributes significantly to the existence of a risk.[108] As such, the existence of the Convention nexus might be, in the above case, linked to the well-founded fear part of the definition, rather than the persecution element. Regardless of the position adopted, it would be less circuitous to argue that the Convention nexus constitutes an additional test, linked to the overall formulation 'well-founded fear of being persecuted', referring either to persecution or to the well-founded fear, depending on the case.

This view has in fact been shared by numerous authors. For instance, Foster considered that the Convention grounds need to be one contributing factor to the whole sentence 'well-founded fear of being persecuted'.[109] Similarly, Hathaway stated that the Convention reasons should constitute a factor 'in creating the risk of being persecuted'.[110] As such, neither of them confined the Convention nexus

107 See Section 2.3.

108 See for instance, Goodwin-Gill Guy and Jane McAdam, *The Refugee in International Law* (3rd edn, Oxford University Press 2011) 100: Goodwin-Gill and McAdam argued that the absence of state protection might well be considered to contribute to the existence of a risk, rather than defining per se the nature of persecution. For them, the correlation between state protection and persecution is 'coincidental' not normative.

109 Michelle Foster, '*Causation in Context: Interpreting the Nexus Clause in the Refugee Convention*' [2002] 23 Michigan Journal of International Law 265, 340, https://repository.law.umich.edu/mjil/vol23/iss2/4.

110 James Hathaway and Michelle Foster, *The Law of Refugee Status* (2nd edn; Cambridge University Press 2014) 390.

to the notion of persecution, but linked it to the overall existence of a risk of persecution. On a similar note, Aleinikoff argued that persecution should not be tied to the Convention grounds but should be given a 'free-standing meaning'.[111] In light of these different views, an interpretive scheme that relies on the Convention grounds as a pivotal element of persecution can unduly heighten the burden of proof on claimants and, as such, appears quite restrictive. This approach, while developing an alternative model to the formalist human rights framework, does not seem able to sufficiently encompass the various types of predicament faced by refugees, in particular when such predicaments are caused by non-state agents of persecution.

Discrimination versus persecution?

Other authors also considered that the reasons for harm are major elements of the persecution definition but they departed from the Convention grounds approach and contended that persecution should be based on the broader principle of non-discrimination. For instance, for Aleinikoff, persecution should be based on a large variety of unjustifiable reasons, not confined to the five reasons of the Convention,[112] thus highlighting the necessity of a broader discriminatory treatment. On a similar note, Bagaric and Dimopoulos argued that the notion of discrimination was the 'touchstone'[113] of persecution. Schoenholtz also considered that the purpose of the 1951 Convention is to provide protection against 'persecutory discrimination'.[114] Durieux contended the same and stated that acts of persecution are considered unjustifiable because they negate diversity in a society and punish individuals for their differences. Durieux uses, as a departure point, the definition of the US Court of Appeal of the 9th Circuit stating that persecution is a form of 'oppression which is inflicted on groups of individuals because of a difference that the persecutor will not tolerate'.[115] In line with this definition, he noted that persecution has a discriminatory character. As per the predominant view,[116] he

111 Aleinikoff (n 98) 13.
112 Ibid. 12.
113 Bagaric and Dimopoulos considered that the concept of discrimination was the touchstone of persecution in cases of harm arising from law of general application in Mirko Bagaric and Penny Dimopoulos, '*Discrimination as the Touchstone of Persecution in Refugee Law*' [2007] 3 Journal of Migration and Refugee Issues 14, <https://search.informit.com.au/documentSummary;dn=477786056215930;res=IELHSS> ISSN: 1832-0643.
114 Andrew I. Schoenholtz, '*The New Refugees and the Old Treaty: Persecutors and Persecuted in the Twenty-First Century*' [2015] 16 Chicago Journal of International Law 81, 124, https://chicagounbound.uchicago.edu/cjil/vol16/iss1/5.
115 *Adela Hernandez-Ortiz* v. *Immigration and Naturalization Service*, United States Court of Appeals, Ninth Circuit 777 F.2d 509, decided 2 December 1985 at [20] quoted in Durieux (n 97) 157.
116 UNHCR Handbook and Guidelines on Procedures and Criteria for Determining Refugee Status under the 1951 Convention and the 1967 Protocol Relating to the Status of Refugees, December 2011, HCR/1P/4/ENG/REV.3, at [54], https://www.unhcr.org/4d93528a9.pdf.

does not believe that a mere discrimination amounts to persecution. He argued, instead, that a certain threshold is necessary to assess the level of harm required under the refugee definition and proposed that the notion of 'violence' be also considered a pivotal element in defining persecution.[117] In his own words, persecution is a 'violent form of discrimination'. It 'supposes the use of coercion towards the suppression of difference'.[118] His model, based on the notion of discrimination, encourages a broad assessment of various harmful measures and, as such, departs from a strict basic human rights narrative. It is also not limited to the five Convention grounds and postulates that numerous discriminatory reasons can underlie an act of persecution. Similarly, Dowd highlighted the broad character of the notion of discrimination. She stated that it can refer both to various forms of serious harm and to human rights violations,[119] and, therefore, encompasses a potentially larger variety of predicaments.

Whilst this narrative permits the development of a seemingly wider analysis of the kinds of harm that amount to persecution, it remains, however, quite vague. Indeed, Dowd pointed to the general character of the notion of 'discrimination' and stated that it has been 'rarely discussed as a concept in itself in refugee law'.[120] In fact, she considered that the concept of discrimination is often used as a 'catch-all' term[121] to deny refugee claims often considered akin to violations of various types of human rights. She demonstrated that, due to this, the notion of discrimination has been interpreted in very inconsistent ways and different standards have been used for different types of claim.[122] In order to minimise the risk of inconsistent interpretations, Dowd proposed that the notion of discrimination should be understood in a broad manner, so as to analyse a large spectrum of measures and not only violations of human rights. For instance, she contended that the consequential impact that certain types of discrimination have on individuals—including the adverse psychological harm that they can cause—should be assessed through a holistic analysis.[123] According to her, the 'purpose of undertaking a cumulative analysis should be to consider the overall impact of discrimination on an individual's life, not merely its impact on a limited selection of narrowly-defined rights'.[124] As such, she stated that the circumstances and conditions of individuals need to be taken as a departure point to assess how discriminations affect a person's life.[125]

117 Durieux (n 97) 157.
118 Ibid.
119 Rebecca Dowd, '*Dissecting Discrimination in Refugee Law: an Analysis of its Meaning and its Cumulative Effect*' [2011] 23 International Journal of Refugee Law 28, 39, https://doi.org/10.1093/ijrl/eeq043.
120 Ibid. 32.
121 Ibid. 35.
122 Ibid. 46.
123 Ibid. 51.
124 Ibid. 53.
125 Ibid. 49.

In contrast to the views of the above authors, it could be said that the concept of discriminatory harm does not always reflect the reality behind certain forms of violence based on personal consideration, such as, for instance, domestic violence. As previously argued, the discriminatory intent can, in some contexts, be imputable to the state rather than the agent of harm when non-state agents of persecution are involved. According to the HRC, an act of discrimination implies 'any distinction, exclusion, restriction of preference which is based on any ground [...] and which has the purpose or effect of nullifying or impairing the recognition, enjoyment or exercise by all persons, on an equal footing, of all rights and freedoms'.[126] In this context, the intention to discriminate is not needed, as long as the act has the 'effect' of discriminating. It might well be argued that acts of domestic violence, although more directly based on personal reasons, might have the effect of perpetuating discrimination against women in certain contexts. As such, there would be an underlying discriminatory element to the infliction of harm. Whilst this is not disputed here, proving this element might be more difficult than proving the discriminatory element underlying the lack or failure of state protection. As such, depending on the context, it remains that considering the notion of discrimination as an inherent part of the persecution test could add an extra burden of proof on certain claimants, in particular in cases of gender-based violence. It remains, nonetheless, a relevant notion to be considered in certain cases of persecution.

In order to understand how the notion of discrimination can be factored into the concept of persecution, reference to Price could be helpful. Indeed, Price interestingly developed the idea of a sliding scale for considering the reasons behind the harm perpetrated. According to him, for grave acts (defined through references to customary law), there is no need to consider the reasons behind those acts, whilst for milder forms of harm, the five Convention grounds become fundamental to the notion of persecution. Although his test seems quite severe because Price considered that only the violations of peremptory norms[127] would remove the need for a Convention ground, his logic brings some insight as to how the degree of persecution is to be articulated with its qualitative aspect. His sliding scale could suggest that various restrictions, when compounded by an element of discrimination (which should not necessarily be restricted to the Convention Reasons) could amount to persecution, whilst other forms of egregious harm could be considered unjustifiable and unacceptable by nature, regardless of the reasons behind the act. In the words of the Canadian Federal Court of Appeal, for certain acts it can be considered that 'brutality in furtherance of a legitimate end is

126 Human Rights Committee, General Comment, No. 18: non-Discrimination (1989) at [7].

127 The nature of such norms is generally debated, which undermines the accuracy of Price's proposed narrative. For example, refer to the: debate on whether rape is considered *jus cogens*. On this see: David S. Mitchell, '*The Prohibition of Rape in International Humanitarian Law as a Norm of Jus Cogens: Clarifying the Doctrine*' [2005] 15 Duke Journal of Comparative & International Law 219, https://scholarship.law.duke.edu/djcil/vol15/iss2/2.

still brutality'.[128] This combination of qualitative and quantitative factors appears indeed relevant to assess the notion of persecution. For more severe acts of violence, for instance domestic violence, no discriminatory intent is needed whilst for milder forms of harm, a discriminatory element might be needed so that the harm qualifies as persecution. In any case, it remains that the Convention grounds have to be attached to the overall formula of a 'well-founded fear of being persecuted'.

In spite of its intrinsic limitations, the above narrative has the advantage of putting a greater focus on the effects of persecution on individuals, in contrast to the various human rights frameworks, that somehow obviate this element by focusing on the formal existence of human rights violations.[129] It demonstrates that both the qualitative and quantitative aspects need to be factored into the assessment of what persecution is, depending on the degree of the harm. This view in turn encourages a more flexible and all-encompassing analysis of the different circumstances of refugees.

In this sense, the UNHCR has proposed a more comprehensive analysis of persecution, factoring in these various elements, including the five Convention grounds, as well as broader qualitative and quantitative criteria, compounded with subjective aspects of the notion of persecution. The UNHCR's view on persecution will be assessed below.

3.2.3 The UNHCR's model for interpreting persecution

The human rights and circumstantial approaches

Before Hathaway formulated his basic human rights framework, the UNHCR published a Handbook[130] in 1979, whereby it proposed a two-tier test for interpreting the notion of persecution. Although the UNHCR's interpretive approach seemed to have gained less influence in the scholarship and in national jurisdictions than the model developed by Hathaway,[131] it nonetheless provides some relevant insights as to how persecution should be interpreted.

Firstly, the UNHCR Handbook stated that serious human rights violations could amount to persecution when based on a Convention ground. Indeed, the Refugee Agency stated that 'a threat to life or freedom on account of [a Convention ground] is always persecution. Other serious violations of human rights [...] would also constitute persecution'. In this first test, the UNHCR firmly relied on international human rights as benchmarks for interpreting the notion of

128 *Cheung v. Canada (Minister of Employment and Immigration)*, [1993] 2 F.C. 314, Canada: Federal Court of Appeal.

129 The QD touches upon this qualitative aspect by saying that some acts are by 'nature' sufficiently serious. However, it does not say much about the nature of the harm as it says that it should amount to 'severe violations of basic human rights', which in turn constitutes a vague threshold as argued above.

130 UNHCR Handbook (n 116).

131 In particular in common law jurisdictions; Chapter 4 will assess the influence of the human rights approach in national jurisdictions.

persecution. This is in line with the official UNHCR's position that the 1951 Convention has a human rights orientation[132] and, as such, human rights should not be ignored when interpreting persecution. This specific test is, however, quite limited because it posits that, to amount to persecution, human rights violations should necessarily be tied to a Convention reason. This therefore restricts the possibilities of interpretation as mentioned above. However, according to the refugee agency, persecution 'should not be defined solely on the basis of serious human rights violations'.[133] In order to balance out this rather formalist approach, the UNHCR considered that if this test fails, an expanded framework should be applied. This second test takes the individual circumstances of refugees as a departure point to assess the various forms of harm that one can face. Storey called it the 'circumstantial approach'.[134]

The UNHCR Handbook affirmed as follows:

> 52Whether other prejudicial actions or threats would amount to persecution will depend on the circumstances of each case, including the subjective element to which reference has been made in the preceding paragraphs. The subjective character of fear of persecution requires an evaluation of the opinions and feelings of the person concerned. It is also in the light of such opinions and feelings that any actual or anticipated measures against him must necessarily be viewed. Due to variations in the psychological make-up of individuals and in the circumstances of each case, interpretations of what amounts to persecution are bound to vary.

132 Paragraph 25 of the UNHCR Handbook: '*The High Commissioner has always pleaded for a generous asylum policy in the spirit of the Universal Declaration of Human Rights and the declaration on Territorial asylum, adopted by the General Assembly of the United Nations on 10 December 1948 and on 14 December 1967 respectively*', see also UNHCR ExCom Conclusion No 50 (XXXIX) 'General Conclusion on International Protection' (1988): 'The Executive Committee [...] (b) *Noted the direct relationship between the observance of human rights standards, refugee movements and problems of protection*'; UNHCR ExCom Conclusion No 103 (LVI) 'The Provision of International Protection including through Complementary Forms of Protection' (2005): 'The Executive Committee (c) *Recognizes that refugee law is a dynamic body of law based on the obligations of State Parties to the 1951 Convention and its 1967 Protocol and, where applicable, on regional refugee protection instruments, and which is informed by the object and purpose of these instruments and by developments in related areas of international law, such as human rights and international humanitarian law bearing directly on refugee protection*'; UNHCR, '*Note on The International Protection of Refugees: Interpreting Article 1 of the 1951 Convention Relating to the Status of Refugees*', [2001] 20 Refugee Survey Quarterly 77, 78, https://www.refworld.org/docid/3b20a3914.html.

133 Statement by Ms. Erika Feller, Director, Department of International Protection, UNHCR, SCIFA (Brussels, 6 November 2002), DIP Statements, Geneva, published on UNHCR website http://www.unhcr.org/42bab1b52.html; see also Storey (n 1) 278. According to Storey, UNHCR considers that there 'is a residual content to persecution uncaptured by the human rights approach'.

134 Storey (n 1) 465.

> 53In addition, an applicant may have been subjected to various measures not in themselves amounting to persecution (e.g. discrimination in different forms), in some cases combined with other adverse factors (e.g. general atmosphere of insecurity in the country of origin). In such situations, the various elements involved may, if taken together, produce an effect on the mind of the applicant that can reasonably justify a claim to well-founded fear of persecution on 'cumulative grounds'. Needless to say, it is not possible to lay down a general rule as to what cumulative reasons can give rise to a valid claim to refugee status. This will necessarily depend on all the circumstances, including the particular geographical, historical and ethnological context.

In this definition, the UNHCR factors in numerous aspects of the notion of persecution. Firstly, this test requires a consideration of the particular situation and vulnerabilities of refugees in order to assess the consequential impact that various measures have on individuals. The UNHCR then highlights the importance of a subjective element in assessing what forms of harm amount to persecution by stating that an 'evaluation of the opinions and feelings of the person concerned'[135] should be conducted. As a result, the persecutory nature of an act will depend on the personal background and conditions of the person claiming asylum and, therefore, the assessment of harm could fluctuate. The UNHCR indeed acknowledged that whether a certain form of harm amounts to persecution 'will depend on the circumstances of each case'.[136] The Refugee Agency justified this position by stating that, 'due to variations in the psychological make-up of individuals and in the circumstances of each case, interpretations of what amounts to persecution are bound to vary'.[137] The UNHCR Handbook added an additional paragraph in which it stated that various other measures can, based on cumulative grounds, also amount to persecution.[138] Overall, the Refugee Agency encourages the adoption of a holistic approach but does not specify the level of harm required for an accumulation of measures to amount to persecution. This omission appears deliberate as the Handbook stated that 'it is not possible to lay down a general rule as to what cumulative reasons can give rise to a valid claim to refugee status. This will necessarily depend on all the circumstances'.[139]

Indeed, according to the UNHCR, all forms of predicament, as a whole, and their consequences on individuals' life should be analysed in order to assess persecution. The UNHCR gave more guidance in another document on the threshold of harm required, by stating that threatening conditions 'mak(ing) life in the country of origin so insecure from many perspectives for the individual concerned, that the only way out of this predicament is to leave the country of origin'[140] constitute persecution.

135 UNHCR Handbook (n 116) at [52].
136 Ibid.
137 Ibid.
138 Ibid. at [53].
139 Ibid. at [53].
140 Feller (n 133).

Interestingly, in the circumstantial approach, the UNHCR did not explicitly correlate the notion of persecution with the Convention nexus, thus seemingly adopting a broader view of what sorts of harm could amount to persecution. The view that the Convention grounds are not always linked to the notion of persecution is repeated in a number of UNHCR guidelines.[141] In particular, when the perpetrator of persecution is a non-state agent, the UNHCR connects the convention nexus to the lack of state protection[142] without necessarily linking the absence of state protection to the notion of persecution. For instance, the UNHCR specifically stated that there are situations 'where the risk of being persecuted at the hands of a non-state actor is unrelated to a Convention ground'.[143] Therefore, for assessing the Convention nexus, the UNHCR seems to establish a separate test that might either relate to the well-founded fear of harm or to the notion of persecution, depending on the circumstances at hand. In light of the foregoing, it appears that the circumstantial approach is broader than the human rights approach that is proposed in paragraph 51 of the Handbook.

A framework leading to inconsistent interpretations?

Whilst the UNHCR's framework encourages a holistic analysis of the notion of persecution, its subjective dimension may raise concern as pointed out by some authors. The subjective element proposed by the UNHCR conflicts with the view of Tobin who believed that the purpose of the interpretive exercise is to maintain some level of coherence within different fields of law. He stated that the 'resolution of any ambiguity within the Refugee Convention should be informed by, among other things, an attempt to achieve coherence or harmonisation with the provisions of international human rights treaties'.[144] Therefore, he considered that for interpreting persecution, a more didactic approach should be adopted by giving primary consideration to human rights standards and the way they should

141 UNHCR, *Guidance Note on Refugee Claims Relating to Victims of Organized Gangs*, 31 March 2010, https://www.refworld.org/docid/4bb21fa02.html, UN High Commissioner for Refugees (UNHCR), Guidelines on International Protection No.2: *Membership of a Particular Social Group Within the Context of Article 1A(2) of the 1951 Convention and/or its 1967 Protocol Relating to the Status of Refugees*, 7 May 2002, HCR/GIP/02/02, https://www.unhcr.org/en-my/publications/legal/3d58de2da/guidelines-international-protection-2-membership-particular-social-group.html.

142 Ibid. in UNHCR, *Guidance Note on Refugee Claims Relating to Victims of Organized Gangs* at [29], and UNHCR Guidelines on International Protection No.2: *Membership of a Particular Social Group Within the Context of Article 1A(2) of the 1951 Convention and/or its 1967 Protocol Relating to the Status of Refugees* at [23].

143 Ibid. in UNHCR, *Guidance Note on Refugee Claims Relating to Victims of Organized Gangs* at [29], and UNHCR Guidelines on International Protection No.2: *Membership of a Particular Social Group Within the Context of Article 1A(2) of the 1951 Convention and/or its 1967 Protocol Relating to the Status of Refugees* at [23].

144 John Tobin, '*Assessing LGBTI Refugee Claims: Using Human Rights to Shift the Narrative of Persecution within Refugee Law*' [2012] 44 New York University Journal of International Law and Politics 448, 455, https://nyujilp.org/wp-content/uploads/2010/06/44.2-Tobin.pdf.

be applied in refugee law in accordance with other legal areas. For him, it would be a 'mistake to selectively import aspects of human rights discourse into refugee law in ways that were not consistent with the entire system of international human rights law'.[145] This view strays away from the UNHCR's approach that rather emphasises the importance of the personal circumstances of refugees to assess the level of harm in combination with human rights norms, only when deemed relevant (selectively imported from the field of human rights). As such, the UNHCR does not seek to reinstate the interpretation of the notion of persecution into the broader field of international human rights law or to achieve coherence between refugee law and human rights law.

The UNHCR's methodology was also criticised by Storey who considered that it was not sufficiently principled.[146] He believed indeed that it 'encourages subjective decision making and [...] divergent jurisprudence'.[147] Storey highlighted that UNHCR's subjective element is mostly contingent upon persons with different characters and thus, the interpretation of persecution might vary greatly depending on individuals. He contended that this component could encourage unfair decisions for people who do not display significant distress or who simply do not reasonably anticipate the danger that they might be at risk of facing upon return to their country. He believes that this is contrary to the universal character of the 1951 Convention. On this point, he stated that 'if Article 1A(2) is to have universal application then it cannot impose a requirement that certain deserving subcategories of persons would often be unable to meet, most notably very young children or disabled people who may not even be aware that they are on a persecutor's death list'.[148] Storey concluded that objective standards are needed to interpret the notion of persecution in all circumstances[149] and, by departing from the human rights approach, he contended that the UNHCR does not adopt an appropriate framework. His view echoes the one held by Hicks and Hathaway who considered that the subjective fear paradigm adopted in the UNHCR Handbook is equivocal and encourages divergent approaches.[150] They called it a 'trepidation'[151] element, which they believe should not be factored into the refugee definition.

Following the contention made by Storey and others, it cannot be denied that the circumstantial approach encourages a case-by-case analysis that can cause inconsistent interpretations of the notion of persecution. However, Storey seemed to place too much emphasis on the role of subjective fear in interpreting the notion of persecution. Firstly, it should be noted that the UNHCR mostly

145 Ibid. 455.
146 Storey (n 1) 468.
147 Ibid. 468.
148 Ibid. 509.
149 Ibid. 467.
150 James C. Hathaway and William S. Hicks, '*Is there a Subjective Element in the Refugee Convention's Requirement of "Well-Founded Fear"?*' [2005] 26 Michigan Journal of International Law 505, 507, https://repository.law.umich.edu/articles/1482.
151 Ibid. 506–507.

referred to this element in order to assess the 'well-founded fear' limb of the refugee definition, which is distinct from the persecution enquiry.[152] As such, the importance of subjective fear in the persecution test itself should be relativised. The view that subjective fear is mostly relevant to the well-founded fear part of the definition has been clearly expressed by Hicks and Hathaway.[153] Similarly, Chimni acknowledged that the UNHCR Handbook posited the existence of a 'subjective test' for assessing the well-founded character of a claim, but he omitted to mention this in his section on persecution, thus suggesting that its role was quite minimal for assessing persecution.[154] Whilst it is true that both tests (well-founded fear and persecution) are closely related, they should, nonetheless, be distinguished for conceptual clarity. The well-founded fear element generally requires an assessment of the likelihood that a certain harm will happen, whilst the test of persecution requires an assessment of the nature and degree of the harm.

It should be acknowledged that the notion of subjective fear is also mentioned in the section on persecution[155] in the UNHCR Handbook. Its importance is, however, minimised as the Handbook considers that subjective fear (or the frame of mind of an applicant) is relevant only when 'supported by an objective situation'.[156] Whilst the UNHCR relativised the scope of this element, the exact role that it should play when assessing persecution is unclear. To clarify that point, reference should be made to the overall wording of the UNHCR Handbook which suggests that subjective fear should not be used to deny refugee status. In this sense, Juss considered that this concept, together with other paradigms, in fact 'adds to and embellishes'[157] the 1951 Convention, thus indicating that it should be interpreted in a manner that is sufficiently in line with the protective purpose of the Convention.

The subjective fear test should indeed be considered relevant for refugees who have certain vulnerabilities so that these fragilities can be taken into account in order to better assess the impact that certain measures can have on the individuals seeking asylum. For instance, some restrictions (such as temporary detention) might have more adverse consequences for someone who has already suffered trauma, than for an able-bodied person without major psychological issues. In this sense, the subjective element of persecution appears relevant to individualise the analysis of the notion of persecution. This view is further

152 The UNHCR Handbook (n 116) paragraphs 35 to 50 deal with the 'well-founded fear' element whilst paragraphs 51 to 53 deal with the 'persecution' analysis.

153 Hathaway and Hicks (n 150) contended that the subjective element should not have a major bearing in interpreting the refugee definition but in their article, they mostly referred to the 'well-founded fear' part of the definition.

154 B. S. Chimni, *International Refugee Law: a Reader* (2nd edn, Sage 2002) 3.

155 The UNHCR Handbook (n 116) at [52].

156 Ibid.: paragraph 52 refers to paragraph 38 whereby the assessment of the 'objective situation' is also required in order to assess whether a fear is well-founded.

157 Satvinder Juss, '*The UNHCR Handbook and the Interface Between "Soft Law" and "Hard Law" in International Refugee Law*' in Satvinder Juss and Colin Harvey (eds), *Contemporary Issues in Refugee Law* (Edward Elgar, Cheltenham 2013) 31–67, 43.

confirmed in paragraph 40 whereby the UNHCR stated that the 'psychological reaction' of individuals is a relevant element to take into consideration when applying the refugee definition. It should, however, not be applied too systematically. Paragraph 52 of the UNHCR Handbook emphasises this point by stating that whether 'prejudicial actions or threats would amount to persecution will depend on the circumstances of each case, *including* the subjective element'. The insertion of the word 'including' is significant in that it confers a minimal importance to the subjective fear and confines it to the analysis of persecution only in certain cases where the psychological element is of relevance. It does not require that all claimants show signs of trepidation to the thought of returning to their country. Consequently, the examination of subjective fear is not posited as a pivotal condition for interpreting persecution in all cases and its importance should not be overstated. The contention that the subjective fear component encourages subjective and divergent jurisprudence appears therefore a bit excessive because this should not be the case, if this notion is appropriately applied in the assessment of persecution.

Practical benefits of the circumstantial approach

Unlike what the above authors have argued, the UNHCR's approach presents positive insights for interpreting persecution. Firstly, it has the advantage of highlighting the personal and psychological aspects of persecution in that it proposes to assess the level of suffering one can experience regardless of whether external human rights have been violated or not. Human rights law is premised on the assumption that all individuals have the same protection needs and conform to one model of 'personhood'. Whilst the standards developed by human rights might be suitable for a large number of individuals, they might inadequately dictate what types of treatment are bearable or unbearable for others. Evaluating the protection needs of individuals necessarily demands that the personal circumstances and psychological make-up of persons be taken into consideration. In contrast, human rights law tends to isolate elements of harm in light of abstract standards and thus, does not encourage an assessment of cumulated circumstances. Whilst it is true that the approach proposed by the UNHCR requires a case-by-case analysis, an objective line of argumentation is nonetheless proposed, that minimises the risk of inconsistent interpretations. Indeed, in encouraging an assessment of the circumstances of refugees, the UNHCR proposes to rely on concrete elements that constitute these circumstances, namely the claimants' profile, vulnerability, past experiences of harm and so on. These factors remain rather objective and provide solid indicators of the level of harm faced by a refugee. Factoring these elements into the assessment of what amounts to persecution would in turn encourage a more transparent assessment of the consequences that certain measures can have on someone's life.

As such, whilst the UNHCR maintains that human rights are important references for interpreting the notion of persecution, they only represent 'one touchstone for determining the existence of persecution'.[158] Supporting this view, McAdam considered that human rights are important standards 'in assessing whether persecution may exist in a given situation' but, for her, 'the additional subjective element of the Convention definition captures a need for protection that is outside the realm of a pure human rights assessment, and cautions against tying the concept of persecution exclusively to human rights law'.[159] Edwards also believed that human rights law does not reflect the different needs of individuals, and although she believed that it 'contributes in some cases to a clearer identification of particular forms of persecution', she considered that 'the 1951 Convention does not require that a human rights violation be acknowledged in order to establish "persecution"'.[160] Through the circumstantial approach, the UNHCR proposes in fact to address the personal aspect of persecution and take the individual situation of refugees in its various aspects as a pivotal element in assessing the level of harm that they might be likely to face upon return to their country.

A case from the Court of Appeal in the UK demonstrated the caveat of a rigid approach based on formalist standards of human rights protection versus a more circumstantial approach such as the one proposed by the UNHCR, in particular in the case of endemic forms of discrimination faced by women. In *AI (Nigeria) v. Secretary of State for the Home Department*,[161] the Court of Appeal denied the asylum claim of a Nigerian woman by considering that the applicant did not have a well-founded fear of being persecuted. The claimant was a single Christian woman, head of a household who used to live in a predominantly Muslim area in Nigeria. She contended that she was at risk of facing harm on account of her profile as a lone woman without male protection. She claimed that she had left her home area due to communal violence against Christians. Following this, she lived alone in charge of her child and in order to meet her basic needs, she had to 'sleep with people'.[162] Whilst the court accepted that discriminations against women were rampant in Nigeria, and such discriminations had most certainly led the applicant to prostitute herself, it was decided that these predicaments did not amount to persecution. However, the reasoning of the court for reaching this conclusion was quite obscure. The court simply interpreted the notion of persecution against formal standards of gender-based violence and considered the concept of 'prostitution' in the abstract by stating that 'prostitution under the threat of violence' can amount to persecution, but 'prostitution per se' does not.[163] The deficiency of this approach is that the Court only analysed grave

158 Cantor (n 17) 385.
159 McAdam (n 3) 12–13.
160 Alice Edwards, 'Age and gender dimensions in international refugee law' in Erika Feller, Volker Turk and Frances Nicholson (eds), *Refugee Protection in International Law: UNHCR's Global Consultations on International Protection* (Cambridge University Press 2003) 80.
161 *AI (Nigeria) v. Secretary of State for the Home Department*, [2007] EWCA Civ 707, 21 June 2007.
162 Ibid. at [7].
163 Ibid. at [12].

forms of harm similar to the ones recognised in international treaties,[164] such as the 'threat of violence' leading to sexual exploitation. The Court considered this form of harm, separately from its context, to conclude that prostitution itself is not a form of persecution because there is no element of violence involved.

Whilst it might be true that prostitution per se does not amount to persecution, it does not mean that the experiences of the applicant considered in the aggregate will not amount to persecution, as the UNHCR's approach would suggest. Indeed, a closer analysis of the applicant's circumstances causing her to prostitute herself would have been useful to reach a more informed decision. The adjudicator could have analysed the harm that the applicant was likely to face against her overall profile as a member of a religious minority (in her home area) who had been displaced without her family due to communal violence and who ended up lacking family and male protection, being a single mother, head of a household who had to prostitute herself to earn her living due to rampant discrimination in her country. As per the UNHCR guidelines on gender-related persecution, 'if measures of discrimination lead to consequences of a substantially prejudicial nature for the person concerned, e.g. serious restrictions on the right to earn one's livelihood, the right to practice one's religion, or access to available educational facilities',[165] such measures could amount to persecution. This case shows that the appreciation of refugees as persons with various circumstances and a complex set of experiences offers a better understanding of what could amount to persecution rather than relying on a rigid approach that compartmentalises the assessment of various types of harm.

In light of the above, it appears that the UNHCR approach encourages a comprehensive analysis of the various circumstances of refugees in order to assess how certain measures could amount to persecution. It adopts a more practical approach, as opposed to the formalist framework that relies on external benchmarks for assessing persecution.

3.3 Concluding remarks

Given the inherent limitations attached to an interpretive framework that only relies on basic human rights for interpreting the notion of persecution, various other models that encourage a more holistic analysis of persecution have been analysed in this chapter. Some models, such as the ones established by the QD, and then by Storey, suggest expanding the basic human rights framework, but still consider external norms of international law as the keystone

164 In this case, the court did not explicitly quote human rights treaties, but it referred to abstract standards developed in international human rights law, and as such followed the same logic as the human rights narrative.

165 UNHCR Guidelines on International Protection No.1: Gender Related Persecution in the Context of Article 1A(2) of the 1951 Convention and/or its 1967 Protocol Relating to the Status of Refugees, 7 May 2002, HCR/GIP/02/01, https://www.unhcr.org/en-my/publications/legal/3d58ddef4/guidelines-international-protection-1-gender-related-persecution-context.html.

of persecution. Whilst these frameworks are broader than Hathaway's narrative, they nonetheless adopt a rather rigid methodology by using objective norms as a departure point for interpreting persecution, which bears the risk of obviating some of the personal circumstances of refugees. They encourage an analysis of different human rights violations, taken in the abstract, and disregard other aspects of individuals' vulnerabilities. In addition to this problem, the recent jurisprudence of the CJEU has demonstrated that human rights frameworks can be very narrowly and variably interpreted. They also do not necessarily resolve the problem of inconsistent interpretations of the refugee definition.

Given these deficiencies, other models have been considered. These models departed entirely from the basic human rights approach and considered that other elements were pivotal for interpreting persecution. In particular, the concepts of 'personhood', 'Convention nexus' or 'discrimination' were advanced by certain scholars. Through the notion of personhood, Firth and Mauthe shifted the paradigm on the individual aspects of persecution by placing a greater emphasis on the profile and experiences of refugees. This model was, however, considered too vague and too subjective. The narratives based on the 'Convention nexus' and 'discrimination' rightly pointed to the qualitative aspect of persecution, namely the unjustifiable infliction of harm, but they also raised some conceptual uncertainty as demonstrated in this chapter.

Finally, the UNHCR has attempted to combine various narratives into a two-tier test, based on a human rights approach on the one hand, and on a circumstantial approach on the other hand. Through this framework, the UNHCR stressed the importance of assessing the consequences that certain restrictions have on individuals rather than focusing on the nature and gravity of the restrictions themselves. The strength of this approach is that it encourages decision makers to better take into consideration the individual circumstances and special vulnerabilities of refugees for interpreting persecution but it also considers that human rights have a role to play in informing an evolutionary understanding of the notion of persecution. It appears particularly relevant to assess the harm faced by individual victims of systematic forms of discrimination in various aspects of their life in order to evaluate the impacts of such discrimination in a holistic manner, rather than through a compartmentalised analysis. In particular, it has been demonstrated that this approach was quite convenient to assess the claim of refugee women as it encouraged a comprehensive analysis of their circumstances rather than considering their profile through a stereotyped understanding of the various forms of harm that they can face.

After a theoretical *tour de table* of the different frameworks proposed for interpreting persecution, the following chapter will engage in a more practical assessment of various approaches adopted in countries with developed RSD systems in order to adjudicate some claims of refugee women. The forms of harm typically faced by women were not considered to be encompassed under the definition of a refugee by the plenipotentiaries but given the 'feminisation' of migration and increased awareness of the endemic forms of discrimination faced by women, it appears necessary to assess how the various theoretical frameworks of interpretation analysed in the previous chapters could apply to the claims of women. This will help to better evaluate whether the notion of persecution remains relevant to their situation or whether the definition of a refugee should be amended.

4 Interpreting persecution in the context of harm faced by refugee women

For a long time, persecution has been perceived as a form of harm perpetrated by state agents in oppressive regimes and consisting in acts that were generally committed in the public sphere.[1] This form of persecution in fact corresponded to the experiences of men, as they were traditionally the ones whose activities tended to unfold in the public and political arena. Until few decades ago, persecution was not considered to encompass private forms of violence, including violence suffered by women within their family or their community as a result of discriminatory practices.[2] This situation led one author to speak of a 'traditionally male centred notion of persecution'.[3] This view, however, progressively changed in the 1980s and 1990s, when an increasing number of women lodged asylum applications based on their fear of violence from non-state agents.[4] In this period, domestic

1 See Chapter 1 and the traditional understanding of persecution according to the plenipotentiaries. See also Jane McAdam, '*Rethinking the Origins of Persecution*' [2014] 25 International Journal of Refugee Law 667, 674, DOI: https://doi.org/10.1093/ijrl/eet048. McAdam mentioned the early League of Nations instruments indicating that 'the men would run the risk of all kinds of persecution, while the women, children and old people would succumb to the hardships of the present economic conditions'.

2 Jean-Yves Carlier, '*The Geneva refugee definition and the "theory of the three scales"*' in Frances Nicholson and Patrick Twomey (eds) *Refugee Rights and Realities: Evolving International Concepts and Regimes* (Cambridge University Press 1999) 37–54, 39.

3 J. Bhabha, '*Demography and Rights: Women, Children and Access to Asylum*' [2004] 16 International Journal of Refugee Law 227, 228, DOI: https://doi.org/10.1093/ijrl/16.2.227.

4 Susan Kneebone, '*Women Within the Refugee Construct: "Exclusionary Inclusion" in Policy and Practice — the Australian Experience*' [2005] 17 International Journal of Refugee Law 7, 9, DOI: https://doi.org/10.1093/ijrl/eei002. See also Florian Francois Hoepfner, *L'évolution de la notion de réfugié, Publication de la fondation Marangopoulos pour les droits de l'homme* (Série 18, Paris Pedone 2014) 265. In James C. Hathaway and Michelle Foster, *The Law of Refugee Status* (2nd edn, Cambridge University Press 2014) 193 Hathaway observed that, around the same period, refugee movements were 'prompted by a risk of harm from persons unconnected to the state, such as insurgent groups, local criminal gangs, or at the hands of members of a family clan, or tribe'. In Walter Kalin, '*Non-State Agents of Persecution and the Inability of the State to Protect*' [2001] 15 Georgetown Immigration Law Journal 415, 432, https://kent.rl.talis.com/items/66C91376-0FD3-C300-0603-6C3B8AE54093.html, the author noted that the 'world-wide decline of State power and the emergence of non-state agents of persecution'

jurisdictions started to adjudicate such claims in a more favourable manner, considering that persecution could occur within the private sphere and be specifically directed at women.[5] In spite of a growing recognition of victims of gender-based violence as refugees, these forms of harm still pose significant interpretive challenges and are inconsistently addressed in domestic jurisdictions. In light of this situation, one might wonder whether the notion of persecution is actually relevant for gender-sensitive claims and which interpretive method is the most desirable in these cases.

Given the rising proportion of refugee women in the world[6] and the conceptual difficulties in addressing their claims, the present chapter will engage in a case-study of decisions involving forms of persecution typically faced by women and that tend to be typically referred to as gender-based persecution. Whilst there is no legal definition of gender-based persecution in international law,[7] the UNHCR defines it broadly as a form of harm that encompasses 'the range of different claims in which gender is a relevant consideration in the determination of refugee status'.[8] Gender-based violence covers a great variety of harms, such as, but not limited to, 'acts of sexual violence, family/domestic violence, coerced family planning, female genital mutilation, punishment for transgression of social mores, and discrimination against homosexuals'.[9] These various types of violence could not be comprehensively addressed in this chapter. However, some of the claims that have been the most regularly lodged in jurisdictions and that have raised contention, will be considered below, namely Female Genital Mutilation (FGM), domestic violence and trafficking in persons (hereunder trafficking) (Section 4.2).[10] Prior to

constituted major 'developments [that] have had the most profound impact on refugee law during the past ten years'.

5 Carlier (n 2) 39. For Carlier, this change of paradigm reflected well how the notion of persecution had evolved in the 20th century.

6 Numbers vary, but women are consistently represented as constituting at least 50 per cent of the entire refugee population. UNHCR, Women, at http://www.unhcr.org/women.html. Kim mentioned estimates reporting that about three-quarters of the refugee population are women and children, in Sunny Kim, '*Gender-Related Persecution: A Legal Analysis of Gender Bias in Asylum Law*' [1994] 2 Journal of Gender and the Law 107, 109, https://digitalcommons.wcl.american.edu/jgspl/vol2/iss1/4/.

7 UNHCR Guidelines on International Protection No. 1: Gender-Related Persecution Within the Context of Article 1A(2) of the 1951 Convention and/or its 1967 Protocol Relating to the Status of Refugees, 7 May 2002, HCR/GIP/02/01, at [1], https://www.unhcr.org/en-my/publications/legal/3d58ddef4/guidelines-international-protection-1-gender-related-persecution-context.html.

8 Ibid.

9 Ibid. at [3].

10 In Kneebone (n 4) 20, the author identified some major categories of gender-related claims including sexual violence, FGM and domestic violence. Anker and Lufkin followed the same line of analysis in Deborah Anker and Pail Lufkin, '*Gender and the symbiosis between refugee law and human rights law*' (Migration Information Sources 2003) online article available at https://www.migrationpolicy.org/article/gender-and-symbiosis-between-refugee-law-and-human-rights-law. See also Heaven Crawley, '*Engendering International Refugee Protection: Are We There Yet?*' in Bruce Burson and David James Cantor (eds), *Human Rights and the Refugee Definition*

this, a theoretical analysis of the nature of gender-based violence will be conducted in order to delineate the contours of the interpretive debate (Section 4.1).

This chapter will demonstrate that decision makers tend to overlook some aspects of the violence faced by women, and this, sometimes, leads to restrictive or inadequate outcomes of their asylum applications. It will be contended that international human rights law had a positive influence on the adjudication of gender-based claims, but the strict application of a human rights framework has not really encouraged protective and consistent approaches. In particular, the role that human rights should play in interpreting persecution has been inconsistently understood. Additionally, decision makers who have relied on a formalist human rights framework have often focused on stereotyped forms of harm[11] and, therefore, have often disregarded diverse circumstances of refugee women. An understanding of the situation of women, involving an intersectional approach, would reveal the complexity of their experiences and encourage a deeper understanding of the various forms of harm they are likely to be exposed to in their country of origin.

4.1 Gender-based violence and interpretive challenges

The following section will demonstrate that the development of human rights on the international scene has encouraged an evolutionary approach to the notion of persecution (4.1.1). In spite of these changes, it will be argued that there are limitations to a human rights approach to the interpretation of persecution in cases of gender-based violence (4.1.2).

4.1.1 The influence of human rights law on the growing recognition of gender-based violence as a form of persecution

In the second half of the 20th century, states started considering that women were facing particular forms of discriminations based on their gender and that, as such, their condition should be regulated through international human rights law. In 1979, the Convention on the Elimination of all Forms of Discrimination Against Women (CEDAW) was adopted as members of the international community proclaimed the necessity to bring 'the female half of humanity into the

Comparative Legal Practice and Theory (Brill Nijhoff 2016) 322–347, 330. The present chapter will roundly adopt the same line of analysis. However, given that the issue of sexual violence is rather broad, this chapter will focus more specifically on one aspect of sexual violence, namely trafficking, due to the conceptual difficulties that these cases raise as it will be analysed below.

11 In Megan Denise Smith, '*Rethinking gender in the international refugee regime*' [2016] 53 Forced Migration Review 65, https://www.fmreview.org/community-protection/smith, the author stated that 'measures to improve RSD and expand the Convention definition for gender-related persecution have tended to portray "essential" refugee women's identities that are constructed by UNHCR, the media and governments but not by refugee women themselves. Key to this victimhood narrative are certain images and categories, such as the lumping together of 'women and children'.

focus of human rights concerns'[12] in order to change 'the traditional role of men [and] women in the society and in the family'.[13] This new focus on women's rights arguably influenced international refugee law. Indeed, a few years after the adoption of the CEDAW, the UNHCR started issuing documents, recommending that the typical predicaments faced by women should also be considered a basis for asylum.[14] In 1991, the UNHCR then released formal guidelines on the protection of women, stating that a gender-based approach should be adopted for interpreting the terms of the 1951 Convention in cases involving refugee women.[15] These guidelines in turn encouraged Canada, the USA, Australia and the UK to develop their own interpretive guidance for claims based on gender-related persecution.[16]

In light of this evolution, some authors pointed out that human rights had exerted a growing influence on the understanding that decision makers had of the notion of persecution. For instance, Anker and Lufkin argued that human rights had a determining impact on the jurisprudence and have led to the recognition of an increasing number of victims of gender-related violence.[17] Kneebone also noted that, even if persecution was traditionally perceived as a form of harm based on ideological differences, the human rights framework positively influenced the way gender-related persecution was interpreted in refugee law.[18] Similarly, Edwards contended that the emergence of specialised treaties had 'advanced

12 Convention on the Elimination of All Forms of Discrimination against Women, 18 December 1979, UNTS 13 Vol 1249, Introduction.
13 Ibid.
14 In 1985 the UNHCR ExCom stated that: 'women asylum seekers who fear harsh or inhumane treatment due to their transgressions of societal mores in their home countries' may fall within the protection regime of the 1951 Convention, UNHCR ExCom conclusion No 39 (XXXVI) – 1985 – Refugee Women and International Protection. Inter alia, see also conclusion defining gender-based violence as a form of persecution; UNHCR ExCom conclusion No 73 (XLIV) – 1993 – Refugee Protection and Sexual Violence; ExCom conclusion No. 77 (XLVI) – 1995; ExCom conclusion No 79 (XLVII) – 1996; ExCom conclusion No 87 (L) – 1999.
15 UNHCR, Guidelines on the Protection of Refugee Women, July 1991, https://www.unhcr.org/en-my/publications/legal/3d4f915e4/guidelines-protection-refugee-women.html.
16 Kneebone (n 4) 15.
17 Anker and Luftin (n 10). See also Deborah Anker, '*Legal Change from the Bottom Up: The Development of Gender Asylum Jurisprudence in the United States*' in Efrat Arbel, Catherin Dauvergne and Jenni Millbank (eds) *Gender in Refugee Law, From the Margins to the Centre* (Routledge 2014) 46–72, 42. See also: Rachel Bacon and Kate Booth, '*The Intersection of Refugee Law and Gender: Private Harm and Public Responsibility: Islam; Ex Parte Shah Examined*' [2000] 23 University New South Wales 135, 142, https://www.researchgate.net/publication/284042711_Bacon_R_Booth_K_2000_Intersection_or_Refugee_Law_and_Gender_Private_Harm_and_Public_Responsibility-Islam_Ex_parte_Shah_Examined_The_UNSWLJ_23_135, 'developments in the international human rights field indicate that a significant shift has taken place in the international community's understanding of gender issues more generally.'
18 Kneebone (n 4) 9.

global trends towards gender inclusion and equal treatment between the sexes', thus leading to more generous approaches to those claims.[19]

In spite of these positive developments, some scholars have argued that there were some inherent limitations existing in the refugee definition that could not be overcome even through the application of a human rights scheme. For instance, in the late 1990s, Haines raised a major concern for the recognition of gender-related persecution cases because of the surrogacy principle. For him, the accountability theory applied by certain European countries regarding the role of the state in acts of persecution was an important obstacle to the recognition of women as refugees.[20] According to these countries, a claimant would be granted refugee status only if the state actively encouraged or tolerated the infliction of harm, thus adding an extra burden of proof on women claimants. This practice had been mostly used in civil law countries such as France and Germany[21] but fortunately has been progressively abandoned since the QD[22] was adopted and is more rarely relied upon in the recent jurisprudence. Whilst some jurisdictions still tend to reject asylum applications by placing an undue emphasis on the role of state protection,[23] the human rights scheme, in particular developed through the QD, had in fact helped to partly overcome this issue, at least in Europe. Although state protection has, at times, been considered in other jurisdictions and used to deny refugee status, an extensive discussion of this element would fall outside the purview of the present analysis. Indeed, as discussed in Chapter 2, the test of state protection should not be considered an inherent part of the persecution test. As mentioned by Kneebone in her analysis of gender-based persecution cases, 'the true position is that the lack of state protection is relevant to the question of the reasonableness of the fear of persecution, but is not a requirement of persecution as such'.[24] The present section will instead focus on the nature of the harm required to amount to persecution as it has also raised major contentions in a number of decisions.

In addition to concerns related to the role of state protection in asylum claims, some authors have observed that the refugee definition is unable to encompass all forms of violence against women due to the absence of 'gender' or 'sex' as a

19 Alice Edwards, '*Age and gender dimensions in international refugee law*' in Erika Feller, Volker Turk and Frances Nicholson (eds), *Refugee Protection in International Law: UNHCR's Global Consultations on International Protection* (Cambridge University Press 2003) 50.
20 Rodger Haines, '*Gender-Based Persecution: New Zealand Jurisprudence*' [1997] 9 International Journal of Refugee Law 129, 139, https://doi.org/10.1093/reflaw/9.Special_Issue.129.
21 Catherine Phuong, '*Persecution by Non-State Agents: Comparative Judicial Interpretations of the 1951 Refugee Convention*' [2002] 4 European Journal of Migration and Law 521, http://dx.doi.org/10.1163/157181602763715064.
22 Article 6 of the QD.
23 Hoepfner (n 4) 318 regarding the practice in Canada.
24 Kneebone (n 4) 39. Similarly, see Hoepfner (n 4) 319 on the view of Canadian jurisprudence.

Convention ground.[25] For them, this omission generally discouraged a gender-sensitive interpretation of the 1951 Convention, and raised concerns regarding the flexibility of the refugee definition and its ability to be interpreted in an evolutionary manner. The UNHCR somehow responded to these arguments by expressing the view that gender-based violence[26] could be easily accommodated within the current definition as women could, depending on the circumstances, fall within the Membership to a Particular Social Group (MPSG) ground. National jurisprudences[27] generally followed the same view.

Some authors, such as Anker, also supported this position. According to her, there was no need for a 'gender' ground to be included within the 1951 Convention because a gender-based approach should be generally applied when interpreting the whole refugee definition.[28] She argued that the development of human rights should be viewed as encouraging a gender-based approach to all the Convention reasons, without the necessity to add a specific ground of 'gender'. In Europe, the recast QD adopted this position by stating that persecution can be of a specific gender-related nature,[29] thus further encouraging states to adopt an overall gender-sensitive interpretation of the 1951 Convention without amending the definition of a refugee. This approach is currently the dominant one, given the absence of concrete prospects to amend the Convention. The interpretive difficulty seems, however, to have been displaced onto the interpretation of the term persecution, rather than the Convention grounds, as will be demonstrated below.

Whilst the influence of human rights has most certainly encouraged an evolutionary understanding of the refugee definition, one might, nonetheless, wonder to what extent this has been the case. In particular, it should be questioned whether human rights have permitted a flexible and adaptable interpretation of the notion of persecution for all refugee women. In fact, in certain situations, human rights seem to have fostered a stereotyped understanding of their condition, which at times has obviated important aspects of their complex experiences. What follows

25 Joanna J. Kallinosis, '*Refugee Roulette: A Comparative Analysis of Gender-Related Persecution in Asylum Law*' [2017] 6 DePaul Journal of Women, Gender and the Law 55, 90–92, https://via.library.depaul.edu/jwgl/vol6/iss1/2. See also Alice Edwards, '*Distinction, Discretion, Discrimination: The new frontiers of gender-related claims to asylum*' European University Institute, Florence, Italy, 18–19 June 2012, 1–13, 13 available at http://www.refworld.org/docid/4ffd430c2.html and Kim (n 6) 108–109 and 113.

26 UNHCR ExCom conclusion No. 39 (XXXVI) – 1985 – Refugee Women and International Protection. UN High Commissioner for Refugees (UNHCR), Guidelines on the Protection of Refugee Women, July 1991, at [72].

27 Inter alia, *Islam v Secretary of State for the Home Department; R v Immigration Appeal Tribunal, ex parte Shah* [1999] 2 AC 629 United Kingdom: House of Lords (Judicial Committee), 25 March 1999; *Minister for Immigration and Multicultural Affairs v Khawar* HCA 14 (11 April 2002); Case No. 0900571, RRTA 303 (16 April 2009); *Matter of A-R-C-G* 26 I&N Dec. 388 (Board of Immigration Appeal 2014).

28 Anker (n 17) 51.

29 Article 9(2)(f) QD.

will highlight some theoretical deficiencies of the human/woman rights narrative in order to assess the limitations that the human rights approach can have in interpreting gender-related forms of persecution.

4.1.2 Human rights: a male-centric paradigm?

The mere existence of a separate set of 'women's rights' in international law indicates that the general system of human rights is not enough to ensure that women live their full life in dignity. The reason why traditional human rights have not been sufficient to guarantee descent standards of life to women is because many of these norms are formulated in a manner that does not adequately match women's needs. Indeed, human rights norms are based on typical males' experiences[30] and, as such, they do not address the specific concerns of women in numerous societies. In this sense, Charlesworth, Chinkin and Wright considered that 'the normative structure of international law has allowed issues of particular concern to women to be either ignored or undermined'.[31]

The main deficiency of the current human rights paradigm is that it operates a distinction between private and public spheres and grant rights that are typically enjoyed by individuals in the public arena.[32] Although, there is nothing preventing women from enjoying these rights, in societies that have been traditionally dominated by males, human rights are, in practice, more easily applicable to men. Therefore, major issues that concern women in the private sphere are left untouched. For instance, the necessity to conform to social mores is relatively ignored by international human rights. It could be argued that there is a right to freedom of expression that could be invoked in cases when women are oppressed by traditions. However, this right is often understood as being of a political nature and, thus, is less easily applied in the private sphere. An explicit right to oppose traditional or family norms in human rights

30 Inter alia see Hilary Charlesworth, Christine Chinkin and Shelley Wright, '*Feminist Approaches to International Law*' [1991] 85 American Journal of International Law 613, DOI: 10.2307/2203269; S. Kim (n 6); C. Romany, '*Women as Aliens: A Feminist Critique of the Public/Private Distinction in International Human Rights Law*' (1993) 6 Harvard Human Rights Journal 87, https://heinonline.org/HOL/LandingPage?handle=hein.journals/hhrj6&div=8&id=&page=; Crawley (n 10) 339: Crawley speaks of the 'gendered nature of IHRL'.

31 Charlesworth et al. (n 30), 625.

32 Alice Edwards, *Violence against women under international human rights law* (Cambridge University Press 2010) 305. See also inter alia, Charlotte Bunch, '*Women's Rights as Human Rights: Toward a Re-Vision of Human Rights*' [1990] 12 Human Rights Quarterly 486, 10.2307/762496. For a general discussion on the distinction between private/public sphere and state/civil society see: Frances E. Olsen, '*International Law: Feminist Critiques of the Public/Private Distinction*' [1993] 25 Studies in Transnational Legal Policy 157, https://conservancy.umn.edu/bitstream/handle/11299/166961/10_02_Symposium_Olsen.pdf;jsessionid=E3CFD0C466DE12DF661359E9E59EDA5D?sequence=1. For a general overview of the debate: Tuuli Karjala, *Sixty Years of Silence: Gender Discrimination under International Refugee Law* (Stellenbosch University, 2016–03) 65.

law would more conveniently fit the experiences of women in many contexts, but such a right does not exist at the international level. Edwards also provided the example of the prohibition of torture, which is still perceived as an act perpetrated by state actors, or by individuals in positions of state authority, for the purpose of extracting information. She explained that these experiences usually relate to men's roles in the society as they have been active in the public sphere more than women.[33] She added that the violence against women has to reach a certain threshold of gravity in order to be considered torture, thus adding an extra burden on women to demonstrate that they have been victims of severe human rights violations.

In spite of this bias, it should be acknowledged that the CEDAW contributed significantly to the advancement of women's rights on the international scene. Nonetheless, it mainly focuses on ending various forms of discrimination between men and women on issues that mainly take place in the public sphere. Therefore, it still perpetuates the dichotomy men/women, public/private sphere. It is not argued that international law should closely regulate private matters as it could end up being liberticide. However, certain issues regarding women that have been traditionally considered to fall within the private sphere are in fact matters of public policy. The distinction between the private and public spheres is indeed misleading because it creates the wrong assumption that harms perpetrated in private are only motivated by personal reasons.[34] A more global understanding of the endemic discriminations and harmful traditional practices that ensure a climate of impunity for gender-based forms of violence in fact shows that although the immediate motivation of the perpetrator can be personal, the harmful act is made possible by a broader system of discriminations and stereotyped understanding of gender roles in the society.[35] This paradigm in turn fails to fulfil the liberal promise of human rights to 'emancipate the individual from the oppression of political structures' as women still need to conform to males' experiences if they want to enjoy human rights.[36,37]

Consequently, using the human rights paradigm to interpret the terms of the definition of a refugee has an impact on how the asylum claims of women are adjudicated.[38] Again, for their asylum application women would have to

33 Edwards (n 32) 237.

34 Anthea Roberts, '*Gender and Refugee Law*' [2002] 22 Australian Year Book of International Law 159, 190, http://classic.austlii.edu.au/au/journals/AUYrBkIntLaw/2002/5.html.

35 On this see, Smith (n 11) 66.

36 Romany (n 30) 90.

37 Crawley (n 10) 341: Crawley noted that the 'ideas of what constitutes human rights follow an androcentric model'. See also Alice Edwards, '*Transitioning Gender: Feminist Engagement with International Refugee Law and Policy*' [2010] 29 Refugee Survey Quarterly 21, 31, https://doi.org/10.1093/rsq/hdq021.

38 Edwards (n 32) 206: Edwards stated that 'men's experiences are posited as the norm of international law and women only gain access to the system by equating their experiences to these masculine norms'.

often conform their experiences to those of men in order to be successful.[39] To assess a refugee claim, a human rights analysis of the situation would only look into the possibility for the survivor to enjoy certain sets of rights upon return to her country, without taking into consideration broader circumstances leading to the oppression of women. For instance, in cases of domestic violence, such an approach would explore the possibility for a claimant to leave her husband, and enjoy protection from the law, to be independent from her family and have equal access to men to work rights and so on. If it is deemed that these rights are in theory accessible to everybody, the claim of the refugee women could simply be rejected. However, for a variety of reasons, it could be more difficult for women than for men to effectively enjoy these rights in societies where they face daily hardships due to a stereotyped understanding of gender roles and stigmatisation attached to this. Rather than isolated rights entitlements, a whole set of various forms of predicaments should be taken into consideration to adjudicate their claims.

Another telling example is how sexual abuse or rape[40] is often analysed in asylum cases. It is now well accepted that sexual violence constitutes a human rights violation. However, other aspects of a victim's life that are also fundamental to understand women's hardships are barely touched upon by human rights or refugee law. On this point, reference can be made to Liberman who highlighted the importance of the notion of shame, as structuring the roles of men and women in certain societies.[41] She described the major implications that this element can have for the safety of women as she stated that:

> in numerous cultures if a woman is raped or subjected to spousal abuse and she tries to seek redress, her family and community may ostracize her and treat her as ruined property, unworthy of remarriage. By the same token, the alternative for a woman who refuses FGM is ostracization, shame, and derision as either a promiscuous woman, or an inadequate, overgrown child.[42]

In spite of this, the element of shame, underlying the acts of gender-related persecution, is rarely acknowledged as a form of violence, let alone a form of

39 Georgina Firth and Barbara Mauthe, '*Refugee Law, Gender and the Concept of Personhood*' [2013] 25 International Journal of Refugee Law 470, 482, https://doi.org/10.1093/ijrl/eet034. 482. According to them, 'there is little space within the dominant discourses for context-specific, accurate representations of refugee women's diverse experiences or agency'. Anker pointed out that some judges adopted the same view, in Deborah Anker, '*Refugee Law, Gender, and the Human Rights Paradigm*' [2002] 15 Harvard Human Rights Journal 133, http://nrs.harvard.edu/urn-3:HUL.InstRepos:11357476. Crawley (n 10) 323.

40 Anker (n 39) 141–144.

41 Irena Liberman, '*Women and Girls Facing Gender-Based Violence, and Asylum Jurisprudence*' [2002] 29 Online Human Rights Magazine of the American Bar, no 3 available at: https://www.americanbar.org/groups/crsj/publications/human_rights_magazine_home.html.

42 Ibid.

persecution in asylum jurisdictions. It is, nonetheless, a powerful tool by which perpetrators keep women in a subversive position in certain social settings. Shame not being a human rights violation, a victim of rape in the context of an indiscriminate criminal violence would often risk seeing her asylum claim rejected as it would be considered that she is unlikely to face the same form of abuse if she goes back to her country. It should not, however, be concluded that she is not at risk of harm upon return. Focusing only on the prospective risk of human rights violation (the rape) would displace the discursive debate onto the wrong form of predicament. The harm that the victim might suffer if she goes back to her community, could be very much attached to the stigma that the rape has bestowed upon the family, leading in the worst cases to honour killings, but also to various forms of ostracism and trauma that can have in turn a major impact on the individual's life. Whilst this aspect of gender-based violence is increasingly discussed in national jurisdictions, it remains too often forgotten.

Overall, a feminist approach to international human rights law highlights the fact that human rights law is based on behavioural standards rooted in men's daily experiences and does not adequately reflect the complexity of women's circumstances. A larger understanding of the public dimension of the violence that they face, and how their roles are shaped by traditional structures of societies, would encourage a more holistic understanding of the nature of gender-based persecution. In fact, the basic human rights narrative runs the risk of simplifying the interpretive exercise of the notion of persecution by identifying only certain forms of harm and overshadowing others. Furthermore, by identifying certain types of formal entitlements, the human rights discourse often disregards the context in which these harms are embedded. Broader circumstances of women refugees should be therefore taken into consideration as encouraged by the circumstantial approach of UNHCR. In particular, this approach is in line with the feminist theory of intersectionality, that indicates that gender in itself is not the only reason for violence but is an element of a more systematic and complex system that particularly exposes women to violence and discrimination. Proponents of this theory have indeed demonstrated 'the need to examine how other forms of inequality and oppression, such as racism, ethnocentrism, class privilege, and heterosexism, intersect with gender oppression'.[43] The concept of intersectionality[44] indeed provides an alternative methodology to demonstrate that gender is an amplifying element of a larger system of oppression that reveals the deeper root causes of the perpetuation of violence. This model points to the importance of considering a larger array of discriminations in women's daily circumstances. A broader understanding of the root causes that structure unequal power relationships would

43 N. J. Sokoloff and I. Dupont, '*Domestic Violence at the Intersections of Race, Class, and Gender: Challenges and Contributions to Understanding Violence Against Marginalized Women in Diverse Communities*' [2005] 11 Violence Against Women 38, 39, https://doi.org/10.1177/1077801204271476.

44 Kimberle Crenshaw, '*Mapping the Margins: Intersectionality, Identity Politics, and Violence against Women of Color*' [1991] 43 Stanford Law Review *1241*, DOI: 10.2307/1229039.

therefore encourage a better understanding of the daily hardship faced by refugee women, rather than focusing on certain stereotyped forms of harm.

It can be concluded that the human rights framework for interpreting the notion of persecution does not sufficiently encourage a holistic assessment of the various circumstances that refugee women could face in their place of origin, which appears in fact in opposition to the arguable intention[45] of the plenipotentiaries to allow for an evolutionary understanding of the notion of persecution. With this theoretical background in mind, the following section will engage in a study of selected cases in order to evaluate how the harms claimed by women have been addressed in various jurisdictions and what evolutions are further desirable.

4.2 The notion of persecution and jurisprudential approaches to gender-based violence

Certain forms of violence perpetrated in the refugee's community or family, such as FGM (4.2.1) coupled with/or domestic violence (4.2.2) have formed the basis of numerous refugee claims. Similarly, criminal activities, perpetrated by transnational networks forcing people into trafficking have been increasingly invoked in domestic jurisdictions (4.2.3). Although men can be trafficked under various circumstances, a very large number of the trafficking victims are women and girls,[46] therefore falling within the category of gender-related violence.[47] The above harms are only a few examples of the forms that gender-based violence can take but they have been adjudicated quite inconsistently, thus raising some legal uncertainty for women asylum seekers. This section will analyse how the notion of persecution has been applied to such claims and argue that this notion remains relevant for these specific cases if a more circumstantial approach is adopted.

4.2.1 The practice of FGM and its persecutory dimension

FGM: a general overview

According to the World Health Organization (WHO), FGM consists in 'all procedures involving partial or total removal of the external female genitalia, or other injury to the female genital organs, for non-medical reasons'.[48] Due to the severe

45 Section 1.2.3.

46 Report of the General Assembly on Trafficking in women and girls A/71/223, 27 July 2016 at [9]. See Saito Kaori, Research Paper No 149, 'International protection for trafficked persons and those who fear being trafficked' Policy Officer Division of Human Resource Management UNHCR, December 2007, Geneva, 9.

47 UNHCR Guidelines on International Protection No 7: The Application of Article 1A (2) of the 1951 Convention and Protocol Relating to the Status of Refugees to Victims of Trafficking and Persons at Risk of Being Trafficked, 7 April 2006, HCR/GIP/06/07 at [21], https://www.refworld.org/docid/443679fa4.html.

48 WHO, 'Eliminating Female Genital Mutilation: An Interagency Statement' (2008) 4; WHO, 'Female Genital Mutilation', Fact Sheet No 241 (Feb 2014) <http://www.who.int/mediacentre/factsheets/fs241/en/>.

medical complications and suffering imposed by the act of FGM, the WHO considers that 'FGM is a violation of the human rights of girls and women'.[49] The practice of FGM is a ritual performed in certain traditional societies in order to mark the passage from childhood to adulthood, and often takes place in the traditional context of arranged or forced marriage. Middelburg and Balta pointed out that FGM is generally 'believed to be a requirement for marriage and necessary to control women's sexuality'.[50] Lewis also highlighted the traditional aspect of FGM by explaining how it structures the role of women within their community.[51] This deep customary imprint and the private dimension of FGM have been viewed by some as a major barrier to the recognition of FGM victims as refugees.[52] For instance, Steinbock rejected the possibility that FGM could be a basis for asylum as he considered that the 1951 Convention was not meant to provide protection against such forms of harms. For him, it was 'hard to justify the application of the refugee definition to this traditional practice of many centuries' standing based on the historical background of the Convention'[53] because he considered that there was 'no evidence whatsoever that the drafters or practitioners of refugee law in the post-war period intended to encompass known, traditional, gender-based inequalities'.[54] His view, however, did not gain major traction amongst decision makers and scholars as FGM became a central concern of refugee women towards the end of the cold war.

FGM as a physical harm: an act of persecution?

As of the 1990s,[55] an increasing number of claims relating to the fear of being subjected to FGM started being lodged in national jurisdictions. This period coincided with the influence of the human rights approach, which arguably had a certain impact on the adjudication of these cases. This evolution led to a growing acceptance that a risk of FGM, due to the extreme suffering that it entails, could amount to persecution. For instance, as early as 1994, Canada acknowledged that

49 'Female Genital Mutilation', Fact Sheet No 241 (updated Feb 2017) <http://www.who.int/mediacentre/factsheets/fs241/en/>.
50 Annemarie Middelburg and Aline Balta, '*Female Genital Mutilation/Cutting as a Ground for Asylum in Europe*' [2016] 28 International Journal of Refugee Law 416, 416–417, https://doi.org/10.1093/ijrl/eew056.
51 In Hope Lewis, '*Between Irua and Female Genital Mutilation: Feminist Human Rights Discourse and the Cultural Divide*' [1995] 8 Harvard Human Rights Journal 1, 30, https://papers.ssrn.com/sol3/papers.cfm?abstract_id=1080248. The author mentions the analysis of Jomo Kenyatta who calls for awareness of the cultural context of FGM. Although caution should be exerted in relying on cultural relativism arguments to justify FGM, the view that FGM is deeply rooted into social structures, is important.
52 Ibid. 8. Lewis mentioned that considering FGM has raised 'complex cultural, gender, and racial questions' and thus is not easily considered a human rights violation.
53 Daniel J. Steinbock, '*Interpreting the Refugee Definition*' [1998] 45 UCLA Law Review 733, 778.
54 Ibid.
55 Hoepfner (n 4) 292.

a risk of facing FGM could warrant refugee recognition.[56] This has remained the interpretive line in the jurisprudence since then, but the methodology for reaching such a conclusion was and remains rather unclear. In some cases, Canadian decision makers seemed to rely on human rights to assess FGM-based claims, although quite implicitly,[57] whilst in other cases, they adopted ad hoc approaches.[58]

The US jurisprudence also adopted a favourable view on FGM claims. For instance, in the landmark case *Matter of Kasinga*, the BIA considered that FGM, 'which results in permanent disfiguration and poses a risk of serious, potentially life-threatening complications, can be the basis for a claim of persecution'.[59] This position has been quite consistent since then in the US jurisprudence. Although no clear line of interpretation is noticeable for those cases, authors have argued that the development of human rights has significantly influenced the decisions of judges. For instance, Hathaway mentioned a series of cases in the US in which FGM has been considered a human rights violation.[60] Anker[61] also noted that the jurisprudence in this field evolved through the influence of human rights law. In line with the above developments, Australia considered that a future risk of FGM, or a risk of being re-subjected to genital mutilation, amounts to persecution.[62] The influence of human rights was notable, for instance, in *Case No 1101038*, where the Refugee Tribunal of Australia (RRTA) considered that FGM involved a 'threat to life'[63] and hence constituted persecution.

A favourable approach to FGM claims has been also adopted in Europe.[64] In particular, in the UK, judges often considered that a risk of FGM can amount to

56 *Khadra Hassan Farah, Mahad Dahir Buraleh, Hodan Dahir Buraleh* [1994] No T93–12198, T93–12199, T93–12199, T12197 Canada: Immigration and Refugee Board of Canada: in this case the Board acknowledged that the risk of FGM would be contrary to the CRC.

57 Ibid. See also *MA1–07929* [2002] Immigration and Refugee Board of Canada (refugee division) 2.

58 *Faustina Annan v Minister of Citizenship and Immigration of Canada* [1995] IMM-215–95 Canada: Federal Court: the Court qualified FGM as a 'cruel and barbaric' practice and granted refugee status to the claimant at [3].

59 *Matter of Kasinga*; 21 I&N Dec 357, 365 (Board of Immigration Appeal 1996); see other cases in the US which adopted the same approach: *Abankwah v. INS*, 185 F.3d 18, 23–24 (2nd Circuit Court 1999); *Abay. Ashcroft*, 368 F.3d 634 (United States Court of Appeals for the Sixth Circuit 2004). *Matter of A-T, Respondent*, 24 I&N Dec (Decided by the US Attorney General 2008); *Khadija Ahmed Mohamed v Alberto R. Gonzales*, Attorney General 400 F.3d 785 (US Court of Appeals, Ninth Circuit 2005): the Court found that FGM amounts to 'continuing and permanent persecution' at 3085.

60 James C. Hathaway and Michelle Foster, *The Law of Refugee Status* (2nd edn, Cambridge University Press 2014) 215.

61 Anker (n 17) 54.

62 Australia: FGM and forced marriage amount to serious harm hence persecution in RRT *Case No 1101038* [2011] RRTA, 307 (14 April 2011); RRT *Case No 0808751* [2009] RRTA 217 (18 March 2009).

63 Ibid.

64 Hana Cheikh Ali, Christel Querton and Elodie Soulard, *Gender-related Claims in Europe: Comparative Analysis of Law, Policies and Practice Focusing on Women in Nine EU Member States* (Directorate General for Internal Policies, Policy department C: Citizens'

persecution.[65] For instance, in *Fornah*, the House of Lords agreed that the harm faced by the applicant consisted in a human rights violation.[66],[67] Similar to the above evolution, France and Belgium also tended to consider that an act of FGM could rise to the level of persecution[68] although they rarely relied on a human rights scheme. In the case of *Melle Diop*,[69] the French judges stated that FGM could be a basis for asylum for reasons of membership to a particular social group. They, nonetheless, restricted the scope of persecution as they posited that refugee status could only be granted if the practice of FGM was condoned or actively tolerated by the state, thus insisting on the necessary public dimension of the notion of persecution. Hoepfner regretted this approach as he noted that the requirement of an active participation of the authorities in these kinds of harm had discouraged claimants from lodging asylum claims on that account until the early 2000s in Europe.[70] Fortunately, the jurisprudence further evolved in France, in particular after the adoption of the QD and the abandoning of the accountability theory. Nowadays, prospective victims of FGM in France tend to be granted refugee status without having to demonstrate that they had sought protection from the authorities before leaving their country.[71]

Regrettably, France has, however, recently developed a restrictive jurisprudential trend for children born after their parents' departure from their place of origin. In *Mlle K*,[72] the CNDA considered that girls born in France and fearing

Rights and Constitutional Affairs, European Parliament, 2012) 36, http://www.europarl.europa.eu/meetdocs/2009_2014/documents/femm/dv/asylum_claims_/asylum_claims_en.pdf.

65 However, a researcher pointed out that very few negative decisions were published in the UK, and efforts to obtain samples remained unanswered, thus relativising this positive observation in Maja Grundler, *The Protection of Asylum Seekers against Female Genital Mutilation in the UK* (Humboldt-Universität zu Berlin Centre for British Studies 2015) 41, https://www.gbz.hu-berlin.de/downloads/pdf/the_protection_of_asylum_seekers_against_fgm_in_the_uk_mbs_thesis_maja_grundler.pdf.

66 *Zainad Esther Fornah v Secretary of State for the Home* [2006] UKHL 46, 18 October 2006: see Baroness Held of Richmond at [94]: 'it is a human rights issue, not only because of the unequal treatment of men and women, but also because the procedure will almost inevitably amount either to torture or to other cruel, inhuman or degrading treatment'.

67 See other cases granting refugee status to victims of FGM: *VM (FGM - Risks - Mungiki - Kikuyu/Gikuyu) Kenya v Secretary of State for the Home Department*, CG [2008] UKAIT 00049, 9 June 2008. *K and others (FGM) The Gambia CG v. Secretary of State for the Home Department*, [2013] UKUT 00062(IAC), April 2013.

68 See *Arrêt n° 61.832*, Belgium: Conseil du Contentieux des Etrangers, 19 Mai 2011; CNDA 21 Décembre 2012 N° 332491; *Arrêt n° 138 876*, Belgium: Conseil du Contentieux des Etrangers, 19 Février 2015.

In France, another case also recognized that FGM amounts to persecution: CRR, 16 Juin 2005, N 492440, *Mlle S.*

69 CRR, 17 juillet 1991, 164078, *Mlle Diop Aminata.*

70 Hoepfner (n 4) 299.

71 Ibid. 300.

72 CNDA, Decision du 12 Mars 2009, *Mme Mariam Diarra ép. Kouyate*, n° 638891; CNDA Décision du 25 mars 2010 *M. S.* n° 08017355 C+.

to undergo FGM in their country would not meet the criteria of the 1951 Convention. According to the French judges, these claimants should instead be granted subsidiary protection. However, no clear framework of analysis has been adopted to justify this position, as the court merely stated that there is no reasonable likelihood that these girls will be individually singled out in their place of origin. This approach clearly disregards important discriminatory elements of FGM perpetrated against women.[73] In another case,[74] the court adopted an even narrower view by rejecting the application of a child born in France on the mere ground of her young age. Hoepfner pointed out that this interpretation was concerning, because the element of 'age' does not normally constitute a bar to refugee status under the 1951 Convention.[75] The above cases exemplify the pitfalls of ad hoc interpretive frameworks that tend, at times, to present little or inaccurate justifications for a decision and disregard a broader system of discriminations faced by women in certain contexts. The French jurisprudence on that point has been qualified as 'ambiguous' by a report of the European Parliament.[76]

Different interpretive approaches have been adopted in national jurisdictions for adjudicating FGM claims, but it can be noted that the general influence of human rights has been positive for claimants and has led to an increasing recognition of individuals at risk of undergoing FGM. However, by focusing on the physical act of FGM and its consequences for the applicant's health and security, decision makers have at times disregarded other aspects of the applicant's claim. For instance, peripheral aspects of FGM such as the claims of parents whose girls are at risk of facing FGM, or girls who themselves can manage to avoid FGM upon return to their country are inconsistently addressed. In these cases, ad hoc methodologies seemed to have been adopted, thus yielding different results.

Peripheral aspects of the harms surrounding the act of FGM

Hoepfner observed the emergence of subsequent waves of FGM claims, involving parents of little girls[77] at risk of genital mutilation in their country. The conceptual difficulties that arise from these types of claim concern the forms of harm that the parents themselves are likely to face in their place of origin. A human rights interpretive framework often fails to address issues of concern, relating to the mental suffering of the parents of the girl who avoided the FGM, as well as the ostracism or stigmatisation of these parents. Indeed, refusing to engage in FGM can have even wider repercussions on the family itself in certain tribal societies, which again engages the notion of shame so rarely considered. Whilst these claims might not always be viewed as being gender-related per se, they are nonetheless tied to a specific perception of the roles of women in the society. Additionally, the

73 UNHCR, Guidance Note on Refugee Claims Relating to Female Genital Mutilation, May 2009 at [1], https://www.refworld.org/docid/4a0c28492.html.
74 Hoefpner (n 4) 305.
75 Ibid.
76 Cheikh Ali et al. (n 64) 37.
77 Hoepfner (n 4) 302.

claims of girls who managed to avoid FGM and are not risk of further FGM acts upon return (i.e. for instance when they are supported by their own parents) also raise concerns that are larger than the mere physical harm, such as for instance risks of stigmatisation or ostracism.

In France, the CNDA usually considers that the parents' opposition to their daughter's excision is not sufficient to establish their fear of persecution. Whilst some cases have granted refugee status to the parents of little girls who escaped their country with their child,[78] the court has more regularly denied these applications. In the view of the court, parents should demonstrate that they had actively expressed their position when they were in their country and that, as a result, they are at risk of being individually targeted.[79] The ad hoc methodology used in France does not provide any justification as to why these forms of harm are not considered persecutory in nature. According to this approach, it can be observed that no consideration is given to the weight of traditional rules in the community, nor to the possible pressure that parents, or children who want to avoid FGM, can face upon return.

In the USA,[80] the Board also denied the application for withholding of removal of a father who refused to return to his country because of the risk of FGM that his child could face. The Board concluded that because the father repeatedly claimed that he was afraid more for his daughter than for himself, there was no risk that 'his life or freedom would be threatened'.[81] The claimant, however, insisted several times that he would be harassed and humiliated upon return. He also referred to the UNHCR guidance stating that, depending on the individual circumstances, parents of children likely to face FGM could have a refugee claim. It should also be pointed out that this claimant further mentioned the possibility of facing 'emotional persecution'. The court rejected this argument and concluded that, in order to warrant refugee status, 'emotional persecution' should be directly and purposely inflicted on the victim. However, this position is not in line with previous jurisprudence[82] as well as with the recommendations of the UNHCR.[83] Additionally, the court stated that no derivative claims could be considered. As such, the court did not consider the existence of a personal claim, resulting from possible harassment, pressure from the community and stigmatisation, therefore adopting a narrow understanding of the different forms of harm that can be caused by the imposition of FGM on a girl child. The refusal of family members to subject their child to the ritual of FGM can indeed have major consequences as it contravenes social norms. Whilst it is not argued that every parent of a child born in the country of asylum and originating from a country where FGM is prevalent

78 Ibid.
79 CNDA SR 12 March 2009 *Mme K.* n° 08019372/638891 R; CNDA 25 mars 2010 *M. S.* n° 08017355 C+.
80 *Kane v Holder*, 581 F.3d 231, 240–42 (United States Court of Appeals for the Fifth Circuit 2009).
81 Ibid. at [23].
82 Matter of *Kasinga* (n 59).
83 UNHCR (n 73) at [11].

should be recognised, a more thorough assessment of the applicant's individual circumstances should be conducted, in order to minimise the risk of arbitrary decisions. The UNHCR, in particular, encourages decision makers to consider different forms of harm that could be suffered by parents who are 'forced to witness the pain and suffering of the child' or 'who are opposed to the practice'.[84]

In recent years, some cases have, in fact, been adjudicated more favourably, although reservations remained in relation to the legal grounds for protection. For instance, in the UK, the Appeal Tribunal[85] dismissed the claims for protection under the 1951 Convention of a family who feared returning to Sudan because their daughter was at risk of facing FGM. In this case, the tribunal adopted a rather narrow understanding of persecution, as the judges seemed to have conflated the Convention grounds with the notion of persecution. The tribunal rejected the fact that young girls at risk of FGM could constitute a particular social group (PSG) and concluded that there was no real risk of persecution.[86] The tribunal, however, considered *non-refoulement* obligations as it stated that the claimants, including the parents, were all at risk of facing violations of rights entailed in the ECHR. To the tribunal, to send the 'first appellant and his family back to a country where circumcision would take place to the first appellant's daughter, would be degrading for the appellant as a family member, and would amount to a breach of Article 3 of the ECHR'.[87] The tribunal's interpretation of both the Convention nexus and the concept of persecution was quite restrictive and inconsistent with the view that victims of FGM can constitute a PSG,[88] and that persecution does not necessarily have to encompass the Convention grounds.[89] However, the idea that parents of FGM victims could face harm upon return is noteworthy, although it was not found to constitute a basis for refugee status under the 1951 Convention. A later case further developed that view and eventually stated that 'given the first appellant's abhorrence of FGM, any infliction of it upon either of her daughters is, we find, reasonably likely to have so profound an effect upon the first appellant as to amount to the infliction on her of persecutory harm'.[90]

Similarly, in another case, the tribunal made a general statement that FGM in 'any of forms 1–4 is persecution for a Convention reason not only of a girl child but also of the parents of a minor child where they are opposed to the procedure and where there is a real risk of its infliction'.[91] In this case, only the claim of the

84 Ibid.
85 *MH and Others (Article 3 – FGM) Sudan CG* [2002] UKIAT 02691, 16 July 2002.
86 Ibid. at [23].
87 Ibid. at [14].
88 As recommended by UNHCR (n 73) and accepted in the Jurisprudence. See, for instance, *Fornah* (n 66).
89 See discussion above, Section 3.2.2.
90 *FM (FGM) Sudan v Secretary of State for the Home Department*, CG [2007] UKAIT00060, 27 June 2007 at [161].
91 *K and others (FGM) The Gambia CG v. Secretary of State for the Home Department* [2013] UKUT 00062(IAC), April 2013 at [13].

child was considered, but the tribunal affirmed a principle that parents of children could have an individual claim, even when they had not actively expressed their opposition in the country of origin as was the case in this situation. This approach was more closely aligned with the recommendation of the UNHCR guidelines[92] and by following this line of argumentation, the tribunal adopted a view that was more protective for the claimants. This decision is not isolated as a few other cases lodged in other countries by parents fearing FGM for their children have been adjudicated in a more favourable manner,[93] albeit quite rarely. Of note, however, is that refugee status tends to be granted when the imposition of FGM appears highly likely. Consideration of what would happen to parents or girls who managed to avoid the act is, however, rarely part of the jurisprudence, although the consequences for their lives could, in certain contexts, be particularly problematic.

Concluding remarks

In all the cases mentioned above, decision makers tended to adopt different approaches that have led to inconsistent results. The human rights narrative has indeed appeared inadequate in these kinds of cases as it mainly focuses on the physical act of FGM and disregards other aspects of the suffering that can ensue from this practice. This situation has led Marouf to regret that the psychological and emotional aspects of FGM are rarely taken into account[94] in courts. It appears, however, that methodologies that are closer to the UNHCR's circumstantial approach, taking into account a broader range of discrimination in the country of origin, have the capacity to yield more protective results by encouraging a holistic analysis of refugee claims, factoring in the above aspects. Although asylum applications involving parents of children at risk of FGM are not particularly frequent in national jurisdictions, they tend to raise contention. These claims reveal important aspects of FGM as a traditional practice that is deeply embedded in certain societies and structures the roles of women in relation to men. As a result, opposing this practice has wider implications than the mere risk of physical harm that this can cause, both for the victims and their relatives.

92 Ibid. at [12].

93 *Arrêt n°45.395* Belgium: Conseil du Contentieux des Etrangers, 24 June 2010: in this case, the fear expressed by the applicant that her daughter could be subjected to FGM was sufficient to consider that she would be perceived as opposing traditions and social mores upon return. See also *Nwaokolo Immigration and Naturalization Service*, 314 F.3d 303 (United States Court of Appeals for the Seventh Circuit 2002): The Court of Appeal returned a case to the BIA as the BIA only assessed the risk of FGM for the main applicant, but failed to consider that her daughter could also face a real risk if she had to return with her mother and did not analyze the impact that this could have on both individuals.

94 Fatma Marouf, '*The Rising Bar for Persecution in Asylum Cases Involving Sexual and Reproductive Harm*' [2011] 22 Columbia Journal Gender and Law 81, 85–86, https://scholars.law.unlv.edu/facpub/788.

It is acknowledged that such claims should certainly be treated with caution as they could potentially concern a very large number of claimants and constitute an avenue for fraud. Nonetheless, for the sake of fairer decisions, a more thorough and transparent analysis of the risk of persecution of the relatives implicated in a potential risk of FGM should be conducted. Similarly, the claims of girls who are not at risk of facing FGM upon return (for instance because the parents are opposed to it) should be more comprehensively assessed so as to take into account various forms of predicaments that they could endure back in their country.

4.2.2 Domestic violence

General overview of the notion of domestic violence in asylum cases

Harmful practices against women can also take the form of domestic violence. Traditionally, asylum judges have been quite hesitant to grant refugee status to victims of domestic violence as they considered that such situations fell outside the ambit of the 1951 Convention[95] because of the perceived private nature of the harm.[96] For instance, a decision of the US BIA in 1975 denied the application of a victim of domestic violence because the motivation behind her husband's alleged actions was deemed 'strictly personal'.[97] However, legal developments on the international scene led to a consideration that the violence perpetrated within the family sphere was in fact in breach of human rights law and that it could fall within the refugee definition.[98,99] In this sense, the UNHCR guidelines on gender-

95 Roberts (n 34) 161–163. See also Anker (n 39) 133.

96 Michael G. Heyman '*Domestic Violence and Asylum: Toward a Working Model of Affirmative State Obligations*' [2005] 17 International Journal of Refugee Law 729, 730, https://doi.org/10.1093/ijrl/eei029. For him, domestic violence 'challenges the common understanding of persecution as an act occurring within the public sphere'.

97 *Matter of Pierre*, 15 I&N 2433 (Board of Immigration Appeals 1975) at [4610]. See also on the same issue *Matter of R-A-*, 22 I&N Dec 906 (BIA 1999).

98 In past decades an increasing number of international instruments addressed the treatment of women in the context of their traditional community and their family. For instance, Article 16 CEDAW laid out measures for eliminating discrimination between men and women in the context of their marriage. See also: Committee on the Elimination of Discrimination Against Women, General Recommendation No 19 (11th session, 1992). In 1993, the General Assembly adopted a Declaration on the Elimination of Violence against Women, stating that reprehensible violence against women encompasses 'physical, sexual and psychological violence occurring in the family, including battering, sexual abuse of female children in the household, dowry-related violence, marital rape, female genital mutilation and other traditional harmful practice', UN General Assembly 48/104. Declaration on the Elimination of Violence against Women, 20 December 1993, A/RES/48/104, Art 2 (a).

99 See Anker (n 17) and Kneebone (n 4) who argued that human rights influenced the way gender-based persecution was interpreted.

related persecution stated that domestic violence can amount to persecution depending on the circumstances.[100]

Whilst domestic jurisdictions have been increasingly inclined to consider that domestic violence itself could constitute persecution, inconsistent approaches have been adopted with regard to the different elements that needed to be considered in assessing such claims, and in particular, in relation to the role of state protection.[101] However, overall, decision makers have not required the active participation of the authorities and granted refugee status as long as there was no reasonable possibility that the state could provide efficient protection to the victims. A general overview of the different interpretive frameworks adopted in cases of domestic violence will, instead, reveal that significant interpretive issues rather lie in the level and nature of harm required to amount to persecution and further question the relevance of this notion in such cases. Whilst the human rights framework remains the dominant one, divergent views have been expressed on what forms of human rights violations could amount to persecution, both between and within jurisdictions, thus reinforcing the legal uncertainty surrounding the adjudication of such cases.

Conceptual confusion regarding the degree of harm in cases of domestic violence in common-law jurisdictions

As noted by Hoepfner, asylum applications relating to domestic violence started to significantly increase in Canada and New Zealand as of the 1980s and 1990s.[102] One of the first landmark decisions to address the issue of domestic violence was *Mayer*[103] where the Federal Court of Canada considered that the risk of ill-treatment faced by the claimant (beating, rape and witnessing the ill-treatment of her children) compounded by the indifference of the authorities, amounted to persecution. The court simply highlighted that the violence endured by the claimant should not be considered as private given the clear indifference of the authorities to her plight. In this case, the court conflated the existence of harm with the absence of state protection, thus seemingly conforming to Hathaway's framework. Whilst the court adopted a rather protective view, no detailed interpretive methodology was applied, and, as such, little explanation was presented as to why these forms of harm constituted persecution.

The view that domestic violence could amount to persecution was later confirmed by the same court in *Narvaez*.[104] In this case, however, the court explicitly adopted a human rights approach as it was stated that the ill-

100 UNHCR (n 7) at [9].
101 Kneebone (n 4) 38; Hoepfner (n 4) 315–324: this element has been particularly discussed in the jurisprudence in Canada and New Zealand.
102 Hoepfner (n 4) 315.
103 *Canada c Mayer* [1992] A-544–92 Canada: Federal Court.
104 *Cecilia Narvaez, Miguel Alexandro Narvaez et Daniel Antonio Narvaez c Ministre de la Citoyenneté et de l'immigration* [1995] 89 F.T.R 94 (TD) Canada: Federal Court, Trial Division.

treatment received by the claimant at the hands of her husband was contrary to the principles enshrined in the UDHR. The court further followed Hathaway's approach by considering that the violation of human rights should be either sustained or systemic. Whilst the above cases resulted in a positive outcome for the claimants, it should be noted that the mistreatment they had faced was particularly severe.[105] Although it became clear that severe instances of domestic violence could constitute a basis for asylum, the bar set by the human rights approach appeared quite high. As a result, question marks remained for interpreting persecution in light of milder forms of ill-treatment. Subsequent jurisprudence did not lift the uncertainty regarding these cases in Canada because, in practice, many cases tend to be rejected on various other issues, in particular on credibility grounds.[106] However, when claimants are victims of severe physical violence and harassment at the hands of their family members, the harm they experienced would usually be considered persecution without much controversy. Unfortunately, high thresholds seem to have been generally applied.

In New Zealand, the jurisprudence is more variable. Judges, who tend to rely on ad hoc human rights approaches, have made inconsistent decisions, adopting either broad or restrictive views of the notion of persecution. For instance, the RSAA[107] granted refugee status to an Iranian applicant who had never experienced individual instances of physical aggression but who was quite outspoken against the patriarchal nature of Iranian society and was deeply affected by the fate her two of cousins who had been killed by family members for not conforming to the society's norms. In this case, the RSAA quoted earlier jurisprudence that referred to Hathaway's definition. However, the RSAA ended up analysing a series of human rights violations, without relying on Hathaway's interpretive modalities. The RSAA also engaged in a more circumstantial analysis, by considering subjective elements such as the psychological state of mind of the applicant and how it impacted the assessment of the harm. Additionally, the notion of shame and its consequences were analysed[108] to conclude that the harm feared was of 'sufficient gravity' to amount to persecution. In this case, the RSAA adopted an expanded human rights approach by referring to multiple aspects of the applicant's situation through a holistic analysis and ended up relying on a rather protective interpretation of the notion of persecution.

105 In *Mayer* and *Narvaez* both claimants faced instances of beating, physical ill-treatment and rape over many years.

106 Hoepfner (n 4) 322. See examples of cases rejected on credibility or IFA: *Canada MA4–07115* [2006] Canada: Immigration and Refugee Board; *X v Canada VB3–02197* [2014] Canada: Immigration and Refugee Board; *X v Canada, MB3–04040* [2014] Canada: Immigration and Refugee Board of Canada.

107 *Refugee Appeal No. 2039/93 Re MN*, New Zealand: RSAA (12 February 1996).

108 The RSAA pointed out that the 'phenomenon of "honour and shame" bears a direct relation to family ties, and to the complex interrelation of social organisation and conduct in Arab society. Once a woman breaks the rules, the whole family will be drawn into a sea of shame'.

Conversely, in later cases, the RSAA seemed to impose a stricter test to assess the notion of persecution, thus departing from its previous approach. For instance, in another decision,[109] the RSAA explicitly adopted the formulation of Hathaway and concluded that the series of predicaments faced by the applicant was not sufficient to rise to the level of persecution. In this case, an applicant was considered at risk of facing harassment, persistent phone calls and extortion. She had also faced one instance of physical assault by her husband. However, according to the RSAA 'such harassment, while possibly extremely unpleasant, does not amount to a sustained or systemic violation of human rights'.[110] Unlike their previously judgments, the RSAA, here, mainly focused on the absence of systematic physical violence and failed to discuss other parameters such as the impact that these events had on the emotional stability of the applicant, and whether this treatment led to other forms of discrimination.

This high threshold was reaffirmed in *Refugee Appeal No. 76501* where the RSAA recognised as a refugee a woman from the Fiji Islands who had suffered ongoing incidents of severe physical violence and harassment for several years. The RSAA concluded that her predicament had met 'the threshold of persecution as it [constituted] a breach of the fundamental human right not to be subjected to cruel, inhuman or degrading treatment or punishment'.[111] Whilst the outcome was positive in this case, the threshold set by the court appeared, again, quite high given the particularly severe forms of harm faced.[112] Overall, it seems that the human rights narrative adopted by some decision makers in New Zealand led to the imposition of different thresholds, depending on the modalities adopted.

Cases in the USA followed the same inconsistent pattern of interpretation, in particular when references to human rights treaties were made. Given that some domestic violence cases in the USA remained unpublished for a long period of time,[113] an exhaustive analysis of the approach adopted by American jurisdictions is difficult. Anker, however, argued that human rights activism had influenced the US jurisprudence in a positive manner leading judges to recognise more often certain forms of gender-based violence.[114] Whilst this element is not denied, it seems that the influence of human rights has its own limitations and has not fostered much clarity in the case law. In particular, published cases of domestic violence victims who have been granted refugee status are rare. Additionally, the

109 Refugee Appeal Nos. *76264, 76265 & 76266*, Nos. 76264, 76265 & 76266, New Zealand: RSAA (16 December 2008).

110 Ibid. at [42].

111 *Refugee Appeal No. 76501*, RSAA (19 November 2010) at [56].

112 On the existence of a high threshold see also *Refugee Appeal No. 75805 and 75806*, RSAA (30 November 2007): claimant was granted refugee status but she had to endure years of physical, psychological and sexual abuse.

113 Anker (n 17) 52. Karen Musalo, '*A Short History of Gender Asylum in the United States Resistance and Ambivalence May Very Slowly be Inching Towards Recognition of Women's Claims*' [2010] 29 Refugee Survey Quarterly 46, 62, https://doi.org/10.1093/rsq/hdq026. Musalo also pointed out that the government does not maintain statistics on gender-claims.

114 Anker (n 17).

victims that have been recognised have usually suffered egregious forms of harm for a long period at the hands of their family members, thus reflecting extreme cases of violence.

For instance, in the case of Rudi Alvaro Pena, the BIA initially rejected the claim of a Guatemalan applicant who had faced severe forms of domestic violence over several years, and who tried to seek protection from the police a few times, but to no avail. Initially, the BIA considered that the harm faced by the applicant was so intense that it could amount to persecution. In spite of this conclusion, the case was rejected due to a lack of Convention nexus[115] but the decision was eventually overturned about 10 years later.[116] This case showed that, whilst some reluctance has been expressed by US judges to recognise victims of domestic violence, individuals who have endured severe forms would tend to be more favourably adjudicated. This high threshold requirement seems to have been later confirmed when the BIA in the USA published a landmark decision in 2014, stating that another Guatemalan woman who had suffered years of abuse at the hands of her husband faced harm amounting to persecution.[117] In this case the abuse that the claimant had faced was quite abhorrent as it included physical beating, burning, rape and death threats. It remains unclear whether milder forms of ill-treatment in the USA would meet the threshold to be recognised as a refugee.

The Australian case law is also marred with uncertainty in that regard. The position of the jurisprudence on gender-based claims was affirmed in the landmark decision, *Khawar*.[118] In this case, the judges considered that the violence experienced by the claimant compounded by the discriminatory attitude of the police towards women, amounted to a violation of her fundamental human rights. Reference was made to Hathaway's framework requiring 'sustained and systematic violations of a basic human right',[119] thus setting again a relatively strict test. It was also considered that the absence of state protection was an element of persecution.

The interpretive methodology developed in *Khawar* has not, fortunately, been scrupulously followed in subsequent cases. Since then, the claims of victims of domestic violence have tended to be more favourably adjudicated, but judges have adopted variable approaches for interpreting persecution. In many cases, they did not use a fundamental human rights framework, but rather focused on the 'serious harm' approach, therefore evaluating the harm more on an ad hoc basis. Unlike the high threshold adopted in *Khawar*, other cases have adopted

115 *Matter of R-A-* 22 I&N Dec 906 (Board of Immigration Appeal 1999) 910: mentioned in Musalo (n 113) 57. See also a positive decision: *DHS's Supplemental Brief, Matter of L-R-* (Board of Immigration Appeal, 2009): https://cgrs.uchastings.edu//sites/default/files/Matter_of_LR_DHS_Brief_4_13_2009.pdf.

116 *Matter of R-A*, Interim Decision, 24 I&N Dec 629 (Attorney General 2008).

117 *Matter of A-R-C-G* 26 I&N Dec 388 (Board of Immigration Appeal 2014) 388.

118 *Minister for Immigration and Multicultural Affairs v Khawar* [2002] HCA 14, Australia: High Court, 11 April 2002.

119 Ibid. at [70].

different views, recognising a wider variety of types of harm as persecution. For instance, it was determined that 'serious physical harm',[120] 'physical harassment'[121] or mere 'threat',[122] could amount to serious harm, and thus persecution. Whilst the above decisions appear more protective of refugees today, the consequential impacts of the domestic violence suffered were not assessed and, therefore, the decision makers did not provide clear reasoning as to why they considered that such acts amounted to persecution. As a result, no consistent pattern of interpretation could be identified, again raising legal uncertainty for survivors of domestic violence who seek asylum.

Domestic violence in the jurisprudence of European countries: inconsistent interpretations of the threshold and nature of harm

The case law on domestic violence in European countries is even more inconsistent both between and within jurisdictions. Indeed, some judges consider that acts of domestic violence amount to persecution if they are sufficiently severe while others consider that such claims simply fall outside the ambit of the 1951 Convention. For instance, in the seminal case, *Islam; Ex parte Shah*, the UK House of Lords examined the claim of two Pakistani women who were both victims of domestic violence at the hands of their husband. Because of the discriminatory treatment of women in Pakistan and the lack of effective protection, the court found that women in Pakistan constituted a particular social group[123] and therefore, victims of domestic violence could be granted refugee status. In these cases, the harm feared by the claimants was quite severe (prosecution on account of false accusation of adultery) and little doubt was expressed as to the fact that such harm amounted to persecution.

In cases of other forms of harm, different views have, however, been noted. For instance, in *DM Albania*, the asylum judges applied a very high threshold in assessing the notion of persecution as they analysed the harm suffered by the claimant against Article 3 of the ECHR. The judges found that the continued life threats and harassment together with one incident of physical violence and one unsuccessful attempt at relocation were not sufficient to conclude that the treatment faced by an Albanian woman by her ex-partner constituted a breach of Article 3 of the Convention. Consequently, they decided that such harm did not amount to persecution and added that, in any case, state protection was available.[124] A recent report published by the European Parliament on the treatment of gender-related claims in Europe lamented the fact that judges in the UK 'do

120 *Case No. 1406045*, RRTA 47 (9 February 2015) at [24].
121 *Case No. 0907337*, RRTA 165 (15 March 2010) at [87].
122 *Case No. 1002606*, RRTA 484 (6 June 2010) at [107].
123 *Islam v Secretary of State for the Home Department; R v Immigration Appeal Tribunal, ex parte Shah* [1999] 2 AC 629 UKHL (Judicial Committee), 25 March 1999.
124 *DM (Sufficiency of Protection - PSG - Women - Domestic Violence) Albania v Secretary of State for the Home Department*, CG [2004] UKIAT 00059, 1 April 2004. At [14] 'We are therefore satisfied that, upsetting though they may have been, the actions of

not always appreciate that where there had been one incident of physical violence in the relationship (irrespective of other forms of psychological abuse) this could amount to persecution'.[125]

Conversely, in another decision, judges considered that the threats and intimidations by the claimant's husband, compounded by a short term of detention (based on false adultery charges that were likely to be dropped) amounted to persecution.[126] In this case, the court relied on the guidance provided by the QD, and seemed to set a high threshold to the test of persecution by referring to Article 3 of the ECHR as a benchmark. This led to considerations that first appeared relatively severe in the sense that the detention experience of the applicant was considered in the abstract and was not found to amount to persecution per se. The court, however, went on to acknowledge that other circumstances, such as the harassment that the applicant was facing at the hands of her husband, should be taken into consideration. All her experiences were found, cumulatively, to reach the level of persecution. It was, however concluded that the claimant could relocate within Pakistan, far from her husband. Although the assessment of the notion of persecution was quite comprehensive in this case, the IFA test was applied in a restrictive manner. For the IFA test, UNHCR usually recommends assessing whether it is reasonable[127] for an applicant to relocate in light of their personal circumstances, but, in this decision, the tribunal considered that in spite of ongoing discriminations faced by single women in Pakistan, the applicant could settle alone in another city, which seems rather strict in light of UNHCR recommendations. This is unfortunate, in particular given the thorough and protective approach initially adopted by the judges when they evaluated the notion of persecution.

The uncertainty of the adequate threshold to apply in domestic violence cases is also exemplified in another case in which the first instance and appeal decision makers reached completely different conclusions by applying different interpretive approaches. The first instance tribunal considered that the treatment faced by an applicant at the hands of her husband, namely a series of physical ill-treatments such as slaps, pushing and on one occasion a punch, constituted 'occasional outburst of violence'[128] and did not amount to persecution as per Art. 9 of QD. According to the tribunal, it simply did not amount to a serious violation of basic human rights. Adopting a very different view on this, the Appeal Tribunal

the former boyfriend did not amount to persecution or prohibited treatment for the purposes of Article 3 as they were not engaging a sufficiently high threshold to do so'.

125 Cheikh Ali et al. (n 64) 39.

126 *KA, AA, & IK (domestic violence - risk on return) Pakistan v Secretary of State for the Home Department*, CG [2010] UKUT 216 (IAC), 22 April 2010 at [260].

127 UNHCR Guidelines on International Protection No 4: 'Internal Flight or Relocation Alternative Within the Context of Article 1A(2) of the 1951 Convention and/or Protocol Relating to the Status of Refugees', HCR/GIP/03/04, 23 July 2003, 5, https://www.refworld.org/docid/3f2791a44.html.

128 *D-D- (Anonymity direction made) and Secretary of State for the Home Department* [2016] AA 12842, Upper Tribunal (Immigration and Asylum Chamber) 12 December 2016 at [17].

considered that the first instance decision makers had erred in concluding that the applicant did not experience persecution. Instead, it was considered that:

> a horrible element of domestic violence is [...] the fact that violence inflicted in a relationship where the victim [...] should be entitled to support and affection. When that is replaced by violence, bullying and controlling behavior it is horrible for her and there is clear evidence here of repeated nasty acts of violence intended to humiliate the victim. This is clearly sufficiently severe as to amount to persecution.[129]

In this case, both tribunals adopted very different lines of interpretation, which led to opposite outcomes. The first instance tribunal relied on a rather formalist human rights narrative, whilst the Appeal Authority did not develop a clear methodology and simply assessed the level of 'gravity' of the act, taking into account various aspects of the Applicant's experiences, which resulted in a more protective approach. In all, the jurisprudence in the UK has generally adopted the view that domestic violence could amount to persecution, but the forms that domestic violence could take remain unclear depending on the interpretive method used.

More significant inconsistencies are notable in French jurisdictions where survivors of domestic violence are not normally considered eligible to refugee protection because domestic violence is deemed a personal act. Therefore, only subsidiary protection is granted to claimants. Further, the threshold for that is rather high, as survivors would be granted protection if the act of domestic violence is accompanied by other elements such as forced marriage or opposition to social mores.[130] The interpretive methodology of the appeal court is rather confusing because little explanation is provided to justify this orientation. For instance, in *Mme T. ép. M.*,[131] the judges considered that a Russian claimant who had experienced ill-treatment from her husband did not meet the eligibility criteria of the 1951 Convention and was granted subsidiary protection. However, no explanation was given for such a decision. Other cases followed the same position.[132] Conversely, in Belgium, a Russian claimant who also experienced violence similar to the one mentioned above was granted refugee status.[133] Unlike the approach in France, Belgian judges took into account all the personal

129 Ibid. at [34].

130 CNDA, *BA*, n°09 023 070, 17 November 2010; CNDA, n°09 006 617, 26 October 2010 mentioned in Cheikh Ali et al. (n 64) 39. See also: Asise Mateo and Elodie Soulard, '*Le Droit d'Asile au Féminin, Cadre Législatif et Pratique*' (Observatoire de L'Asile et des Refugies) Les Cahiers du Social, No 32, 36.

131 CRR 2 Novembre 2007 412955, *Mme T. ép. M.* Cour Nationale du Droit d'Asile, *Contentieux des Réfugiés: Jurisprudence du Conseil d'État et de la Cour nationale du droit d'asile*, 15 April 2008.

132 CNDA 26 Fevrier 2009, n° 23.825; CNDA 9 juillet 2008, n° 13.874; CNDA 6 Septembre 2011 *Mme V.* n° 10023173 R; CNDA 12 Mars 2013, *Mme H.K., épouse G*, n°12017176 C.

133 CNDA 9 juillet 2008, n° 13.874.

circumstances of the claimants in order to evaluate the risk of harm upon return, including the trauma suffered and mental distress caused by the experience of mistreatment and considered that such violence is based on a convention ground.[134] This approach has been reiterated in a recent case[135] and has been labelled as a 'good practice' by researchers of the European Parliament,[136] making the notion of persecution more adapted to these cases. As such, victims in Belgium are more generally entitled to refugee status under the 1951 Convention.

Concluding remarks

In spite of inconsistent decisions amongst domestic jurisdictions, we observe an increased tendency to consider domestic violence as a form of persecution. Although this trend had perhaps been encouraged by the development of women's rights on the international scene, as some authors have argued, the application of a human rights framework for interpreting persecution has not revealed itself to be particularly protective of the interests of women in a number of cases, thus undermining the relevance of the notion of persecution in certain situations. Additionally, the vagueness of human rights standards has caused inconsistent interpretations of the Convention with a particular focus on physical harm. Whilst extreme forms of harm do not seem to raise debate, milder breaches of human rights or other complex situations are more problematic so that the degree of harm required to amount to persecution remains unclear in most cases, as exemplified in the above analysis. Ad hoc approaches adopted by civil-law countries have also led to very divergent outcomes. As a result, a more coherent interpretive approach in order to evaluate the harm faced by an applicant appears necessary to reassert the importance of the concept of persecution for cases of domestic violence. Psychological as well as physical mistreatment and other various forms of discrimination need to be taken into consideration, in addition to the different protected interests of the claimants and the consequential impact that the violations of such interests can have on their lives. In particular, the political view that domestic violence is based on the traditional perception of women's roles in certain societies or communities, leading to possible ostracism or stigmatisation, should not be ignored as is too often the case in certain decisions.

4.2.3 Trafficking in persons and the conceptualisation of persecution

Definition and legal framework

Trafficking is a complex phenomenon that has been defined internationally in the Protocol to Prevent, Suppress and Punish Trafficking in Persons, through a

134 CRR 14 December 2006 n°06–0817/F2548, mentioned in Cheikh Ail et al. (n 64) 39.

135 *X v Commissaire général aux réfugiés et aux apatrides*, Case No 177 178, Conseil du Contentieux des Etrangers, 27 Octobre 2016; see also *Arrêt n° 72 002*, Belgium: Conseil du Contentieux des Etrangers, 16 Décembre 2011, at 5.5.7.

136 Cheikh Ali et al. (n 64) 39.

lengthy formulation, pointing to the importance of the means and purpose of the act of trafficking.[137] According to the UNHCR, trafficking involves 'interrelated actions'[138] such as 'abduction, incarceration, rape, sexual enslavement, enforced prostitution, forced labour, removal of organs, physical beatings, starvation, the deprivation of medical treatment'.[139]

The causes and consequences of trafficking are multiple and have raised interpretive challenges in the jurisprudence. As pointed out by Dorevitch and Foster, the harm faced by survivors of trafficking 'is inflicted by multiple actors across a temporal and geographical continuum' and therefore raises complex issues.[140] In particular, given the numerous forms of harm that trafficking entails, confusion has emerged as to the types of predicaments that are involved in a situation of trafficking and whether such predicaments should amount to persecution. The absence of a nexus[141] or the availability of state protection have often constituted elements on which decision makers have relied for rejecting asylum applications of survivors of trafficking. A comprehensive analysis of the Convention nexus or the availability of state protection would fall outside the purview of the present analysis as previously argued but the qualification of the harm faced by victims of trafficking as persecution has also raised major contention that will be assessed below.

137 Article 3: of Protocol to Prevent, Suppress and Punish Trafficking in Persons, Especially Women and Children, supplementing the United Nations Convention against Transnational Organized Crime, New York 15 November 2000, UNTS, Vol. 2237, 319, Doc.A/55/383: 'For the purposes of this Protocol: (a) "Trafficking in persons" shall mean the recruitment, transportation, transfer, harbouring or receipt of persons, by means of the threat or use of force or other forms of coercion, of abduction, of fraud, of deception, of the abuse of power or of a position of vulnerability, or of the giving or receiving of payments or benefits to achieve the consent of a person having control over another person, for the purpose of exploitation. Exploitation shall include, at a minimum, the exploitation of the prostitution of others or other forms of sexual exploitation, forced labour or services, slavery or practices similar to slavery, servitude or the removal of organs. (b) The consent of a victim of trafficking in persons to the intended exploitation set forth in subparagraph (a) of this article shall be irrelevant where any of the means set forth in subparagraph (a) have been used; (c) The recruitment, transportation, transfer, harbouring or receipt of a child for the purpose of exploitation shall be considered "trafficking in persons" even if this does not involve any of the means set forth in subparagraph (a) of this article'.

138 UNHCR (n 47) at [10].

139 Ibid. at [15]

140 Anna Dorevitch and Michelle Foster, '*Obstacles on the Road to Protection: Assessing the Treatment of Sex-trafficking Victims under Australia's Migration and Refugee Law*' (2008) 9 Melbourne Journal of International Law 1, 40, http://www5.austlii.edu.au/au/journals/MelbJIL/2008/1.html.

141 Satvinder S. Juss, '*Recognizing Refugee Status for Victims of Trafficking and the Myth of Progress*' [2015] 34 Refugee Survey Quarterly 107, 116, https://doi.org/10.1093/rsq/hdv003. See also French jurisprudence rejecting claimants on the absence of a nexus: Décision du Conseil d'État, Arrêt du 7 Novembre 2011, n°348228; Décision du Conseil d'État n° 350661, recueil Lebon, lecture du 25 Juillet 2013.

Firstly, it should be noted that the causes of trafficking are an important element that can have a major importance in assessing the notion of persecution and should be factored into the analysis of the refugee definition. Some international instruments have emphasised the vulnerability of victims of trafficking by pointing to the root causes of this phenomenon. For instance, the Beijing Declaration considered that major barriers to the security of women were 'systematic or de facto discrimination, violations of and failure to protect all human rights and fundamental freedoms of all women, and their civil, cultural, economic, political and social rights, including the right to development and ingrained prejudicial attitudes towards women and girls'.[142] The UN General Assembly also highlighted the underlying causes of trafficking by mentioning 'gender inequality, poverty, unemployment, lack of socio-economic opportunities, gender-based violence, discrimination and marginalization'.[143] Similarly, the UNHCR considered that 'scenarios in which trafficking can flourish frequently coincide with situations where potential victims may be vulnerable to trafficking [as it is the case for instance in states] prone to increased poverty, deprivation and dislocation of the civilian population'.[144] Finally, in 2002 the Office of the United Nations High Commissioner for Human Rights (OHCHR) issued Recommended Principles and Guidelines on Human Rights and Human Trafficking, identifying inequality, poverty and discrimination as major causes of trafficking.[145] As such, the social and economic situation of the victims prior to the trafficking experience is an important aspect that can have an impact on the condition of victims upon return to their country and, therefore, should have a major relevance for assessing the notion of persecution.

Moreover, in addition to the physical violence endured by the victims, certain consequences of trafficking are also important to evaluate what types of harm amount to persecution. In particular, various documents have highlighted the medical and psychological effect that trafficking has on the victims. For instance, the Beijing Declaration affirmed that 'exploitation places girls and women at high risk of physical and mental trauma'.[146] The UNHCR also insisted on the 'ongoing traumatic psychological effects'[147] of trafficking experiences. Some UN resolutions insisted on the necessity of adopting a gender- and age-sensitive approach to the problem of trafficking[148] by noting the 'heightened vulnerability'[149] of women

142 Beijing Declaration and Platform for Action, Fourth World Conference on Women, 15 September 1995, A/CONF.177/20 (1995) and A/CONF.177/20/Add.1 (1995) at [42].
143 Resolution adopted by the United Nations General Assembly on 19 December 2016, [on the report of the Third Committee (A/71/477)] A/RES/71/167, 4/13.
144 UNHCR (n 47) at [31].
145 Office of the UNHCHR, Recommended Principles and Guidelines on Human Rights and Human Trafficking (HR/PUB/02/3), 2010, 1.
146 Beijing Declaration (n 142) at [100].
147 UNHCR (n 47) at [16].
148 Resolution adopted by the General Assembly (n 143) at [34].
149 Ibid. 4/13; see also Resolution adopted by the General Assembly on 30 July 2010 (A/64/L.64) 64/293, A/64/PV.109, United Nations Global Plan of Action to Combat Trafficking in Persons that promotes a 'human rights based, gender- and age-sensitive approach in addressing all factors that make people vulnerable' at [50].

and girls who have been trafficked. These instruments all pointed to the various forms and intensity of harms resulting from trafficking.

From the normative framework described above, a series of vulnerabilities and predicaments can be identified as the root causes and consequences of trafficking. Prior to being trafficked, most victims would have generally experienced situations of gender discrimination and socio-economic disadvantage and, after being trafficked, they often suffer the psychological and physical consequences of their traumatic experience. It should be, therefore, expected that these elements, including the socio-economic position of the claimant, which has been described by one author as the 'most pervasive'[150] reason for trafficking, would be taken into account to understand the profile of victims when interpreting the notion of persecution. Persecution being a forward-looking test, not all victims of trafficking might be entitled to refugee status but it will be necessary to assess whether the vulnerable profile of a claimant, compounded by other risk factors, can lead to further persecution. In this view, the UNHCR considered that even when the trafficking instance was a 'one-off experience'[151] and is not likely to be repeated, other forms of harm could be faced by former trafficking victims upon return to their country. In particular, they could suffer from severe psychological difficulties arising out of past persecution,[152] potential reprisals[153] or ostracisms and discrimination.[154]

A large variety of parameters therefore need to be taken into consideration when interpreting the notion of persecution in order to make this notion relevant in the context of trafficking cases. Unfortunately, decision makers in national jurisdictions have adopted inconsistent approaches on these issues, as will be demonstrated below.

The risk of (re)trafficking as a form of persecution

Saito observed that the risk of being trafficked itself (or re-trafficked) is consensually considered persecution in national jurisdictions.[155] Given the egregious forms of violence that trafficking entails, such as rape, forced labour, organ removal, beating and other forms of ill-treatment, the qualification of persecution has raised little debate. According to Saito, 'cases show a general consensus in considering trafficking as a human rights violation that could amount to persecution'.[156] Dorevitch and Foster also considered that these types of acts clearly 'are

150 Theodore R. Sangalis, '*Elusive Empowerment: Compensating the Sex Trafficked Person under the Trafficking Victims Protection Act*' [2011] 80 Fordham Law Review 403, 41, https://ir.lawnet.fordham.edu/flr/vol80/iss1/10.
151 UNHCR (n 47) at [16].
152 Ibid.
153 Ibid. at [17].
154 Ibid. [18].
155 Saito Kaori, Research Paper No 149, 'International protection for trafficked persons and those who fear being trafficked', Policy Officer Division of Human Resource Management UNHCR, December 2007 Geneva, 16, https://ir.lawnet.fordham.edu/flr/vol80/iss1/10.
156 Ibid. 11.

flagrant violations of international human rights'[157] and, therefore, are sufficiently serious as to amount to persecution.

In opposition to the above views, some early cases in Canada have adopted quite a narrow understanding of the harm that could be faced by the victims of trafficking by considering that when the consent of the claimant was initially given, the subjection to forced labour did not amount to trafficking. Therefore, in the cases of trafficking of Chinese minors, the Court disregarded the trafficking elements and simply analysed the penalty imposed on individuals for leaving a country illegally.[158] The applicants were rejected as it was considered that receiving a penalty for illegal departure did not rise to the level of persecution. The trafficking element was not taken into consideration, because the victims (who were minors at the time) had voluntarily left their country through illegal means and, therefore, it was not accepted that they had been trafficked against their will. Fortunately, this approach was overturned in *Li v Canada* as the court considered that 'applicants were persecuted by virtue of their being "trafficked", regardless of their initial consent to resort to an agent'.[159]

Whilst these cases concerned boy applicants, the principles posed by the court, namely that the consent of the victims should not have a negative impact on the case, is valid in most trafficking cases for female applicants as well. In *Li*, the court adopted a human rights approach as it considered that it could not be concluded that the victims had provided their consent to the journey proposed by traffickers given their young age as per the standards set out in the CRC. The court referred the case back to the Immigration and Refugee Board for a redetermination of the facts 'taking into account the values reflected in international human rights law as aids to help inform the contextual approach to interpretation of the definition of the Convention'.[160] In this context, references to external human rights norms have been conducive to a rather protective understanding of the terms of the 1951 Convention.

Similar views have been expressed in the jurisprudence examined in Australia,[161] the United Kingdom,[162] France,[163] the United States,[164] whereby the harm arising out of the risk of being trafficked or re-trafficked would easily rise to the level of persecution. In these cases, the human rights narrative constituted a convenient

157 Dorevitch and Foster (n 140) 19.
158 *Bian v (Minister of Citizenship and Immigration)* [2000] IMM-1640–00, Canada: Federal Court; see also *Zhu v Canada (Minister of Citizenship and Immigration)* [2001] F.C.J. No 1251, 2001 FCT 884, Canada: Federal Court.
159 *Li v Canada (Minister of Citizenship and Immigration)* [2000] IMM-932–00, Canada: Federal Court at [23].
160 Ibid. at [27].
161 *Case no NO3/47757* RRTA 355 (11 May 2004). *VXAJ v Minister for Immigration and Another* [2006] FMCA 234 (20 April 2006); *Case No. 0903290*, [2009] RRTA 727 (4 August 2009).
162 *AM and BM (Trafficked women) Albania v Secretary of State for the Home Department* [2010] UKUT 80 (IAC) 18 March 2010.
163 CNDA, 24 Mars 2015, n°10012810, *Mlle J.E. F*; CNDA, 29 Avril 2011, n°10012810; CNDA, 12 Juillet 2012, n°11026228; CNDA, 29 Avril 2011, *Mlle E.*, n°10012810.
164 *Matter of O-*, CGRS Case No 275 (Russia), (Board of Immigration Appeal 2003) cited in Saito (n 155), 12.

approach because it clearly identified violations of basic protection standards. However, more complex situations in which the claimants are not likely to be re-trafficked (either because they can benefit from state protection or because they have been trafficked in a different place than their place of origin) have raised more uncertainty.

Inconsistent approaches regarding the peripheral harms surrounding the trafficking experience

Whilst international guidance indicates that a variety of factors should be taken into consideration for adjudicating claims of trafficking victims, the jurisprudence has remained inconsistent in considering these elements.

Some decisions in the UK followed a narrow line of analysis, by simply assessing the level of safety that the former victims could face upon return to their country.[165] For instance, the Upper Tribunal recently rejected a Vietnamese claimant who was trafficked from Vietnam to Hungary and sexually exploited. The tribunal concluded that:

> Vietnam is a large country of some 90 million people with a number of large cities in it. If the appellant were able to return, a matter to which we shall have to return, she would not be a person of any adverse interest to the government, and the chance of coming across her traffickers is very slight.[166]

The court, however, did not assess other harms, such as the impact of a possible trauma,[167] or the risk of being ostracised or stigmatised. On another occasion, the Upper Tribunal also rejected the appeal application of a trafficking victim by considering that there was no real risk of being re-trafficked and the claimant would have the opportunity to benefit from the protection of available shelters in her country.[168] In this case, the appeal authority did not consider that other forms of harm could impact the applicant's daily life upon return,[169] thus failing to engage in a more circumstantial and holistic assessment of her circumstances. Fortunately, this restrictive

165 Inter alia, *VD (Trafficking) Albania v Secretary of State for the Home Department*, CG [2004] UKIAT 00115, 26 May 2004; *MP [Trafficking - Sufficiency of Protection] Romania v Secretary of State for the Home Department* [2005] UKIAT 00086, 21 April 2005; *NA (Kyrgyz Woman) Tajikistan v Secretary of State for the Home Department*, CG [2004] UKIAT 00133, 28 May 2004.

166 *Nguyen (Anti-Trafficking Convention: respondent's duties) v. The Secretary of State for the Home Department* [2015] UKUT 00170 (IAC), 25 March 2015, at [51].

167 Although in this case a medical report attesting to the fact that the applicant suffered from PTSD was produced.

168 *PO (Trafficked Women) Nigeria v Secretary of State for the Home Department*, CG [2009] UKAIT 00046, 23 November 2009, at [212].

169 It was considered that an NGO could provide support for her trauma but further consideration would have been desirable regarding her chances of reintegration as a single mother with a child (presumably born out of her trafficking experience). She had no family network and had been subjected to child labour.

approach was abandoned in *D (Trafficked women) Nigeria CG*[170] as the tribunal conducted a detailed analysis of the claimant's individual circumstances by relying extensively on the UNHCR guidelines[171] for victims of trafficking and concluded that 'if the appellant is met by NAPTIP shelter on arrival in Nigeria [...] [although] she would not be at risk of being trafficked [...] she would in effect be locked up for the duration of her stay and only allowed out with a chaperone'. It was further stated that 'in this appellant's case such restriction on her movements would [...] cause significant re-traumatisation'.[172] The importance of the trauma faced, compounded by the lack of family support, was the basis for granting refugee status to this applicant. To reach this conclusion, the tribunal adopted a circumstantial approach by acknowledging 'the need for critical and close analysis of the particular personal circumstances of a victim of trafficking in the context of the evidenced background material'.[173] A rather similar view was adopted in the case of a Congolese applicant in the US as the decision makers accorded significant weight to the psychological harm faced by the applicant.[174]

In light of the above, it can be observed that when decision makers take into account the psychological element for assessing the risk of persecution, the outcome tends to be positive for the applicants.[175] However, the risks of ostracism, stigma and alienation are rarely considered, which is an unfortunate approach because these aspects could further inform the interpretation of the notion of persecution. For instance, in Australia, in *Appeal No. 1105325*,[176] the Appeal Tribunal rejected the asylum application of a Korean applicant who had gone to Australia to seek better opportunities but who was eventually forced to work in a brothel by her agent. The tribunal noted that the applicant had been unable to present a psychological report attesting to her fragile mental state and that she was not at serious risk of being re-trafficked. Her claim was therefore rejected. The tribunal then acknowledged that the claimant's 'family may have learned about her sex work and drug use in Australia, and, as a result, will reject her'. It was further

170 *D (Trafficked Women) Nigeria CG* [2016] UKUT 00454 (IAC) October 2016.
171 Ibid. at [21].
172 Ibid. at [212].
173 Ibid. at [70].
174 *Matter of X*, United States Executive Office for Immigration Review, 9 August 2011, available at: http://www.refworld.org/cases,USIC,4ea6e2a62.html: in this case, the psychiatrist who performed an evaluation in preparation for the hearing of the claimant before the Court determined that it would be 'highly detrimental' for her to return to her country because she had no family members who could provide her with emotional or financial support and returning her to the DRC would force her to relive her traumatic experiences, which would be very damaging, especially if she were not able to obtain mental health care (p. 13). Given the nature of the respondent's past persecution and her particularly vulnerable position as a young woman with no familial connections and limited income, the Court found it very likely that she would suffer serious harm if removed to the DRC.
175 *AM and BM (Trafficked women) Albania v Secretary of State for the Home Department* [2010] UKUT 80 (IAC), March 2010: The Tribunal granted refugee status to a claimant acknowledging that victims of trafficking were likely to suffer PTSD syndromes that could affect their ability to reintegrate in the society.
176 *Case No.1105325* [2012] RRTA 272 (20 March 2012).

stated that there was a 'possibility that such knowledge may reach her family, and that they may disapprove or even reject her because of that activity'.[177] However, the tribunal concluded that such a reaction or rejection would not amount to 'serious harm'.[178] While the mere fact of being rejected by one's family might not indeed amount to persecution, the evaluation of this element would have required a more thorough examination of her various circumstances. In particular, the claimant's ability to meet her needs alone in Korea and the potential ostracism that she could face without family support could have also been assessed to reach a more transparent conclusion. Foster pointed out that, for instance, 'a trafficked woman may face isolation from traditional support networks, leading to destitution, which may itself constitute persecution'.[179] This aspect was not sufficiently taken into consideration in this case.

Conversely to the above, a recent evolution has been noted in France in such cases. In some trafficking cases, the appeal court has taken into account not only the risk to applicants of being re-trafficked and facing reprisals, but also the possibility of 'social alienation',[180] ostracism from the family and community as well as discrimination.[181] This has led to more positive outcomes for applicants. In certain traditional and paternalistic societies where a family or community network is essential, the position that the victim of trafficking will have in her society upon return might indeed be important in order to assess the level of harm that she could face.

A singular approach pertaining to mental harm is the one adopted in the US, whereby an applicant can be granted asylum if her past experience has been deemed particularly atrocious, even when no prospective risk of physical harm is identified.[182] In this sense, the US legislator has introduced the possibility to recognise an applicant for 'compelling reasons' based on past persecution.[183] UNHCR considers, that in extreme cases, forms of mental suffering could amount to persecution when the extremely fragile psychological state of mind of the applicants could render their return to the country unendurable.[184] Gauci distinguished this aspect from the concept of 'continuing persecution'[185] caused by a trauma that makes an applicant more vulnerable to other forms of harm such as the ability to reintegrate into the society. This is different from considering the trauma itself as a form of mental persecution, as suggested by the UNHCR guidelines. Whilst the difference is slight, this option has rarely been adopted by national courts, save for the USA. This unfortunately

177 Ibid. at [75].
178 Ibid. at [75].
179 Dorevitch and Foster (n 140) 2.
180 CNDA, 24 March 2015, Décision n° 10012810, *Mlle JEL.*
181 CNDA, 12 juillet 2013 n° 13003859, 4.
182 *Matter of Chen*, 20 I&N Dec 16 (Board of Immigration Appeal 1989) and *Matter of B-*, 21 I&N Dec 66 (Board of Immigration Appeal 1995).
183 Title 8 Code of Federal Regulations, para 208.13(b)(1)(iii)(A).
184 UNHCR (n 47) at [16].
185 Jean-Pierre Gauci, *Trafficked Persons as Refugees* (King's College London 2013) 224–225, https://kclpure.kcl.ac.uk/portal/en/theses/trafficked-persons-as-refugees(d764272f-d6a4-4125-a15e-1148df0bbc5b).html.

demonstrates the reluctance of domestic jurisdictions to accept mental harm as a form of persecution per se as courts usually require that applicants also demonstrate a risk of facing other forms of predicament in addition to the trauma experienced.

Concluding remarks

Apart from the above-mentioned cases, the previously discussed decisions generally fail to consider the individual circumstances of the trafficked claimants, their role in the society as well as the stigmatisation, isolation, shame and ostracism that they could face upon return to their country. A strict interpretation of persecution would only assess the risk of experiencing continuous instances of trafficking while a broader understanding of the notion, which is more desirable in these cases, would take into account an accumulation of different elements and the adverse impact that they have on the physical and psychological integrity of the claimants. In particular, Kneebone pointed out that the phenomenon of trafficking reveals the deficiencies of certain social systems whereby some women are in a position of vulnerability.[186] These aspects are important elements that need to be evaluated in order to adopt a more holistic approach to persecution so as to facilitate a better understanding of this notion in trafficking cases.

4.3 Concluding remarks

This chapter has analysed how claims arising out of situations of gender-based violence, often perpetrated in the private sphere, have been addressed in the jurisprudence. Whilst some jurisdictions have been quite reluctant to consider that private individuals could be agents of persecution, this position has progressively evolved, making the notion of persecution more relevant to the claims of refugee women in the 21st century. Regrettably, the interpretation of the various forms of harm that non-state agents of persecution can cause still raises dissension because gender-based persecution cases are usually complex and involve a wide array of harms that are inconsistently taken into account. Whilst acts of physical violence such as FGM, domestic violence and trafficking in persons are generally found to amount to persecution, 'milder' forms of violence peripheral to those harms are more variably addressed, causing a 'degree of uncertainty about how to approach matters in which issues of gender and refugee law intersect'.[187] This state of the jurisprudence led Kallinosis to speak again of a 'refugee roulette'[188] for the 'refugee woman' and tends to set an undesirably high threshold.

Overall, inconsistent approaches are partly due to the fact that different interpretive patterns have been used by decision makers as observed in this chapter. It

186 Susan Kneebone, '*Human Trafficking and Refugee Women*' in Efrat Arbel, Catherin Dauvergne and Jenni Millbank (eds) *Gender in Refugee Law - From the Margins to the Centre* (Routledge 2014) 197–219.

187 Kneebone (n 4).

188 Kallinosis (n 25) 80.

appears that most common-law jurisdictions have often relied on human rights as interpretive benchmarks for assessing the notion of persecution but they have done so through divergent parameters. Other jurisdictions have adopted ad hoc narratives, on a case-by-case basis, thus creating further uncertainty for asylum seekers and refugees. More consistency should, therefore, be fostered in national jurisdictions in order to provide decisions that are better adapted to the protection needs of refugee women. For this, a holistic assessment of their different circumstances should be conducted, taking into account the complexity of their experiences in both the public and private spheres and recognising that both spheres, in fact, closely intersect.

In this sense Crawley called for a 'contextual analysis [of refugee claims] that includes gender relations and gender equality and moves beyond discrete monolithic categories of men and women that flatten out the complexity and diversity of experience'.[189] An absolute harmonisation of jurisprudential practices is rather difficult to achieve, but lending more weight to the personal circumstances of refugees and their individual profile for interpreting persecution could encourage fairer and more transparent outcomes and reassert the relevance of the notion of persecution in these cases.

189 Crawley (n 10) 348.

Conclusion

The present book demonstrated that the notion of persecution progressively emerged in international refugee law after World War I to finally become the cornerstone of the definition of a refugee in 1951. However, persecution was never defined in international instruments, thus creating some uncertainty as to the scope of the notion and raising risks of inconsistent and restrictive interpretations. This has, in turn, led to variable applications of the Convention and questioned the relevance of this notion in new types of refugee claims, in particular in refugee claims lodged by women.

Concerns of interpretation are, in fact, quite recent as, for a long period of time, the concept of persecution did not raise particular debate. In the aftermath of World War II, persecution was almost always understood as a form of harm occurring in the public sphere, perpetrated by repressive states, persecuting members of the political opposition or minorities. Whilst scholars seemed to have always considered that persecution could take various forms beyond state repression, in practice the notion was almost always perceived as a political act. The way it was interpreted was serving interests of recipient countries, viewing refugees as individuals who were voting with their feet to disavow their own state's officials and policies. Given that this notion was generally applied in male-dominated societies, where the condition of women was not yet a concern of the public powers, the notion of persecution seemed to have mainly fitted the profiles of men, whose experiences unfolded in the public sphere and political arena. Women persecuted for political reasons constituted a minority of individuals granted refugee status. In this context, women were more often recognised refugees as part of a family unit, rather than in their own right.

The interpretation of persecution, however, started raising contention in the past few decades when refugee claims progressively diversified and when people started claiming new forms of harm at the hands of non-state actors. Members of communities, members of the family, local or criminal groups came to the fore as possible agents of persecution, which had been not anticipated by the plenipotentiaries. Additionally, the emergence of a new phenomenon, called the 'feminisation' of forced displacement, started questioning the traditional paradigm of the asylum system, as a larger number of women were claiming asylum independently, based on their personal experiences and often involving sexual and other gender-related forms of violence.

In this new context, it was observed that, at the end of the cold war polarity, national jurisdictions gradually moved away from a political application of the refugee definition and started interpreting its terms in a manner that better reflected contemporary concerns. Different legal approaches, influenced by grassroots human rights activism and legal scholarship, had been adopted for applying the notion of persecution, thus giving rise to new methodologies of interpretation. As principled approaches started being developed, it appeared that the application of the 1951 Convention entered a new judicial phase in the 1990s, leading to more favourable interpretations of persecution for refugee women and recognising that certain forms of violence were of a gender-related nature or at least different than what was typically experienced by male refugees. However, these new approaches emerged in a rather inconsistent manner, which shed some light on the difficulty in defining the meaning of persecution in contemporary contexts. In particular, persecution appeared to be a general and malleable concept, which could be variably understood through different views shaped by cultural, gender, religious or social influences. This led many authors to point out that the notion itself had tainted the international regime of refugee protection with a strong gender bias, raising concerns of inadequate or even inconsistent applications of refugee law. One author in particular described the condition of women in the urban asylum system as a 'refugee roulette',[1] highlighting the uncertainty of their legal circumstances.

The quest for the right meaning for the notion of persecution has been both encouraged and challenged, in recent decades, by the continuing diversification of refugee situations and the surging number of displaced individuals on the international scene. The multiplicity of women profiles has continued to question the relevance of the notion of persecution for them in the 21st century. It has made the necessity to interpret it in an evolutionary manner even more pressing in order to ensure the 'enduring relevance'[2] of the 1951 Convention. UNHCR expressed these concerns at the 60th anniversary of the Convention by stating that there were now significant 'gaps in the scope of the existing refugee protection framework'.[3] It was noted that, today, numerous displaced individuals, in need of some form of assistance were often falling outside the ambit of the international protection regime, in particular because they have difficulties in demonstrating that they fit the persecution criteria. As a result, they are left without protection. Whilst this issue concerns numerous individuals with various profiles, the specific condition of refugee women and girls was highlighted in the Global Compact for Refugees as an area where major developments were needed.

1 Joanna J. Kallinosis, '*Refugee Roulette: A Comparative Analysis of Gender-Related Persecution in Asylum Law*' [2017] 6 DePaul Journal of Women, Gender and the Law 55, 90–92, https://via.library.depaul.edu/jwgl/vol6/iss1/2.

2 Jane McAdam, '*The Enduring Relevance of the 1951 Refugee Convention*' [2017] 29 International Journal of Refugee Law 1, https://doi.org/10.1093/ijrl/eex017.

3 UNHCR, Background Paper, 2010 High Commissioner's Dialogue on Protection Challenges, 'Protection Gaps and Challenges', 22 November 2010, available at: http://www.refworld.org/docid/4cef89242.html.

The present book has, therefore, attempted to assess whether these protection gaps could be overcome through an evolutionary understanding of the notion of persecution or whether a shift of paradigm is needed to adapt the current refugee law regime to the protection needs of forcibly displaced people on the international scene and in particular to the needs of refugee women.

In order to address the risk of inconsistent and inadequate applications of the Convention, scholars have developed principled frameworks for interpreting persecution. The dominant one, as analysed in the present book, relies on basic human rights norms to define what persecution is. Human rights criticisms have, however, pointed to the rigidity of this approach, highlighting its unduly formalistic character. It has been demonstrated, in the preceding chapters, that this paradigm, whilst providing objective benchmarks of interpretation, also fosters a compartmentalised assessment of persecution, at times obviating certain aspects of the harms experienced by refugees. This framework is opposed to a more holistic understanding of persecution, based on the personal circumstances of each individual as proposed by the UNHCR in its 'circumstantial approach'. Whilst the UNHCR's model requires a case-by-case analysis, and, as such, raises concerns of inconsistent and subjective interpretations, the refugee agency nonetheless proposed objective indicators to minimise such pitfalls by taking into account the individual circumstances of refugees.

In spite of the existence of theoretical models for interpreting the notion of persecution, the preceding chapters have also observed that national jurisdictions have still not applied consistent methodologies of interpretation. Although some judges have formally acknowledged the relevance of basic human rights as adequate interpretive tools, most of them have, in practice, adopted variable modalities of interpretation. Whilst human rights have, to a certain extent, allowed for an evolutionary understanding of persecution in particular in cases of gender-based violence, they have not abided by their promise to foster greater consistency in the international system of protection. Additionally, unduly restrictive interpretations of the notion of persecution have been noted in the case of asylum applications lodged by women due to the generally male centric character of the human rights paradigm, adding an additional burden of proof on women in many cases. As such, a fragmentary system of protection seems to have arisen on the international scene, with the risk of undermining the coherence of the international refugee law regime and creating both legal uncertainty and incentives for asylum shopping.

In order to fill these gaps, more coherence in interpreting the terms of the refugee definition, and in particular the notion of persecution, would be desirable, not only between jurisdictions but also within them. Attempts to define persecution have been met with little success,[4] as defining this notion would most probably confer too much rigidity on the 1951 Convention.

4 UNHCR, Handbook and Guidelines on Procedures and Criteria for Determining Refugee Status under the 1951 Convention and the 1967 Protocol Relating to the Status of Refugees, December 2011, HCR/1P/4/ENG/REV.3 at [51].

Given the constantly evolving circumstances of refugees, a flexible approach remains desirable, but consistent methodologies of interpretation should be adopted. Whilst the basic human rights model has proven to be useful and has advanced to a certain extent the condition of women, it should not be applied in a rigid manner. The UNHCR's proposal to complement this mode of interpretation with a more circumstantial approach appears to be both sufficiently principled and flexible in order to adapt to the evolving protection needs of refugees and capture the complexity of women's experiences. It adequately assesses the thresholds of harm required to fall under the purview of the 1951 Convention and encourages decision makers to factor in various elements of women's daily circumstances, rather than confining its analysis to formal and abstract entitlements such as international human rights. As pointed out by the Refugee Agency, a 'balanced and holistic application of the definition, incorporating human rights law principles, has the best chance of yielding the correct result'.[5]

Conclusively, it is contended that a proper understanding of the notion of persecution, based on a holistic approach, factoring in a human rights and circumstantial analysis as proposed by the UNHCR, with elements of intersectionality, would foster a better understanding of the conditions of women and make it possible to better evaluate the risk that they are likely to face upon return to their country. As pointed out by one author, a 'broad reading'[6] of a (seemingly) narrow definition appears desirable because it allows for a broad application of the 1951 Convention, beyond the confines of current states' practices. It also clarifies the duties of states towards refugee women and the nature of the assistance required. At this stage, therefore, the notion of persecution does not appear to be obsolete but still has the capacity to fit the experiences of women in the 21st century.

5 UNHCR, '*Note on The International Protection of Refugees: Interpreting Article 1 of the 1951 Convention Relating to the Status of Refugees*' [2001] 20 Refugee Survey Quarterly 77.

6 Matthew Lister, '*Who are Refugees*' [2013] 32 Law and Philosophy 645, 671.

Index

For Product Safety Concerns and Information please contact our EU representative GPSR@taylorandfrancis.com
Taylor & Francis Verlag GmbH, Kaufingerstraße 24, 80331 München, Germany

www.ingramcontent.com/pod-product-compliance
Ingram Content Group UK Ltd.
Pitfield, Milton Keynes, MK11 3LW, UK
UKHW022122190926
475702UK00013B/1602

9780367528256